ENJOYING CANADIAN PAINTING

L'Enfant au Pain, c. 1892-1899
oil on canvas
19-7/8″ x 22″ (50 cm x 56 cm)
Ozias Leduc (1864-1955)
The National Gallery of Canada, Ottawa

PATRICIA GODSELL

Enjoying Canadian Painting

General Publishing Co. Limited
Don Mills, Ontario

Published 1976 by
General Publishing Co. Limited
30 Lesmill Road
Don Mills, Ontario   M3B 2T6

Designed by Allan Fleming and Peter Maher

Canadian Cataloguing in Publication Data

Godsell, Patricia, date
    Enjoying Canadian painting

Bibliography: p.
Includes index.
ISBN 0-7736-0053-1

    1. Painting, Canadian. 2. Painters — Canada.
I. Title.

ND240.G63   759.11   C76-017106-8

Printed and bound in Canada

1 2 3 4 5 BP 80 79 78 77 76

For Jack

and

Jennifer, Janet, Sally, and David

Preface

I have written this book mainly because I enjoy looking at paintings and talking to people about art. I also take great pleasure in learning as much as I can about the language of painting – and it *is* a language that takes time and effort to learn. But this is a fact that is easy to forget, because paintings are also 'pictures' that seem to speak for themselves.

Works of art, though, are not just pictures that fill galleries or hang forgotten on the walls of our homes. Rather, they are places where we can meet each other and share our ideas and feelings. The artist gives, and we respond; the painting is the meeting-ground. But if we cannot understand the artist's language, we will not be able to grasp his meaning. All we will see is the surface subject, the picture.

This is the problem that so many people face when attempting to respond to contemporary abstract art and the language of painting in its purest state. When forms, spaces, light and shadow, colour, line, and texture are the only 'words' an artist uses to communicate his feelings and ideas, we can no longer escape into a surface subject. The meaning of abstract painting is not in a story or in a landscape view but in the forms and colours themselves.

Yet the statements artists make through their art have remained fairly constant over the years. Human beings remain much the same even though their circumstances may change greatly. In a letter to Emily Carr, Lawren Harris once wrote, 'Great works of Art are the same yesterday, today and forever. We but endeavour to be ourselves, deeply ourselves....' This is true. If it were not, no one would read Shakespeare any more, or listen to Beethoven, or look at Rembrandt.

But it is also true that we learn from each other. Each generation looks back on past achievements and builds on them or adapts traditions to suit new circumstances. Art is a continual process of re-creation, of saying the same basic things over and over again in many different ways.

Because of this, I think it is easier to understand the painting of today by seeing the changes that have taken place over the years, and so the works I have chosen are arranged in an approximate chronological order. Occasionally this order has been slightly changed, but no work of art has been taken far out of its context.

Neither life nor history is as tidy as we might like. New styles may be introduced, but old ones continue, and some artists combine many at the same time. Thus, when changes in historical order have been made, they have been made to make the meaning of progression clearer.

In the modern period, with its many styles and directions, only the paintings dependent on each other have been arranged by date. Otherwise, meanings and relationships have been the guiding factors.

The selection of paintings and other works, such as maps, prints, and drawings, has caused some problems. Obviously, it is impossible to include every artist who has painted in Canada. Many excellent painters are, in fact, not represented. This applies particularly to the contemporary period, where some of Canada's best-known modern artists have been omitted. This is not because their work is not recognized for its quality, but because my choice was made to include as wide a range of artistic expression as possible within a limited number. In fact, in some cases I have selected variety over quality, believing that the wider our experience of art, the easier it becomes to recognize excellence.

To balance this situation, I have chosen to limit myself to looking at one work, or occasionally two, at a time. I myself believe that more can be learned from looking at a single painting carefully than by seeing many superficially. I also believe in looking, and looking, and looking again.

It seems to me that there are several stages a person goes through in experiencing a work of art. The first stage is instantaneous; it happens in a flash. This is the moment when, in a gallery, we might hear, 'Oh! Isn't that beautiful!' or 'Ugh! Do they call that Art?' Sadly, for many people that is the end, and they move on to the next work. It is not at all unusual to sit in an art gallery and watch a crowd pass by twenty paintings in about twenty seconds.

This is a pity, because the next stage of understanding and the one after that are often much more rewarding. By degrees, through looking and looking, the painting projects its own character, and it is then that we are really meeting and getting to know each other.

Because art is a personal expression of an individual artist, the meeting between the viewer and the work of art is also personal. Each individual is completely free to respond to a work in his own way. His opinions, beliefs, loves, and hates will obviously affect his relationship with the painting. There is no *right* way to respond to a work of art, and no one should feel embarrassed or shy about his response.

But in making a judgement, it is only fair that the person has sufficient knowledge and experience to make it, and this again reinforces the necessity of learning the language of painting. For it is a language that can be learned by anyone who takes the time and trouble.

In this book I have tried to set a selection of Canadian paintings in the context of their history, and, because most art does not emerge isolated, from a vacuum, I have also set them in the general context of the art of the Western world. Necessarily, this could only be done in a very simplified way but will, I hope, help to show how painting has developed in Canada.

I have also taken the liberty of suggesting ways in which the paintings may be 'read'. Because these interpretations are my own personal reactions to the works of art, everyone may not agree with them. I hope, though, that they may at least act as a springboard, a jumping-off place into a pool that some may feel too timid to enter alone. There is such great satisfaction and pleasure to be gained from enjoying paintings that no one should be held back merely through the lack of some helping hand.

So many people have helped me in the preparation of this book that it is impossible to name them all individually. There are, however, some to whom I particularly want to express my gratitude.

Both the Canada Council and the Ontario Arts Council gave me generous grants towards my research. This allowed me to travel from coast to coast in Canada, visiting all the major galleries. As a result, I have been able to include works that can be seen in the original in almost all the major centres. With the assistance of these grants, I have also been able to have paintings photographed that have never been reproduced in colour before.

Many artists have most graciously allowed me to reproduce their works without a fee, and many galleries have generously loaned their colour transparencies.

Gallery directors, curators, and registrars across the country have been consistently helpful and enthusiastic about the book.

I have also received a great deal of help with the necessary photographic material. Helen Clark, photograph editor for the Reproduction and Rights Department of the National Gallery, has assisted me most courteously on numerous occasions. Toni Smialowski has also kindly provided me with some excellent photographs.

Betty Cunningham and Shirley Kane have helped me overcome my typing problems, and Kay Burgess has kindly assisted with the numerous letters concerning reproduction permissions.

My particular gratitude, though, goes to my editor, Susan Gaitskell. To her I give my thanks for the superb way in which she has helped me clarify my thoughts into a simple and direct form, using constant tact and good humour.

And, finally, there is my family. To them I shall always be grateful for their continual help, encouragement, and patience, despite the many cold dinners and buttons left hanging by a thread.

PATRICIA GODSELL

Contents

ENJOYING CANADIAN PAINTING

PART I

THE EXPLORERS

circa 1546 to 1715

The earliest visual records of Canada, before the land had divisions or boundaries, are maps dating from the sixteenth and seventeenth centuries.

This was the great age of exploration and discovery. Men like Cabot, Cartier, Frobisher, Hudson, and Champlain sailed west from Europe in search of a shorter route to the rich spice lands of the East. Equipped with sturdy wooden ships, armed with guns, and spurred on by the ambition of their monarchs to find new lands and wealth, a new breed of explorers emerged. Not only were they practical leaders with knowledge and strength of purpose; they were also imaginative, intelligent men who dared to challenge the geographical theories of the Middle Ages.

The medieval mapmakers had reduced the oceans to puddles and condensed the continents into the northern hemisphere in the belief that Jerusalem was the centre of the world. They also believed that any person venturing south of the equator would certainly turn black from the scorching heat of the sun.

But the new explorers made new maps, basing them on those of Ptolemy, the Greek astronomer and geographer of the second century, and on their own more scientific information. From these early records the shape of the world as we know it today has gradually emerged.

As well as being articles of practical use, sixteenth-century maps are beautiful objects that display a high quality of craftsmanship and imagination. In the many illustrations that decorate them, fact and fantasy mingle freely. Strange and wonderful creatures stand among closely observed animals. Monstrous men with heads on their chests or oversized ears take their place beside historical figures; dolphins and mermaids play in the sea. Events were recorded with little concern for accuracy but plenty of scope for imaginative design. And all these fantasies were imposed on maps of ever-increasing geographical precision.

The notebooks kept by some of the explorers are also interesting visual records. Artistically many of the drawings are stiff and crude, though they have an appealing quality of simplicity and directness, whether they are accurate or not. Others are highly imaginative sketches with a remarkable quality of design.

Strictly speaking, some of the works in this section are neither 'Canadian' nor what is normally called 'painting'. But each one does have its own particular role to play in this book – besides supplying an interesting and attractive record of Canada's earliest days.

1

Pierre Desceliers

Mappemonde, 1546 (North American section only)
25-3/4″ x 32-1/4″ (65 cm x 82 cm)
John Rylands Library, Manchester
lithograph by M. Jomard, 1854
Public Archives of Canada, Ottawa

Detail of Mappemonde

After returning from their voyages, some explorers made maps of their own. Others gave information to mapmakers such as Pierre Desceliers, a French parish priest from the village of Arques, near Calais.

Based on information from English, Spanish, Portuguese, and French explorers, Desceliers made several large world maps. Sixteenth- and seventeenth-century mapmakers often gathered their information from many different sources, and this might partly explain the rather odd combination in their work of precise geographical accuracy and extremely fanciful decoration.

Pierre Desceliers's *Mappemonde* of 1546 is very large, measuring approximately eight feet by four feet. Although here we see only the North American section, the entire work is lavishly illustrated with figures of men and animals, both factual and fanciful; little scenes of the explorers arriving; and descriptions of particular events and customs. Among the animals are bears, wild boars, stags, and a unicorn. Among the human population the artist has included several 'noble savages' standing like Greek gods, soldiers in armour, and hunters with bows and arrows.

It is interesting that in this map the outlines of the continents in the northern hemisphere are designed to be read from one direction, while the illustrations and lettering are meant to be read from the other. In this southern hemisphere, though, everything is arranged in the same direction.

Looking at this detail, Labrador is at the bottom left and the Gulf of Mexico at the top right. But if we were viewing the whole map, the continent would be reversed and the lettering and illustrations would be upside down.

The *Mappemonde* might have been created in this way for the convenience of people sitting on opposite sides of a table with the map between them. On each side there would be some information to read,

though it would be necessary to exchange places to get the whole picture.

There are several little scenes and figures here that are especially interesting. In the centre of the map there is a seated, lightly-clad, bearded figure — resembling Moses — around whom several other figures are kneeling. This group probably represents a missionary preaching the Gospel to his pagan followers.

Though acquiring new lands and wealth was undoubtedly the main reason for voyages of discovery, there was also a sincere desire to spread the Christian faith. Even Columbus wrote of 'what I conceive to be the principal wish of our most serene king, namely the conversion of these people to the holy faith of Christ.'

There are two other small details that are particularly interesting because they have a long artistic history. One shows a reclining figure and can be found on the map below and to the left of the missionary group; the other, on the lower left of the map, depicts a pair of horsemen.

3

Detail of Mappemonde

The position chosen for the reclining figure – one knee bent, shoulders half turned, and head looking sideways – has a Classical Greek origin. It was a pose used many, many times in the decoration of Greek vases and in Greek and Roman sculpture. In the original Greek form, it was often used for nymphs and river gods, but later it was transferred to all types of figures. Through the centuries, the pose has become a type of formula for reclining human forms. This semi-nude figure is an example of the revival of Classical art in France by the artists of the Renaissance. That even a mapmaker would use the style shows how widespread the practice had become.

The detail of the riders on horseback again shows the method of borrowing a format. Equestrian figures in this pose also date back to Classical Greece and Rome. Among the most famous are the relief sculptures of galloping horses in the Parthenon temple in Athens. Since the fifth century B.C. when these sculptures were completed, many other sculptors have chosen this position as a basis for their own variations – particularly to suggest conquering heroes. It has also been used again and again in painting. For example, years later Paul Kane, a Canadian artist, used this very formula to present his Indian warrior (p. 62).

Detail of Mappemonde

Nicolas Vallard's Atlas

Detail of Map of Canada, 1546

Jacques Cartier Landing with Colonists
in 1541 at Stadacona (Quebec)
The Huntington Library, San Marino, California

Although the name Vallard is used to identify this particular map, there is no record of a mapmaker by that name. But since 'Nicolas Vallard' is inscribed on the map, it is assumed that this may be the name of the original owner of the atlas. Possibly he was a Norman merchant.

At one time the atlas belonged to Prince Talleyrand, the noted French politician and diplomat who served under Napoleon. Later it was in the collection of Sir Thomas Phillips in Cheltenham, England. From there it was brought to the United States by an American collector.

The scene shown here is Jacques Cartier's landing at Stadacona, Quebec, in 1541. The figure in the short cloak to the right of the centre of the group is probably Sieur de Roberval, the leader of this expedition. His right arm is stretched towards a man in a long black robe who is believed to be Jacques Cartier. It looks as though Roberval is attempting to calm the group's fears as he encourages them to follow the guide and meet the band of Indians on the right.

The place names on the map are a mixture of French and Spanish, though the map and decorations resemble earlier Portuguese works. This fact again suggests that the artist-cartographers who made the maps used information from several sources. In this case the artist probably added to the material that Cartier provided after his third voyage to Canada.

There are a number of interesting differences between this map and Pierre Desceliers's *Mappemonde* (p. 2) of 1546. Desceliers's figures, small and crude though they may be, are often clothed and posed in a Classical manner. In the Vallard map the artist has dressed his colonists in the clothing of the day and his Indians in animal skins, a fact that shows he received little accurate information about Indian costume. Instead, it is likely that he substi-

tuted his own ideas, based on what he knew of the European Barbarians.

The design and composition of the Vallard map are tighter and better balanced than in Desceliers's *Mappemonde*. Here the artist has emphasized the group of French gentlemen and their ladies gathered around the figures of Roberval and Cartier. The soldiers guarding them also form part of this group. The smaller group of Indians on the right balances the design and is held into it by the pointing arm of the guide. The single Indian on the left who shows the way to the newcomers is also a part of the artistic scheme.

The colours of the map are rich and alive. They have a clarity that would do justice to a stained glass window or the exquisite paintings that decorated handwritten books of the fifteenth century. The reds, yellows, and black of the central group look even brighter against the green trees and the blue in the distance.

The strong and brilliant colours of the Vallard map are very different from the pastel greens and blues that characterize Desceliers's work. Generally, up to the sixteenth century, the maps produced by the Portuguese cartographers tended to emphasize warm reds and golds, while the Italians used quieter greens and blues. The French, who did not begin painting highly decorated maps until the sixteenth century, tended to follow the Italian style.

This detail of Jacques Cartier's arrival in Canada, though only a small part of a much larger whole, is a delightful example of the art of the sixteenth-century cartographers. It is also an interesting visual record of a historical event. How unfortunate that we do not know the name of the artist.

Attributed to

Abbé Louis Nicolas

1634 – ?

from *Les Raretés des Indes (Codex Canadiensis)*
c. 1674
Thomas Gilcrease Institute, Tulsa, Oklahoma

These sketches are taken from a watercolour sketch-book dated about 1674. Though the artist is unknown, the text accompanying the sketches was written by Abbé Louis Nicolas, a French Jesuit missionary who was in New France between 1664 and 1675.

Louis Nicolas was born in Aubenas, France, in 1634 and arrived in Quebec in the summer of 1664. For three years he worked with the Algonquins at Trois-Rivières and then moved to several other missions. In 1673 he was asked to go to Sept-Iles, and there he opened the mission of St-Vital in the Saguenay district. In that area, he explains, there were seven rocky islands where the Indians would go to trade with the French after they returned from hunting. It was barren land, and life was difficult for the French missionaries.

Abbé Nicolas wrote an account of the conditions at St-Vital that was meant to be a guide for the missionaries who followed him. He also wrote *Mémoires sur le Canada*, a journal of his voyage, including a grammar of the Algonquin language. The sketches of *Les Raretés des Indes* that illustrated his experiences were probably done by him too.

Today, since natural history is based on scientific fact, some of Louis Nicolas's animals seem comical. We may even think he was deliberately exaggerating in order to catch the attention of his audience, but this is most unlikely. Much that he wrote about he actually saw, and his more fanciful sketches were probably based on information he completely believed.

Until the time when scientific statements were based on proven facts alone, natural history books were amazing blends of fact and imagination. Nicolas's book is very similar to the natural history books of the Middle Ages called bestiaries. These are delightful works containing information about many animals as well as illustrations of them.

For example, in a translation of a twelfth-century Latin bestiary there is this description of an elephant.

The Elephant's nature is that if he tumbles down he cannot get up again. Hence it comes that he leans against a tree when he wants to go to sleep, for he has no joints in his knees. This is the reason why a hunter partly saws through a tree, so that the elephant, when he leans against it, may fall down at the same time as the tree. As he falls, he calls out loudly; and immediately a large elephant appears, but it is not able to lift him up. At this, they both cry out, and twelve more elephants arrive upon the scene; but even they cannot lift up the one who has fallen down. Then they all shout for help, and at once there comes a very Insignificant Elephant, and he puts his mouth with the proboscis under the big one, and lifts him up. This little elephant has, moreover, the property that nothing evil can come near his hairs and bones when they have been reduced to ashes, not even a Dragon.

In another place we hear about the whale.

This animal lifts its back out of the open sea above the watery waves, and then it anchors itself in one place; and on its back, what with the shingle of the ocean drawn there by the gales, a level lawn gets made and bushes begin to grow there. Sailing ships that happen to be going that way take it to be an island, and land on it. Then they make themselves a fireplace. But the Whale, feeling the hotness of the fire, suddenly plunges down into the depths of the deep, and pulls down the anchored ship with it into the profound.

This bestiary was written in the twelfth century, six hundred years before Nicolas collected his information and made his drawings of the men, animals, birds, reptiles, and plants in New France. His 'scientific' information is not quite as colourful as that of the earlier bestiary, but it still shows a delightful blend of fact and fiction. He draws a sea

from *Les Raretés des Indes (Codex Canadiensis)*

horse that has the front end of a horse and the tail of a fish; he speaks of 'a mountain rat as large as a spaniel dog' (probably a beaver); he shows a mermaid and states that it 'was killed by the French on the Richelieu river in New France'. On another page he sketches these beautifully decorative whales, but makes it perfectly clear that mother whales feed their young on milk as other mammals do. This scientific accuracy means that either he, or those who gave him his information, observed nature carefully.

Many other drawings of animals, birds, and plants show close attention to scientific facts. He includes a lively drawing of one of the stallions sent from France by Louis XIV to breed with local horses and improve stock. There are also many detailed and accurate sketches of Indian tribes, their dwellings, and objects they used.

The *Codex Canadiensis*, as it has since been called, is one of the first books on Canadian natural history; it is also a careful study of Indian life. But the illustrations were not merely records of what the artist saw. Each sketch shows his strong natural feeling for design, and many of them are delightful little works of art.

Each animal displays a variety of patterns and is given a character of its own by the changing designs. There are wide, wavy bands on the sea horse, circus patterns on the galloping stallion, and a mosaic of shapes on the whales.

Nicolas also creates a wonderful feeling of movement. The stallion actually bounces along, its spots and stripes and flowing mane strengthening the rhythm. The whales, which could have been shown separately, are linked together by the sweeping stream of water curling over their backs and flowing around them. Whales they may be, but to Nicolas they are also a perfect opportunity to enjoy the effects of line and pattern.

from *Les Raretés des Indes (Codex Canadiensis)*

Hermann Moll

? – 1732

The Cataract of Niagara
insert on his map of 1715, engraving
9-1/8″ x 9-1/8″ (23 cm x 23 cm)
Public Archives of Canada, Ottawa

The Cataract of NIAGARA, some make
this water-Fall to be half a League while
others reckon it no more than
a hundred Fathom.

A View of ẙ Industry of ẙ Beavers of Canada in making Dams to stop ẙ Course of a Rivulet, in order to form a great Lake, about w.ᶜʰ they build their Habitations. To Effect this; they fell large Trees with their Teeth, in such a manner, as to make them come Cross ẙ Rivulet, to lay ẙ foundation of ẙ Dam; they make Mortar, work up, and finish ẙ whole with great order and wonderfull Dexterity. The Beavers have two Doors to their Lodges, one to the water and the other to the Land side. According to ẙ French Accounts.

Hermann Moll was born in Holland but came to England in 1680 and died there in 1732. A bookseller by trade, he was also an engraver of maps and during his lifetime made many kinds of these: miniatures, medium-sized English county maps engraved with thick black lines, and larger country and world atlases.

The works seen here are sketches that Moll inserted along the sides of his maps to decorate them. Using sketches and plans in this manner was a technique adopted by several mapmakers, though Desceliers and the artist who painted the Vallard map placed such decorations within the main body of their maps.

Hermann Moll, like other artist-cartographers, received his information from the explorers and was never actually a witness to the scenes he painted. Once again, then, his sketches display a mixture of fact and fiction. This is particularly true of his delightful scene of beavers building a dam, since the beaver had always been a source of interest and amazement to the European travellers. Exaggerated descriptions of its appearance and habits encouraged artists to sketch their own interesting, and often fanciful, ideas about this animal.

Artistically Moll's engraving is no masterpiece. But it does give us a good idea of the sort of information about the New World that a curious European public was receiving at this time. The full title of Moll's work is *The Cataract of Niagara, Some make this Water Fall to be half a league while others reckon it to be no more than half a fathom.* Below the engraving is written this gem of scientific accuracy.

A view of ye Industry of ye Beavers of Canada in making Dams to stop ye Course of a Rivulet, in order to form a great Lake about wch. they build their Habitations. To Effect this: they fell large Trees with their Teeth in such a manner as to make them Cross ye Rivulet, to lay ye foundation of ye Dam: they make Mortar, work up and finish ye whole with great order and wonderfull Dexterity. The Beavers have two doors to their Lodges, one to the Water and one to the Land side. According to ye French Accounts.

The sketch shows the beavers so remarkably well organized that they would surely impress a modern time and motion expert. Each fellow has his own job to keep the production line moving, and, at the rate they are going, it looks as if they could make a dam across the base of Niagara Falls itself. As for the appearance of the beaver, it would be hard to decide whether the animal looked more like a grizzly bear with a large, flat tail or a lion with an appetite for wood.

The small drawing on page 14 is a much more accurate, if less lively and appealing, diagram of a Newfoundland cod-fishing operation. Here we see the whole process from the arrival of the catch to the drying of the fillets on the wharf. Each stage is carefully labelled.

A. The Habit of ye Fishermen
B. The Line
C. The Manner of Fishing
D. The Dressers of ye Fish
E. The Trough into which they throw ye Cod when Dressed
F. Salt Boxes
G. The Manner of Carrying ye Cod
H. The Cleansing of ye Cod
I. A press to extract ye Oyl from ye Cod Livers
K. Casks to Receive ye Water and Blood that comes from ye Livers
L. Another Cask to receive ye Oyl
M. The Manner of Drying ye Cod

By 1718, when Moll made this sketch, the New-

The Newfoundland Cod Fishery
insert on his map of 1718, engraving
6-3/4″ x 9″ (17 cm x 23 cm)
Public Archives of Canada, Ottawa

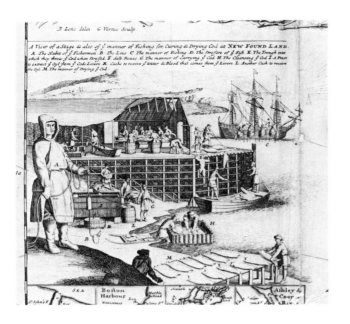

foundland cod-fishing industry had been active for almost two hundred years since Jacques Cartier first referred to it in 1534. On page 184 there is a painting by a Newfoundland fisherman who recounts his early days on the island and reminds us that, in many ways, little has changed since the time of Moll's sketch.

PART II

THE EARLY YEARS IN FRENCH
CANADA

circa 1670 to 1810

In 1608 Samuel de Champlain built the *habitation* of Quebec at the foot of the great rock on the St. Lawrence River. Constructed of wood, it served as a fort and a fur-trading post. Three years later Champlain cleared land at the meeting-place of the Ottawa and St. Lawrence rivers to establish the settlement of Montreal. And thus the colony of New France was founded, a centre for fur-trading and further exploration, as well as a base for missionary work.

It was not until 1663, twenty-eight years after the death of Champlain, that Louis XIV of France decided to give full recognition to the colony. Three leaders were appointed: a governor, Daniel de Rémy Courcelle; an intendant, Jean Talon; and a bishop, François-Xavier Laval-Montmorency. Quarrels raged among them and the governors were frequently changed. But despite their many problems, Jean Talon and Bishop Laval succeeded in establishing the roots of a French culture in Quebec.

In 1663 Bishop Laval founded the classical college of the Grand Séminaire, which later became the Université Laval. He also built many churches that were elaborately decorated by sculptors, gilders, and French-trained artists whom he brought to the colony. He founded an arts and crafts school at St-Joachim, near Quebec, where painting and sculpture were taught along with carpentry, gilding, and other skills. During this period every effort was made in New France to encourage education in the arts.

For many centuries in Europe, the church had used art as an important tool for teaching the Christian faith. It was found to be of particular value in communicating with the uneducated and illiterate, since art could teach both facts and faith by appealing to the mind and emotions. For missionaries, who had problems of language as well, paintings and sculpture were a great asset. So, in

France's new colony, where the church was strong and one of the principal aims was to convert the native Indians to Christianity, art was of considerable importance.

There was also a growing demand for decoration and paintings to fill the new churches being built in the larger centres for the European settlers. Most of the trained artists who did this work were members of the various church orders – Frenchmen who came to New France for a short time and then returned to Europe. Their abilities and talents varied. Some had received a sound training in Europe; others had had little formal art education. None were leading masters by European standards, but they brought with them a knowledge of styles and techniques that was important to the developing artistic community.

The artists born in Canada during this period were untrained. Many of them were priests or nuns. Yet much of their work has a simple charm that is appealing because of its direct and honest approach.

Other than a few non-religious works that were imported from France by the wealthier families, most of the paintings were of a religious nature. Portrait painting was popular, but, with a few exceptions, it too depended mainly upon the church. Nuns and churchmen, preserved on canvas either while alive or on their deathbeds, became examples of holiness for their younger followers.

By the end of the eighteenth century great changes were beginning to take place in the art of French Canada. The Treaty of Paris in 1763 brought an end to the war between the French and English on this continent. With the coming of peace, a new interest in painting began. Canadian artists began travelling to France to study, and European artists began settling in Canada.

Portrait painting became very popular. A new and wealthy group of merchants in Montreal and

Quebec were now commissioning portraits of themselves, their wives, and their children.

Despite the growing popularity of portraiture, the early works were generally quite simple in composition and rather stiff, though they were decorative. At this stage there was less concern with portraying the character of the sitters than with showing their outward appearance. Great attention was paid to the detail of the elaborate clothing of the day. Frilled hats and bonnets, lace cravats, and dainty fichus draped around the women's shoulders gave artists endless opportunities for fine brushwork.

Although artists were now receiving more commissions for portraits than they had in earlier years, the church was still their main patron. And the more churches that were built, the more demand there was for religious paintings to fill them. Many of these were copies of the works of the Old Masters, known from prints or older oil copies that had been imported from Europe.

There is still much to be learned about the work of these early artists in French Canada. Many of their canvases are unsigned, and little is known of them from the documents that remain. Nevertheless, it is clear that a firm foundation was laid in a remarkably short time for the fine painting to be produced during the next fifty years.

Attributed to
Frère Luc
1614–1685

La France Apportant la Foi
aux Indiens de la Nouvelle France
undated (c. 1675), oil on canvas
89-1/2" x 89-1/2" (227 cm x 227 cm)
Ursuline Convent, Quebec City

17

Frère Luc was born in Amiens, France, in 1614 and was given the secular name of Claude François. He received his early training in France under Simon Vouet, an influential Court artist and painter of small religious works. From him Claude François would have received a solid academic training, and, in keeping with the fashion at the time, François went to Rome in 1635 to complete it. There he copied the works of Raphael and other leading masters.

On returning to France he received the title of Painter to the King, Louis XIV, while working with a group of artists on the decorations for the Louvre. For some time this group worked under the direction of Nicolas Poussin, one of the greatest French artists of the seventeenth century.

After his death of his mother in 1644, Claude François gave up his secular life and entered the Recollet order as Frère Luc. He chose this name after St. Luke, the patron saint of painters, and devoted the rest of his life to painting and supervising religious works for his order.

In 1670 Frère Luc came to Canada, where he remained for fifteen months. He and five other Recollet brothers had been sent to re-establish the order in Quebec and rebuild the monastery that had been abandoned since 1629. Frère Luc designed the chapel and completed it in 1671. It is still in use in the Hôpital-Général. He was also responsible for the large altar-piece of the *Assumption of the Virgin,* which he signed and dated.

Other than the altar-piece, only four canvases are definitely thought to be his. One, the *Holy Family* at Ste-Famille church, Ile d'Orléans, was painted while he was still in Quebec. Three other works that he signed were sent back to Canada after his return to France.

Since he borrowed characteristics of style from several sources, including Poussin and his master Simon Vouet, and since he had varied training and wide interests, it is difficult to determine which paintings Frère Luc actually did. A number of unsigned and undated works have been attributed to him – probably more than he could possibly have painted during the time he was in Canada.

La France Apportant la Foi aux Indiens de la Nouvelle France (p. 17) is one of the paintings attributed to Frère Luc. At present it hangs in the inner chapel for the nuns at the Ursuline Convent in Quebec City. This work, like most religious paintings of the time, was intended to help the missionaries teach the Christian faith to the Indians, but it was also designed to avoid a serious problem that had caused arguments within the church since its earliest days.

Some churchmen believed that art was a valuable tool to teach the faith; others believed that paintings and sculpture could too easily become objects of worship instead of objects of instruction. They feared that the Fourth Commandment (Thou shalt not make unto thee any graven image) was broken by those who knelt before paintings and sculpture, forgetting that they were only works of art. But Frère Luc's painting is allegorical, designed to show that we must worship God above and not the painted canvas.

The use of allegory in painting and literature is an old tradition. Basically, its method is to present one thing but to mean another. Some allegories, like parables, are designed to simplify a subject in order to teach it. In such a case, an idea is presented in familiar terms that will be understood easily by the viewer. In other cases, allegories are deliberately complicated in order to tease the viewer into working out the hidden meaning.

Though allegory was used as far back as the Middle Ages, it became a favourite type of painting in the sixteenth and seventeenth centuries. Frère Luc undoubtedly knew of, and probably saw, Peter Paul Rubens's series of allegorical paintings that hung in the Luxembourg Palace in Paris. In these works, painted for Marie de' Medici, the widow of Henry IV and mother of Louis XIII, Rubens glorified his subject with skill and splendour.

Frère Luc's painting is a humbler cousin of that ambitious series. It is a beautiful painting, soft in colour and rhythmic in design, though there are some obvious technical weaknesses. The figures are stiff and the perspective inexact; nevertheless, it is an appealing work.

The female figure, France, stands before the ship that brought her as Queen to her colony. It is decorated with her flags, and she wears a robe embroidered with fleurs-de-lis, as does the Indian subject kneeling before her. Behind him two simple huts displaying crosses suggest the primitive dwellings of the mission settlement. France is presenting the Indian with a painting, a symbol of the faith.

The device of a picture within a picture, also used by Rubens in his Marie de' Medici cycle, is a skilful way of contrasting the material world with the spiritual one. The small painting shows a holy scene presided over by God the Father, but France points upwards to the real spiritual gathering of the Holy Trinity in Heaven. The warning is clear: a work of art is merely a symbol of faith in the Eternal Truth; in itself, it is not an object of worship.

Pierre Le Ber

1669–1707

Marguerite Bourgeoys, 1700, oil on canvas
24-1/2″ x 19-1/2″ (62 cm x 50 cm)
Congrégation de Notre-Dame, Montreal

One of the most remarkable paintings we have from the early days of French Canada is this portrait of Marguerite Bourgeoys, painted on her deathbed. It is the work of Pierre Le Ber and is the only painting among the many resembling his style that has definitely been attributed to him.

Le Ber came from a wealthy Montreal family. His sister Jeanne Le Ber was a famous recluse who lived for nineteen years in a chapel of the church of the Congrégation de Notre-Dame. While she was there, she embroidered many exquisite vestments and altar-hangings, many of which still survive. She had learned her craft from the Ursuline sisters, who also taught this skill to the Indians. It has been suggested that the Huron taste for richly decorated costumes is largely the result of the sisters' teachings.

Le Ber was not only a talented artist; he was also a very generous man who contributed his money and talents towards the founding of a charitable home in Montreal for the old and the destitute. He also designed a chapel and a stone house for the community of Les Frères Charon or, more formally, Les Hospitaliers de St. Joseph de la Croix, which was established in 1700.

Marguerite Bourgeoys, the subject of the painting, was the foundress of the great teaching order of the Congrégation de Notre-Dame, one of the most influential institutions for women in New France. In 1657 she opened the first school in Montreal, and later, because of her good work, the church officially recognized her as a saint. Her portrait, originally commissioned by the sisters of the Congrégation, is still in the collection of that order.

Although it is one of the earliest portraits painted in New France, it has great appeal for us today as one of the most 'modern'. The artist has rejected the temptation of depicting his subject as some sort of ideal of goodness or piety, although many artists of his day would have done exactly this. Instead, Le Ber has chosen a stark, dramatic presentation that borders on abstraction.

He uses no literary props or stage scenery to present his subject. Relying solely on his own artistic talent, Le Ber carefully reveals the character of Marguerite Bourgeoys. His composition is strong; his lines are sensitive and expressive, and his colours of black, white, and ochre are sombre. All these suggest the strength of the character he depicts. We can sense the hardships that she endured in her sharp and angular features. Le Ber has used the jagged movement of the white cloth surrounding her face to emphasize this idea.

The bold white areas of her garments also have an emotional effect rather than a descriptive one. They tell us little about her actual costume. But there is drama in the shapes, and they too contribute to the feeling of austerity that plays so central a role in this painting.

But just as much a part of the sister's character as her severe self-discipline is her humility and faith. The artist has skilfully suggested these qualities in his gently curving arrangement of her hands. Together with the cross over which they are clasped, they form a soft oval unit, echoing the shape of her head. In combining line and shape, softness and harshness, Le Ber has revealed the dual nature of Marguerite Bourgeoys.

Sister Marie Barbier

c. 1663 – 1739

The Christ Child, late seventeenth century, oil on canvas
15-3/4" x 13-3/4" (40 cm x 35 cm)
Congrégation de Notre-Dame, Montreal

This little painting is thought to be the work of Sister Marie Barbier, who was the first Montreal woman to enter the Congrégation de Notre-Dame under Marguerite Bourgeoys. From the age of fourteen she had lived with the sisters of the Congrégation and later became a full member of the order.

It is said that while she was a novice, Sister Barbier was especially devoted to the Infant Jesus. From Him she sought forgiveness for the sins of her youth that had haunted her with guilt. She spoke to Him regularly and always asked His help in her daily duties. She even hung this little painting above the bread ovens so that the loaves made in His honour would not be burned. The image of the Christ Child, crude though it is in many ways, has a forcefulness that comes from Sister Barbier's simple, stylized method.

Like the details of the *Mappemonde* by Pierre Desceliers (p. 2), the pose of this figure also has a long history. In the early days of the Christian church, Christ was often painted in this position – standing upright with the palms of His hands turned forward, displaying the nail wounds He received on the cross. Because this pose symbolized Christ's suffering for man's redemption, even this little figure, painted in the simplest fashion, carried a powerful message.

Anonymous

Ex-Voto de Monsieur Edouin, 1712, oil on canvas
64″ x 44″ (163 cm x 112 cm)
Commemorative Chapel, Ste-Anne de Beaupré

An ex-voto is a work painted 'out of gratitude' to St. Anne, mother of the Virgin Mary, for the outcome of a miracle. Often these pictures were painted after an escape from sudden death in an accident or after recovery from an illness. They were then hung in the entrance vestibules of village churches, where they served to remind the congregation of the grace and mercy of St. Anne.

During the seventeenth and eighteenth centuries a number of ex-votos were painted in French Canada; many were done by untrained artists whose names have not been recorded. Several of them may be found at Ste-Anne de Beaupré, the major shrine to the saint in the province of Quebec.

Because the ex-votos told a story and because they were painted by untrained, or naïve, artists, they have a simplicity and directness that give them a special charm. But the better ones, and they do vary greatly in quality, are also interesting because of their style.

The ex-votos belong to a large group of paintings variously called primitive, folk, or naïve art. While differences can be noted among these three categories, the style of untrained artists, who painted in different times and in different places all over the world, remains curiously similar. We shall be looking at several examples, produced in different parts of Canada at different times, not only for the sheer pleasure of enjoying them, but also to observe the special qualities that all naïve paintings share.

The *Ex-Voto de Monsieur Edouin* (p. 23) is much larger than most, not only because of its physical size, but also because of the artistic presentation. The design is bold and fills the canvas with a sense of conviction. It has been suggested that it was painted by Michel Dessaillant de Richeterre, a painter who used similar physical and artistic dimensions in another ex-voto showing a miracle at sea. But as yet

there is not definite proof that he was the artist.

Monsieur Charles Edouin was the captain of the barque *Sainte Anne,* which had been sent to report on the English plans to attack the French in 1709. A terrible storm overtook the ship on its journey, but the prayers of the ship's priest were answered and no lives were lost. In gratitude for their rescue from danger, M. Edouin commissioned this work, which he gave to Ste-Anne de Beaupré in 1712.

When we first look at the painting, our attention is instantly attracted by the three most important aspects of the story: the ship, the huge waves, and St. Anne. On closer inspection, we can see the details that add to the drama: the broken bowsprit, the falling masts and rigging, the frightened men on board, and most important, the priest praying and pointing upwards to a concerned St. Anne.

Three bodiless cherubs float above the saint. Possibly the foreshortening of their bodies would have caused problems for the artist, who does not seem to show a trained knowledge of drawing. We can see that the perspective of the stern of the ship gave him trouble and that St. Anne's hands are deliberately placed parallel to the canvas to avoid further difficulties.

But none of this destroys the direct force of the painting. Not knowing how to reproduce his ideas in a realistic form, the artist has relied on the power of design and pattern. The waves, for example, have been arranged in repeated curling shapes that reach a climax in the centre. They are echoed by the curves of the clouds and even by the little angels' wings. In this way the artist has given a sense of unity to the canvas.

Monsieur Edouin is one of the most impressive examples of French-Canadian ex-voto painting. But there are many others, some of them quite small, that are also delightful.

The *Ex-Voto des Trois Naufragés de Lévis* was

painted after a tragic canoe crossing from Lévis to Quebec. The St. Lawrence was very rough, and the canoe overturned. Two boys and a young girl managed to climb on top of it, but two other girls were drowned. The ex-voto, though rather crude artistically, gives a vivid description of the scene, which is observed by a motherly St. Anne cushioned upon woolly clouds.

Another ex-voto was painted as the result of a woodsman's accident. A tree he was chopping fell in the wrong direction and pinned him to the ground. After praying to St. Anne, she appeared to him in a vision and instructed him to soak a piece of the bark in his blood, give it to his dog, and order the dog to take it back to the village as a sign of his misfortune. After he was rescued by the villagers, the woodsman had an ex-voto painted in praise of the mercy of the saint.

In each case the ex-votos referred to specific incidents. For this reason they are very human documents, painted with faith and sincerity. What some may lack in artistic skill, they gain in an appealing story. Yet the *Ex-Voto de Monsieur Edouin* is a fine naïve painting, a type of art that is at last receiving the serious attention it deserves.

Attributed to
Michel Dessaillant de Richeterre
active 1701 – 1723

Ex-Voto de l'Ange gardien, c. 1707, oil on canvas
46-1/2″ x 33″ (118 cm x 84 cm)
Hôtel-Dieu, Quebec City

As is the case with other artists painting in these early days, little is known about Michel Dessaillant. A number of works that he may or may not have painted have been attributed to him. He is credited, though, with having done several other ex-votos, including that of *Monsieur Edouin* (p. 23).

Monsieur Edouin and *L'Ange gardien* differ so completely in style that it seems most unlikely both were done by the same artist. Still, they do share a feeling of monumentality, a sense of grandeur and scale regardless of the actual size of a canvas.

It is known that Dessaillant based *L'Ange gardien* on an earlier French Baroque engraving. This practice of copying a painting from an engraving was a common one and was in no way thought to be unethical. The process of transformation is actually rather fascinating to study. Just as the entire style of a painting can be altered by an engraver, so an engraving, in the hands of an artist, can blossom into a complete oil painting.

In *L'Ange gardien* there is no evidence of the dry, mechanical repetition that can result from copying. Dessaillant has borrowed a form and used it creatively, giving his painting a moving contrast of strength and tenderness.

The huge angel dominates the scene. He is more symbolic than real, representing a supernatural power that seems to engulf the little girl. His immense legs, though actually out of proportion, are as solid as stone columns, yet his arm curves around the child with controlled gentleness. Her lovely, softly modelled face and her hands, held together in prayer, are touching in their innocence. Yet they lack any of the cloying sweetness that so often spoils the portraits of children.

L'Ange gardien is a Baroque painting. Unfortunately, the term Baroque is very difficult to define, and many critics believe it should not be used at all. Yet like the terms Classical and Romantic, which we

shall consider later, it is useful to describe a variable set of feelings and a general state of mind. It is unwise, though, to use such terms rigidly in order to make history tidy.

Baroque art was the product of the seventeenth century in Europe. But all seventeenth-century art is not Baroque, and the style is not confined to this period alone. It is an art of strong emotions, both felt and displayed. Size, weight, and swinging movement are expressed in grand diagonal compositions that reject the quiet completeness of the circle. Life is portrayed in action, within time that is passing. Events are caught as they are actually happening; they are not frozen into a moment of timelessness.

Michel Dessaillant's enormous angel, his wings outspread and his robes swirling as he arrives on earth, has a quality of strength and emotion that is typically Baroque.

This Baroque quality is further strengthened by the composition of the painting, which is organized on a strong diagonal. Starting from the lower left, it moves up through the child's red sash and the grouping of her hands and head, along the arms of the angel who points upwards, and finally ends in the sun and the heavenly seat of God. A series of weaker diagonals in the opposite direction balance the force of the main diagonal and hold the painting within its canvas. The angel's wing, his flying robes, the angle of his head and left foot, the little girl's hands and the sloping rocks beside her, all have a stabilizing effect.

L'Ange gardien is a powerful painting that is more a symbol of faith than an attempt to be realistic. Technically it is naïve in many ways, but it does show the sincerity of emotion that is the one necessary quality of all true art.

François Beaucourt

1740-1794

Portrait de Marguerite Mailhot, épouse
d'Eustache-Ignace Trottier dit Des Rivières, 1793
oil on canvas
31-1/2″ x 26-5/16″(80 cm x 67 cm)
Musée du Québec, Quebec City

François Beaucourt was born in Laprairie, near Montreal, in 1740. He received his earliest instruction from his father Paul Beaucourt, a principal ex-voto painter of the late eighteenth century, and later studied in France. At the age of about forty-six, Beaucourt returned to Canada and undertook various commissions for the church. In about 1792 he settled in Montreal, where the following advertisement appeared in the *Gazette* of June 28.

BEAUCOURT, Canadian Painter. Member of the Academy of Painting, Sculpture and Civil and Naval Architecture of Bordeaux, aggregated to that of Paris. Begs leave to inform the amateurs of those arts, that he paints Portraits in oil; also executes historical, and landscape painting. He undertakes to paint theatrical scenery. Having made geometrical and aerial perspective his particular study, he has met with considerable encouragement in several Cities of Europe, viz. Paris, Petersburg, Nantz, Bordeaux, & c, in which he followed his art as a profession. He understands the art of ornamenting, in the newest stile and taste, apartments, by painting to imitate either architecture, baso-relievos, flowers, or the arabesque stile. He will undertake to teach a few students in any branch of drawing agreeable to their wish and taste.

Apply at Mr. Belair, near St. Laurent's Gate No. 9 Montreal, June 4, 1792

This portrait of Madame Des Rivières matches one of her husband Eustache-Ignace dit Des Rivières; both works delightfully portray a moment of leisure in the lives of well-established French-Canadians. Madame Des Rivières is seen opening a gold caddy in order to prepare tea in her elegant samovar, while her husband, in his velvet coat and lace cravat, passes his time wagering at cards.

The style of the portrait of Madame Des Rivières was undoubtedly influenced by Beaucourt's experiences in Paris. While he was there, he would have seen the work of the leading French Rococo artists and met many of their pupils. Boucher, one of the principal Rococo painters, was dead by that time, and Fragonard, his most famous pupil and successor, had completed his major works. Nevertheless, while Beaucourt was in Paris, there was still a demand for the decorative portraits and light-hearted pieces that were typical of the Rococo style.

The term Rococo comes from the French word *rocaille,* meaning 'rock-work'. It was probably suggested by the arrangements used around simple fountains and in informal gardens. But the word Rococo itself refers to a particular style of decoration where small curves and lightly curling forms ornament furniture, porcelain, gold and silver work, and tapestries. In fact, Rococo affected all the visual arts, including painting. Pretty curving forms were combined with pastel colours, mirrors, and light, airy spaces to create an atmosphere of liveliness and gaiety.

Beaucourt's portrait of Madame Des Rivières, while rather stiff, is delightfully decorative in the true Rococo manner. The artist has obviously enjoyed painting the patterned folds and dainty pleats of the lady's bonnet. The spots on her fichu, the ruffled lace, and the clarity of the miniature around her neck suggest a strong love of detail.

The little still life of the dainty samovar, cup, saucer, and jug is particularly fascinating. When Beaucourt was in Paris, he would have seen many portraits in which small lifes had been introduced. This custom, which originated in fifteenth-century Flemish painting, had remained popular in European portraiture. The still life that Beaucourt has introduced into his painting places the work in a long historical tradition. It also shows how, even in small details, European art affected developments in Canada.

PART III

THE BRITISH ARMY VISITORS

circa 1757 to 1840

In 1756 England formally declared war on France. The following seven years of hostilities between the two countries brought many British troops to the shores of North America. Among them were a number of topographical artists whose job it was to make accurate drawings of towns and land forms for military records. Since photography had not yet been invented, this was the only means the armies had of making visual records for official use. Thus, army cadets with a talent for drawing were trained at British military academies by professional artists.

Topographers, such as Hermann Moll, had been working in Canada long before the arrival of the English military artists. But it was not until the arrival of these artists at the outset of the Seven Years' War that topographical watercolours were produced in large numbers. While most of the topographers were British officers, there was one important Canadian topographer. He was Joseph Bouchette (1774–1841) of Montreal, who eventually became Surveyor General of Canada and published topographical books illustrated with his own sketches.

Watercolour painting was becoming very popular in England at this time. The eighteenth century was the age of the Grand Tour, when fashionable English gentlemen and their ladies travelled through Europe absorbing the culture. As souvenirs of their travels for themselves and their less fortunate friends, they brought home pictures of the places and things they had seen. Just as we buy coloured postcards, they bought oil and watercolour paintings.

Two very different artists, Canaletto, who painted large, very accurate views of Venice, and Salvator Rosa, who painted more imaginative scenes, both sold well to the British tourists. They and other leading French and Italian landscape artists also had a great influence upon the development of topographical painting. But among amateurs and professionals alike, it was the watercolour medium that was particularly favoured in England.

The English army topographers who came to Canada were trained to make accurate visual records, not works of art. Yet their teachers were professional artists, sensitive to changing styles in painting, and as a result many differences of style can be found among the works of the British topographers. Some, of course, are simply individual characteristics, but others are undoubtedly the result of changing fashions.

The best of the topographers went beyond the influences of fashion to produce true works of art; the less talented painted according to certain accepted rules. A comment in the official records of the Royal Military Academy at Woolwich rather nicely protected the reputation of the artist-teachers.

As drawing is an accomplishment which depends in a great measure upon genius, it should not be expected that every Gentleman Cadet should be an expert draughtsman.

But to prevent disastrous results, they added that to pass the course '...it is intended to strictly require certificates of diligence from the Drawing Master'.

Many of the paintings of the military topographers were not produced for official purposes but were painted for pleasure in their spare time. Some were later made into engravings and aquatints and used as illustrations for books. As a result, the subject matter covers a wide range of topics from landscapes to scenes of social gatherings and events in the rural life of Canada. Birds and animal studies, scenes of Indian encampments, and an occasional interior view were also painted.

There were a number of amateur artists among

the wives of the military officers and among other visitors to the British North American colonies. Victorian ladies were expected to be able to draw and paint in watercolours, and many of them would spend hours recording their surroundings and experiences. Groups of friends would gather for sketching parties as a means of relieving the monotony of their confined daily lives. Few masterpieces emerged from these events, but the results were treasured as mementos of the colony. Today they are also valued as interesting and important historical records of life in Canada in the early nineteenth century.

The works of four British army topographical artists are included in this section of the book. The paintings have been selected not only for their quality, but also for their variety of style and subject matter. Of course, there are other military watercolourists whose work deserves equal attention.

Hervey Smyth, aide-de-camp to General Wolfe, and Richard Short, purser of H.M.S. *Prince of Orange,* were both amateur artists who came to Canada in the early stages of the Seven Years' War. Colonel J.F.W. DesBarres illustrated a set of naval maps that were published in the *Atlantic Neptune.* James Peachey, who became Surveyor General of Canada, painted a number of scenes of the Loyalist refugees making their encampment in Canada. These men, together with the four represented here, are among the best known of the British military topographers.

Thomas Davies

c. 1737–1812

A View of the River La Puce near Quebec,
North America, 1789, watercolour
13-1/4″ x 20-1/4″ (34 cm x 51 cm)
The National Gallery of Canada, Ottawa

Of all the British army topographers working in
Canada at this time, Thomas Davies was the best
artist. He looked at the world with sharp, clear eyes
that saw every detail around him. But he also had
the gift of selecting his details and organizing them
into general patterns. In spite of the artistic training
that he received, Davies retained a style of his own.
In many ways it was closer to that of the best naïve,
or untrained, painters than it was to the soft and
gentle landscapes that were painted by many English artists of his time.

Davies was born about 1737 of parents who were
probably Welsh. When he joined the army at the age
of eighteen, he entered the Royal Military Academy
at Woolwich. There he studied under Paul Sandby,
who is sometimes called the father of English
watercolour painting. Sandby influenced the styles
of many of the young topographers, but he had little
effect on Davies's work. Perhaps, though, he did
encourage him towards the sense of breadth and
spaciousness that is evident in his later paintings.

In 1756 Davies was appointed Lieutenant-
Fireworker, the lowest rank of an officer in the
Royal Artillery. The next year he was sent to

33

A View of the Bridge on the River La Puce, 1790
watercolour
13-3/8″ x 20-1/4″ (34 cm x 51 cm)
The National Gallery of Canada, Ottawa

Halifax and spent much of his military career in different parts of North America. During his travels Davies painted many landscapes in watercolour. A keen student of nature, he also did a number of wildlife studies and was particularly noted for his knowledge of birds.

In 1787 he began a watercolour series of Quebec scenes in which some of his finest work is included. All of the paintings but one were bought by the National Gallery of Canada when they were sold in England in 1953.

These two views on the Rivière-Sault-à-la-Puce near Quebec were part of this series. They show Davies's ability to combine a strong sense of design with a deep understanding of nature. He has searched every object for its underlying pattern and has combined them all into a broad design. Though each tree and leaf can be seen separately as a particular object, it is also a part of one overall scheme.

This is what gives Davies's work its feeling of timelessness. He shows us a world that is eternal because it has a form and pattern that will be repeated over and over again. When this set of leaves drops from these trees, another set will come and form a similar design. The ripples on the water will constantly change, but as long as there is a river, patterns like these will continue to form.

Davies also introduces delightful little details into his paintings, which add interest and character to each one. In the view of the river (p. 33) there are a number of small figures that are barely noticeable until we look closely at the scene. On the right a bear is coming out of the woods, and on the left a hunter and his dog come down to the water's edge. Farther up the river a man stands looking out over the scene from a high rock.

The view of the farm is also rich in small details that are part of everyday life. A horse and cart are used to move a canoe up from the river, perhaps to portage some rapids. A couple passes the time as they look over the bridge. A buggy brings a man and woman home. Each one is an individual episode, but, taken together, they all describe the events of a day on that farm.

It is this relationship of parts to a whole that gives a universal quality to a work of art. It suggests that all things in all times and in all places are related. Painted in bright, clear colours and bathed in light, Davies's pictures are both beautiful and thoughtful. Far from being mere topographical illustrations, they are true works of art.

Davies has often been compared with Henri Rousseau (1844–1910), one of the most famous of all amateur, or naïve, artists, whose works now hang in galleries throughout the world. Both artists share the same strong feeling for design, and both create the same kind of dream-world atmosphere. Yet strangely enough, neither could have known of the work of the other.

We are left, it seems, with an interesting puzzle, involving not only Davies and Rousseau, but also the history of art itself. While we may ponder the question of how an artist develops his style, we must accept that there are no final answers, and that in the end this process still remains a mystery.

James Cockburn

1778–1847

The Falls of Montmorency, 1829–1830
coloured aquatint and etching
17-1/3" x 26-1/3" (44 cm x 67 cm)
Royal Ontario Museum, Toronto

James Cockburn, like Thomas Davies, received his training in military topography while he was an officer cadet at the Royal Military Academy at Woolwich. There, between 1793 and 1795, he studied the art of drawing and landscape painting under the direction of Paul Sandby.

Having published several books of European views, Cockburn is one of the better-known topographical artists. Wealthy Englishmen of the eighteenth century who undertook the Grand Tour of the Continent were anxious to purchase souvenirs of their journeys. A rapidly expanding reading public with romantic tastes also wanted to see pictures of far-away places. As a result, Cockburn's

book, *Quebec and its Environs,* written and illustrated while he was serving in Canada between 1826 and 1832, sold well in England and Canada alike.

Davies and Cockburn both studied under Sandby at Woolwich, but their styles and choice of subject matter differed greatly. Davies preferred to paint almost pure landscapes, introducing figures as details rather than subjects. Cockburn, on the other hand, evidently enjoyed society, and his watercolours are full of interesting and distinctive characters, tiny though they are.

Yet in comparison with Davies, Cockburn tends to be more an illustrator of what he saw than an

36

artist with a strong personal vision or creative imagination. Cockburn obviously enjoyed depicting scenes of life around him and did so in a delightful manner. But it seems that, unlike Davies, he seldom penetrated his subject in order to find its universal and timeless qualities. Even so, his watercolours have great charm and tell us much about the life of the British visitors in Canada.

Here, for instance, a group of elegant ladies and gentlemen admire the view of Montmorency Falls. Visits to Montmorency were popular social events in winter and summer alike and were a common subject for every artist and writer. No diary or description of Quebec would have been complete without an account of a picnic or sleighing party at the Falls. Perhaps in keeping with his interest in people, Cockburn painted many more street scenes than Davies, who produced only one.

To help him with perspective and topographical detail, it is said Cockburn used a *camera lucida.* This was a darkened box-like device that contained a prism and mirrors. Any view could be reflected through the *camera* onto a sheet of paper, where an outline was revealed that the artist then traced. Canaletto, the famous eighteenth-century Italian painter of topographical views, had used the *camera obscura,* a similar but simpler device that had been invented in the sixteenth century.

Cockburn illustrated his books with watercolours. But for publication, since photography was not yet available, prints had to be made from the original paintings. Engraving and etching were the most popular printing methods, though many pupils of Paul Sandby were using aquatint (p. 39), a process introduced by him into England.

Engraving and etching are both intaglio methods of printmaking where the lines of the design are carved into the printing plate. These differ from relief methods where the surrounding material is removed, leaving the design above the surface.

To engrave, the artist inscribes his lines directly onto a metal plate, which is usually made of copper. He uses an instrument that makes a V-shaped trough. The quality and tone of the lines depend upon the depth and width of the cut. The deeper the line, the more ink it holds, and therefore the darker it will be. This technique demands great control, since the surface of the plate is slippery and the engraving tool has to be pushed ahead of the hand.

To etch, the artist covers his plate with an acid-resisting surface, usually wax. This surface is then blackened with candle smoke, and on it the artist draws his design with a sharp instrument like a needle. This allows the artist greater freedom and control than he has when engraving on the slippery plate. When the design is complete, the underside and edges of the plate are protected with lacquer, and the whole plate is immersed in a shallow bath of acid. The acid eats into the lines that have penetrated the wax surface. The plate is then removed, and those areas that are to be light in tone are covered with lacquer. Again the plate is immersed and the acid bites deeper into the remaining lines. The process is repeated again and again. The lines that are left open until the final bath will be the deepest and therefore the darkest in tone.

In printing, the plates that are engraved and those that are etched are treated in the same way. Ink is spread across them, and then the surface is wiped clean. Dampened paper, more absorbent than dry, is laid on the plate that is then put through a press. The damp paper will draw the ink from the lines, and the design, with its varying tones, will be printed on it.

Because Cockburn produced so many watercolours that were later copied as engravings and etchings, he is one of the best known of the military topographers. His lively style and individual treatment of each tiny character also give a vivid and delightful description of his personal experiences in Quebec.

George Heriot

1766–1844

Lake St. Charles near Quebec, c. 1800, watercolour
10-11/16" x 17-1/2" (27 cm x 44 cm)
The National Gallery of Canada, Ottawa

George Heriot also attended the Royal Military Academy at Woolwich, where he trained under Paul Sandby. But unlike many other topographical artists, he came to Canada as a civilian in the army paymaster's department rather than as an officer.

In 1800, nine years after he arrived in Canada, he was appointed Deputy Postmaster General of British North America, a post he held for sixteen years. In this capacity he travelled extensively through Upper and Lower Canada and the Maritime colonies, sketching many views and collecting material for his books. One volume of *A History of Canada* appeared in 1804, and *Travels Through the Canadas* was published in 1807. Both

books were illustrated with aquatints made from his own sketches. In 1816 Heriot resigned his position and returned to England after a serious disagreement with Sir George Drummond, Administrator of Lower Canada.

Of the many topographers who received their training from Paul Sandby, George Heriot was one of his closest followers. Sandby himself had studied topographical draftsmanship in the first half of the eighteenth century. His training had been strict, and so he was critical of the new methods that he thought were becoming a 'wild rumble-tumble (or anything else you please) of pencilling'. But these new methods did inspire some of the greatest

38

English watercolour painters, and Sandby did much to influence them. It is for this reason that he is sometimes called the father of English watercolour painting.

Sandby was a close observer of nature and made many studies of trees to learn their individual characteristics. But, in general, he based his style on that of Claude Lorraine (1600–1682), the great French landscape painter who recorded nature in a more ideal than realistic way. Claude's gentle pastoral scenes, framed by trees and quietly fading into the horizon, were very popular in England. In fact, they were so popular that landscape gardens were deliberately planned and planted in order to improve on nature as Claude had done in his paintings.

George Heriot's style, as seen in *Lake St. Charles,* owes much to Claude, or at least to Claude as he was interpreted by Paul Sandby. Heriot's composition is close to one that Claude used repeatedly. A large group of trees on one side is balanced by a smaller group on the other; both frame the scene. In the foreground a few figures, here a boat with fishermen, seem to belong to the landscape itself. A middle distance is emphasized by the lightness of the lake, a few more figures, and the suggestion of other trees. The far distant mountains fade away into a misty light. Heriot used his watercolours fluidly, gradually lowering the strength of his tones from foreground to background. It is this treatment of watercolours that sets Heriot's work apart from that of the other topographers we have seen.

In order to reproduce the graded, translucent effect of watercolour washes in printing, Paul Sandby adopted the technique of aquatint. The method is said to have been invented in France around 1750, but Sandby was the first artist to use it effectively in England. George Heriot's two books were illustrated with aquatints made from his watercolour originals.

The aquatint process is basically a tonal one, whereas engraving and etching are more linear. As we have seen (p. 37), tones can be achieved very skilfully in engraving and etching. But these techniques depend upon cutting lines into an even surface, and because of this the lines tend to look more obvious than they do in the aquatint process.

In aquatint, as in etching, the surface of a metal plate is covered. But in aquatint the artist applies a layer of fine particles of resin, or another similar material. The way in which the acid penetrates this surface depends on how fine or how coarse the particles are. After the resinous layer is applied, the plate is heated. The warmth melts each particle into an acid-resisting dot, and on this surface the artist inscribes his design. When the plate is submerged in the acid bath, the acid eats around the melted dots. As in etching, the areas that are to be the lightest are the first to be covered with lacquer. In printing, the darkest tones are produced by the areas exposed to the acid bath the greatest number of times. Since tones can be blended gradually by using the aquatint process, it was an excellent method of translating Heriot's wash drawings and liquid watercolours into prints.

Sir Richard Levinge

1811 – 1844

Salmon Fishing by Torchlight,
New Brunswick, c. 1836
watercolour
9-5/8″ x 15″ (24 cm x 38 cm)
Public Archives of Canada, Ottawa

Sir Richard Levinge was an officer in the Forty-third Monmouthshire Light Infantry and was sent to Saint John, New Brunswick, in 1835. In 1837 rebellion broke out in both Upper and Lower Canada, and that winter Levinge's regiment marched to Montreal. In 1840 he left the infantry with the rank of captain and returned to England, where he retired from the army three years later.

As well as painting many watercolours while he was in Canada, Levinge also wrote several books. In one, *Echoes from the Backwoods* (1846), he gives a colourful and detailed account of life in the Canadian bush, including a description of the custom of salmon fishing at night. The salmon gathered in

deep pools at the foot of waterfalls, and the Indians lured them to the surface, using torches that they carried in their canoes.

Nothing can be more exciting than this scene – the canoes hurled about in all directions by the foaming tides, the skill displayed by the Indians in forcing them up the rapids, and fending them off the rocks, or allowing them to plunge head-foremost downstream, when they suddenly bring them to, and transfix their fish. The eagerness of the chase, the contrast of the flaming torches with the black masses of the woods, and the fine attitudes of the men, dashing at the salmon with their long spears, form a wild and most animating picture.

First view of the River St. Lawrence by
the leading Company 43ᵈ Reg.ᵗ on March from
New Brunswick to Canada
across the Madawaska Portage, 23ᵈ Dec.ʳ 1837.
watercolour, 8″ x 10-3/8″ (20 cm x 26 cm)
Public Archives of Canada, Ottawa

Levinge was so impressed by this sight that he painted it in watercolour.

In another of his books, *Records of the 43rd Regiment Monmouthshire Light Infantry* (1868), Levinge describes the long winter march from New Brunswick to Montreal. The march continued despite temperatures as low as thirty degrees Fahrenheit below zero and must have been a terrible ordeal for the men. Levinge describes the experiences of a friend who arrived cold and tired at

a wretched log camp...open at the top, smoking so dreadfully that we could not open our eyes; a bed of pine branches, a supper of salt pork, biscuit and unmilked tea in a tin pot, the heat of the fire singeing our moccasins, whilst our fur caps were frozen hard to the walls of the hut, the snow on the roof melted by the fire, dripping through on our luxurious couch.

As part of his account of the march Levinge included this watercolour, depicting the arrival of the infantry at the St. Lawrence River.

Both works reveal a dramatic style that is totally different from that of the other topographical artists. Davies's sense of design tends to control even his dramatic scenes; Cockburn's character sketches are interesting, but not exciting; and Heriot chose to tame and refine his subject matter.

Levinge, though, often seems to have searched for the excitement in a situation. In *Salmon Fishing by Torchlight* this is very clear. Perhaps the drama is less obvious in *First View of the River St. Lawrence*, but it is still present.

Levinge has organized the foreground of this painting into a strong V-shape by placing a line of soldiers on the right and a row of houses and chimney smoke on the left. Row upon row of ice ridges slash across the painting in the middle ground. Behind are mountain peaks, arranged in another series of repeated forms.

The composition alone creates a forbidding scene, but Levinge has further emphasized the feeling of starkness by his treatment of the figures. The soldiers silhouetted along the ridge seem to have lost their human quality and are reduced to triangular shapes. The central figure, his cape flying in the wind, also looks more symbolic than real.

Although it is easy to over-analyze such a tiny watercolour, it is interesting to see what powerful effects can be achieved through composition, even on a scale this small. It is also fascinating to see the considerable differences in style among the works of these four army officers, whose basic artistic training was directed towards accurately recording places and events, rather than creating works of art.

PART IV

THE SECOND HALF OF THE
NINETEENTH CENTURY

circa 1840 to 1910

In 1840 Upper and Lower Canada were united by the passing of the Act of Union. This brought an end to the open rebellions that had torn both colonies during the 1830s. The threat of further warfare between the United States and Canada had also been removed, and both countries turned their attention towards internal development. Once peace had been restored, immigrants arrived from all parts of Europe. Among them were artists who brought to Canada the styles and subject matter popular in their homelands.

Montreal, Quebec City, and York (now Toronto) were the three centres of wealth and power in Canada. But, except in Quebec City, where painting had reached a high level of quality and popularity, it was difficult for an artist to make a living from his commissions alone.

There was continued interest in portraiture in Protestant Ontario. And even in Quebec, where religious works were still in demand, portrait painting was a significant source of income for many artists.

By the middle of the nineteenth century, the choice of subject matter was becoming much wider. Pure landscapes of town and country scenes, still lifes, historical and allegorical subjects, scenes of local disasters, ship and train 'portraits', canvases depicting the lives of the peasants, all these and more became popular.

In Quebec the standard of painting reached one of its great peaks. In fact, this period has been called the Golden Age of French-Canadian art. In portraiture particularly, great advances were made.

The portraits of the 1790s, though they had their own particular charm and 'Canadian' character, were stiff, stylized, and decorative. But by the middle of the next century, Antoine Plamondon and Théophile Hamel, two of the most important artists in Quebec, were painting their subjects as living

people in full three-dimensional space.

Joseph Légaré, another of the great Quebec artists, painted the first truly Canadian landscapes and was noted for his dramatic scenes of local disasters.

Elsewhere in Canada the immigrant artists, many of whom had been trained in Europe, were producing a great portion of the best and most popular work. Local artists, in the meantime, were painting local subject matter. On the East Coast they chose the sea, ships, and harbour scenes, while farther inland, farms and events of village life were popular subjects.

With the building of the great railways, artists began to travel, and their subject matter widened. Indians and the Indian way of life, now threatened by extinction, were appealing subjects for some artists and popular with the viewing public. The grandeur of the Rocky Mountains and the lure of the West also provided a wealth of subject matter.

Surprisingly, Confederation in 1867 did not have a great impact upon the art or artists of Canada. There was no great wave of patriotism or any attempt to produce a national Canadian style. Rather, throughout the nineteenth century, the styles and subjects popular in Europe, and later in the United States, had the strongest influence in Canada.

The artistic styles of France had always been a major influence and continued to be well into the twentieth century. The two main movements, Neoclassicism and Romanticism, were the foundations of Canadian painting in the nineteenth century. They arose from two opposing ideas about life and were expressed not only in the visual arts but also in literature and music. Both styles were adapted by the painters of this country and served their purpose according to the local situation.

Neoclassicism was a new form of the ancient style

43

of Greece and Rome. The ideas and artistic methods on which it was based were taught at the French Academy. This institution, founded in the seventeenth century, exercised great control. An artist could only be recognized by showing his paintings at the official salon.

The Academy laid down strict rules for the teaching and practice of art. The style it taught was based on skill in drawing, controlled colour, and clear, ordered composition. There was also a scale of importance laid down for subject matter. Historical and religious subjects, for example, were considered more important than portraits, landscapes, and still lifes.

Classical art was a visual way of expressing a belief in an order and purpose in the world. It also supported the philosophy that man's mind and reason were his greatest gifts.

In contrast, Romanticism was a movement that rejected the order and discipline of the Neoclassicists. The Romantics expressed the idea that the truth of life lies in the imagination and the emotions rather than in the mind.

Because it has so many characteristics, it is difficult to describe all the feelings that Romanticism expresses in a few sentences. Basically, though, Romantic art involves escape – escape from a world that was becoming more and more industrialized and less and less concerned with church and social strucure.

While there was injustice in the old religious and social systems, there was also stability. Now everything was open to question. With a loss of faith in God and society, people started to look into themselves. They sought relief from the outside world in the world of the imagination.

But looking inward can produce pain as well as pleasure. Thus Romantic art is often a mixture of opposite feelings. Excitement and mystery are mingled with fear and confusion. Artists tempt us with visions of far-away places and sadden us with deathbed scenes. Ruins of castles and temples recall days of splendour but are also reminders of decay. The imagination can turn dreams into reality, but it can also create nightmares. In the words of Goya (1746–1828), the famous Spanish painter, 'The Sleep of Reason produces Monsters.'

Most early and mid-nineteenth-century painting by trained artists was based on one or the other of these two movements.

In the latter part of the century many Canadians trained at the Ecole des Beaux-Arts, the official school of the French Academy in Paris. Others received instruction at the private art schools there that also taught the academic style. But the Romantic outlook was accepted and widespread, and other styles and theories were also developing.

As a result, the end of the nineteenth century and the early years of the twentieth became a period of transition in Canadian painting. Some artists developed personal styles that showed various trends; others painted some canvases in one style, others in another. It was not until after the First World War that clearer directions became evident.

Joseph Légaré

1795–1855

Portrait of Josephte Ourné, c. 1840, oil on canvas
51-3/4″ x 37-3/8″ (131 cm x 95 cm)
The National Gallery of Canada, Ottawa

Légaré's *Portrait of Josephte Ourné* (p. 45) is one of the treasures of early Canadian painting. With her slanting eyes and mysterious expression, the Indian girl is a symbol of the wild world from which she came. Dressed in a glowing scarlet tunic, she stands at an angle to the viewer, holding her fish and rod in one hand and her bird in the other. Behind her are the dark woods where she has been hunting.

Joseph Légaré invites us into her world, with its sense of mystery and excitement, and encourages us to wander through it, responding with our eyes and imaginations. In this painting he has captured the spirit of Romanticism, a spirit new to Canadian art but present in nearly all Légaré's work.

The *Still Life* has the same sort of music. The shining grapes, glowing in the dark cave, are spread before us like a gift from the underworld. They are beautiful. But there is something almost evil in their beauty, as if some spirit were tempting us to taste the fruit that would charm us into the unknown land beyond the cave.

Joseph Légaré is remembered as the first Canadian-born landscape artist, and he is also well known for a series of canvases he painted showing local disasters.

In 1845 a terrible fire swept through St-Roch in Quebec, destroying a large part of the town. Légaré made several paintings of this event. In one he shows the raging fire; in another, the grim ruins of houses standing like gravestones in the flickering moonlight. In yet another dramatic canvas Légaré depicts a crowded street at night during a cholera plague. Horrified people watch as the dead are carted away and others are overcome with sickness. The terror of the scene is increased by the moonlight and the flaming torches in the darkness.

All these subjects and the style in which they are painted are Romantic in spirit. Yet at this time Romanticism was still very new, even in Europe,

and in Canada it was hardly known. It is believed that Légaré never went beyond Quebec for his artistic training. Instead, he taught himself by copying the works of European painters whose style appealed to his active imagination. The results are the first examples of Romantic art in Canada.

Légaré, who was born in Quebec of a wealthy family, seems to have shown a great interest in painting from an early age. He also took an active part in politics throughout his life, and after the Rebellion of 1837, he was arrested for associating with *Les Patriotes,* the followers of Papineau.

Early in his career Légaré painted portraits and religious subjects. When he was twenty-two, he bought a collection of European paintings that had originally belonged to French noblemen fleeing from the Revolution. The canvases had been brought to Canada by a priest named Louis-Joseph Desjardins and were eventually put up for auction. Légaré exhibited many of the paintings he bought in a section of his studio where he also sold his own works. While the Desjardins collection contained few masterpieces, it did serve to introduce styles and subjects that had not been seen before in Canada.

Six of these works were thought to be by Salvator Rosa, an Italian artist who painted wild landscape scenes. Horace Walpole, an eighteenth-century English writer, captured the sense of excitement and imagination that the Romantic painters tried to create in their landscapes when he said, 'Precipices, mountains, torrents, wolves, rumblings – Salvator Rosa.'

Another artist included in the collection was Hubert Robert, a Frenchman whose paintings of ruins in the moonlight sold well to tourists.

These artists and others made a great impression on the young Légaré, and he painted many copies. Perhaps his own style developed from his study of these European Romantics; perhaps it evolved from

Still Life with Grapes, undated, oil on canvas
37-3/8″ x 49-3/4″ (95 cm x 126 cm)
The National Gallery of Canada, Ottawa

his own imagination. Perhaps it was a combination of both, and this new approach to painting gave Légaré a way to express his own emotional character.

It is strange, though, that despite a successful career in which he established his individual style, Légaré's manner of painting had little effect upon his students. His work, unique in its imaginative qualities, makes an interesting comparison with that of Antoine Plamondon (p. 48), the most famous of his pupils.

Antoine Plamondon

1804–1895

Portrait of Soeur Saint-Alphonse, 1841
oil on canvas
36″ x 28-1/2″ (91 cm x 72 cm)
The National Gallery of Canada, Ottawa

Still Life with Apples and Grapes, 1870
oil on canvas
38-1/2″ x 30-1/2″ (98 cm x 77 cm)
The Art Gallery of Windsor

Like Légaré's *Josephte Ourné,* Antoine Plamondon's *Soeur Saint-Alphonse* is a beautiful painting, but the styles of the two portraits could hardly differ more. The Indian girl is mysterious and exciting; the young nun, calm and peaceful. The styles of Légaré and Plamondon, like those of all great artists, convey the sense of their subject. And it is here, where style and subject meet, that we may find the meaning of their paintings.

Plamondon received his early training from Joseph Légaré. He worked with Légaré on restoring and copying the European paintings that were bought from Abbé Desjardins. In 1826 the church raised funds to send Plamondon to study in Paris, and he remained there for four years. During this time he studied with Paul Guérin, a portrait painter who had been a pupil of Jacques Louis David, the most famous Neoclassical artist. On his return to Quebec Plamondon opened a studio and became a successful painter of portraits and religious and allegorical works. Plamondon was also noted for his pride and short temper, which he often directed at those he thought to be poor artists.

Plamondon's style of painting was based on the Neoclassical training he received at the French Academy. He himself said that his aim as a painter was to 'instruct, edify, and ornament'. Painting was a serious profession. It tried to teach men to live good lives and to control their emotions with their minds. The Neoclassicists believed that truth and beauty could be found in thought and reason. The Romantics, on the other hand, believed that these things lay in the heart and soul.

Plamondon's portrait of the young nun and his still life both have a quality of calm and completeness. They are visual statements of a belief that there is order in the world. In contrast, Légaré's works convey a sense of mystery and the unknown.

Plamondon has organized his forms logically. It is

his way of showing that there is reason and purpose in life. Everything is controlled: the colours are quiet; the shapes of objects are clear; the forms are rounded and complete; the composition stays within the canvas. We are not invited to move into the picture or to travel through it to far-away places. Instead we are asked to consider that peace comes to man through order and that beauty lies in control.

We have looked at Légaré's still life and the way in which he seems to tempt us into a magical cave. Plamondon has no desire to create this feeling. Everything in his still life is arranged so that it holds together in a composition of order and balance. The top, the bottom, and each side of the subject is evenly weighted. The eye is encouraged to follow a

49

circular movement, upwards from the curved table-top, through the vase, and around the arc of the fruit. The apple on the table at the left and the shadow on the right balance the weight of the fruit above. Thus Plamondon keeps his whole design within his canvas. He carefully fixes the balance of his painting: light against shade, colour against colour, shape against shape. Each part contributes to one complete whole.

The portrait of the young nun is just as skilfully composed and logically ordered. It glows with a feeling of peace. The quiet and thoughtful personality of the sitter is shown in the style of the painting itself. Here, as in the still life, the artist praises the order of nature in his balanced and confident composition.

The painting styles of Plamondon and Légaré were influenced greatly by the artistic movements of the nineteenth century. Neoclassicism was a direct result of the teaching of the Academies, while Romanticism began as a revolt against strict tradition. But both these approaches to art, the Neoclassical and the Romantic, are timeless. More than styles, they are attitudes to life. One does not have to exclude the other, but there will always be a difference between the expression of feeling and the expression of thought.

William Berczy

1744–1813

The Woolsey Family, 1808–1809, oil on canvas
23-3/4" x 34-1/4" (60 cm x 87 cm)
The National Gallery of Canada, Ottawa

William Berczy did not come to Canada until he was about forty-eight years old, and even then he came rather by accident. His youth and early life were spent travelling throughout Europe, where he was able to experience many different cultures.

Berczy was born in Saxony but was brought up in Vienna, where his uncle was the German ambassador. He went to Leipzig University, married a girl from Switzerland, and then spent five years painting in Italy. From there he moved to England and found work as drawing master to the daughters of the Marquis of Bath.

He must have been a restless man, for in 1792 he decided to come to the United States. Working as a land-agent for the Marquis, he brought a group of German settlers to New York. After an argument with the authorities, he and the settlers moved to York, the capital of Upper Canada. He remained there for about eleven years before moving to Montreal, where he settled down and opened a studio. In these last eight years of his life, he painted a number of portraits. Three of these were of Joseph

Brant, the famous chief of the Mohawks.

Berczy's masterpiece, though, is his portrait of the Woolsey family (p. 51). It is a delightful family study, soft in colour with a gentle, flowing rhythm that holds the group together.

The quiet landscape view, seen through the window, is balanced by the figure standing in the angle of the wall. But these are the only parts of Berczy's painting that suggest a feeling of depth. Instead, Berczy links his figures together in a graceful horizontal composition that resembles the patterns on Greek vases or the flat relief sculpture on temples.

This organization is not the result of the artist's inability to create a feeling of depth. In fact, Berczy's handling of the floor design shows that he is perfectly able to work with perspective. Berczy is obviously more concerned with patterns created by line than with patterns created by solid shapes.

It is fascinating to see the types of curves that Berczy has used. Some swinging one way and some the other, the lines build up rhythms, like individual themes in a musical composition. Yet they are all held together by one theme that flows through the piece. The artist has emphasized the effect by contrasting his curves with straight lines set at different angles. These similarities and contrasts make the design interesting and rhythmic.

When he prepared a painting, Berczy made individual sketches of each figure. He then put these together, adjusting them until they were all related in one complete composition. The little girl in the sketch shows how the artist was more concerned with the linear design of a figure than with the creation of a solid form.

The arrangement of this painting is typical of a kind of Neoclassical design that Berczy would have seen in England. In 1775 John Flaxman, an English sculptor, was employed by the Wedgwood china company to design their new Etruscan series. He was sent to study in Italy and to copy designs from original Roman and Etruscan vases. While in Italy he was inspired by the simple and pure lines of the carvings on gems and cameos based on Greek designs.

Founded on these, Flaxman began a series of illustrations for Homer's *Iliad* and *Odyssey*. His line drawings had a great influence on several artists, and, since Berczy was in England at this time, it is likely that he too would have been influenced by Flaxman's style.

For his portrait of the Woolsey family, Berczy received the sum of ten pounds for each member of the family included in the painting. He generously contributed the dog, whose collar bears the name of Woolsey, free of charge.

It was partly for the sake of economy that group portraits had been popular for so long. As far back as the seventeenth century, Rembrandt, for example, had painted large canvases of groups where each character was individually portrayed. His famous *Night Watch* shows a military company in which each member contributed his share for the privilege of being recognizable.

By the mid-eighteenth century a new type of group portrait, the conversation piece, was being produced. These works were smaller in size than the older portraits. They were also less formal, showing families or small groups in relaxed settings: having tea, sitting in a garden, or, as we see here, sitting together in a corner of their drawing room.

These conversation pieces were particularly popular in England, where they were frequently painted by Johann Zoffany, a friend of William Berczy. Perhaps their friendship might explain why this new type of portraiture appeared at such an early date in Canada.

Study of Eleanor Woolsey as a Child, undated
graphite
16-3/4″ x 12-1/4″ (43 cm x 31 cm)
The National Gallery of Canada, Ottawa

Théophile Hamel

1817−1870

Self Portrait, c. 1837, oil on canvas
42″ x 40″ (107 cm x 102 cm)
Musée du Séminaire de Québec, Quebec City

Théophile Hamel's *Self Portrait* was painted when he was only about twenty years old. By that time he had worked for three years as apprentice to Plamondon and had remained with him for another seven. Because of the older man's fiery nature, it is surprising that Hamel stayed for so long, but he probably realized he was receiving valuable training.

When he was twenty-six, Hamel left his home town of Quebec to study in Europe. Unlike Plamondon, who stayed in Paris, Hamel spent most of his time working in Rome and visiting major centres in Italy. Before returning to Canada three years later, he visited Paris and Antwerp briefly. There he was very impressed by the richness of the paintings of Rubens (p. 19). He also made copies of the works of van Dyck, Jordaens, and other Baroque masters who painted portraits in a grand, extravagant manner.

Hamel's own style never came close to the liveliness of this seventeenth-century spirit. But by nature and training, he was less concerned with strict Neoclassical controls than his early master Plamondon.

From the time of his return to Quebec in 1846 until his death twenty-four years later, Hamel painted many portraits of the leading men and women of the church, state, and society in Upper and Lower Canada. He also painted studies of children and some religious and historical works.

His *Self Portrait* is a youthful work, painted before he left for Europe, but already there is evidence of the style he was later to develop. Hamel was still studying under Plamondon, a Neoclassicist who thought that painting should 'instruct, edify, and ornament'. Plamondon thought that a good painting should present a clear scale of moral values in order to teach the viewer to copy and praise good men and to pity and condemn bad ones.

In Hamel's *Self Portrait* the scene is more poetic than moral. This is not to say that he has abandoned all Neoclassical ideas about art. Indeed, the artist is shown quiet and calm, suitably well-dressed, and he is painted in a balanced composition.

Hamel, though, has created a gentle mood of introspection. He seems to be wondering about himself and his future life. There are no firm statements of beliefs here; instead, there is a feeling of dreaminess, which comes both from the figure of the artist and from the quiet landscape setting. The river behind him, flowing through the valley, moves off towards the unknown, like a symbol of the young man's future life.

Many of the earlier Canadian portaits were set in a shallow space and often had plain backgrounds to emphasize the sitter. But Hamel has followed the European practice of placing the central figure in a landscape setting. This practice, like the custom of introducing small still lifes into portraiture (p. 29), has a long history. Both date back to fifteenth-century Flemish art.

Beside the sitter, or behind his shoulder, artists often painted little views of the countryside or street scenes shown through an open window. This added a greater feeling of space to the portrait and allowed the artist to describe the place where he painted it. As well, these fine little landscapes made the whole work more interesting and lively.

Although this practice evolved in northern Europe, landscapes were also introduced as backgrounds for a wide range of subjects in Italian painting from the sixteenth century onward. In portraiture, Leonardo da Vinci, for example, painted many of his sitters in very beautiful and imaginative landscape settings. In fact, portraits like the *Mona Lisa,* where the landscape seems to reflect the mysterious quality of the sitter's character, reveal the same sort of method that Hamel used in his own *Self Portrait.*

Anonymous

Micmac Indians, c. 1820–1830, oil on canvas
18" x 24" (46 cm x 61 cm)
The National Gallery of Canada, Ottawa

Indian Voyageurs Hunting, c. 1820s, watercolour
12-1/2" x 18" (32 cm x 46 cm)
Beaverbrook Art Gallery, Fredericton

These two paintings of Micmac Indians make an interesting comparison. One, in the collection of the National Gallery, is an oil; the other, belonging to the Beaverbrook Art Gallery, is a watercolour. In some ways the two works differ considerably, but there are sufficient similarities to suggest that they were both painted by the same person. At the Beaverbrook Art Gallery there is also another watercolour of a scene that resembles part of the oil painting. It too appears to have been done by the same artist.

Since these three works are unsigned, painted in two different media, and have no documentary proof of authorship, they pose an interesting problem of identification. Careful comparison of style must be made in order to determine whether they were actually painted by the same artist.

There are obvious differences between the two paintings reproduced here. In the oil, the composition is more crowded and details are introduced more freely than in the watercolour. The smooth, glazed surface of the oil painting emphasizes the precision of the drawing and the clarity of colour.

In the watercolour, though, the artist seems to have felt a greater sense of freedom, which is expressed in a more flowing and graceful treatment of line. Here too there is more emphasis on texture, particularly in the branches and needles of the trees.

But there are also striking similarities between the two works. Both, of course, are of Micmac Indians, and both are hunting scenes. The treatment of the figures in profile is similar, particularly in the awkward drawing of the arms and shoulders. Various animals (foxes, geese, and dogs) are also introduced as details into each work.

But the most noticeable likeness between the two paintings is the design of the group of flying geese. Though there are six geese in the oil painting and only three in the watercolour, the relationship of

one group to the other in line and rhythm is very strong. It is so strong, in fact, that this is the main reason for suggesting that both works were done by the same artist.

Attribution, the term used for assigning a work of art to a particular artist, is a specialized skill. To make an accurate attribution three main factors are considered: the style of the work, documents related to the work and/or the artist, and information based on refined methods of scientific analysis.

Early Canadian painting presents difficulties in all these areas. For example, there are many problems in tracing works by their style. Early Canadian painters received little formal training in the major artistic traditions. As a result, they tended to become eclectic artists, picking up ideas and methods from many sources. When an artist has no strongly defined style, it is difficult to attribute a painting to him. The historian, in constantly comparing canvas after canvas, must develop a particularly keen eye for detail.

It is also difficult to collect documentary evidence, which is very scarce for artists painting in Canada before the middle or end of the nineteenth century. Until that time, interest in art, even in major centres like Toronto and Montreal, was very limited. There are few records concerning professional artists and their work and even fewer concerning amateur artists, such as the painter of the works shown here.

As a result, it is often hard to trace the progress of an artist's career and the provenance, or history, of an individual painting. Through lack of interest, carelessness, destruction by neglect, fire, or any of many reasons, valuable records have been lost.

Analysis of paintings by chemical and x-ray methods may aid the historian in determining authorship, but scientific means alone are insufficient. Thus, in the field of early Canadian art the experts are faced with many problems: inconsistencies of style, shortage of documentation, and a great number of lost or missing paintings. Exact identification, or even attribution, is a long, slow task.

These two paintings were purchased quite independently of each other by galleries located far apart. There is still no positive identification of the artist, though on the basis of other works dealing with Micmac Indians, some suggestions have been made. But until proof can be found either from documents or a signed painting linked to these works by style, they can only be attributed to an anonymous artist.

Cornelius Krieghoff

1815–1872

Merrymaking, 1860, oil on canvas
34-1/2" x 48" (88 cm x 122 cm)
Beaverbrook Art Gallery, Fredericton

If every night at the Jolifou Inn were as lively as the one Cornelius Krieghoff depicts in *Merrymaking* (p. 59), the innkeeper must have done a roaring trade. And many a sore head there must have been among the merrymakers returning at dawn.

The frolics of the night are over, and the balcony of the old stone house is crowded with people preparing to leave. A woman covers her head as a fat man blows his horn in her ears; a group of small boys pelt snowballs at the departing guests, and in an upstairs dormer window an old crone, unable to sleep, peers down upon the rowdy scene. Outside the inn the sleighs are arriving and the passengers pile in, ready for the chilly ride home. While one sleigh pulls up to the steps, another tips over, throwing its occupants into the snow.

Detail by detail Krieghoff has built up his canvas. Each individual scene contributes to his depiction of the night's merrymaking and in turn contributes to the overall composition of his painting.

Scenes of the everyday life of simple farming people, called genre scenes, were fairly rare in Canadian painting at this time. Genre painting, though, was an old and established tradition in Europe. It was particularly important in the northern countries, where Krieghoff had been born and brought up.

In the sixteenth century Pieter Bruegel, for instance, had painted many canvases of rural life and country customs, which earned him the nickname 'Peasant Bruegel'. By the seventeenth century this type of subject matter was very popular. Middle-class merchants and burghers, who now had the money to buy paintings, enjoyed viewing scenes of daily life and everyday objects. They much preferred these to the paintings of intellectual classical subjects that appealed to the scholars.

There was a wide range of material available to the genre painter: tavern scenes, farm life, festive occasions, country occasions, country customs, and endless others. Packed with details and crowded with figures, each canvas was unified by its theme or narrative.

Cornelius Krieghoff was born in Amsterdam in 1815. His father was German and his mother was Dutch. Though not much is known of his early life, he seems to have spent his childhood years in Düsseldorf and may also have received his training at the famous academy there. When he was about eighteen, he left home and travelled through Europe, painting and working as a musician, since he had also been trained in this art.

In 1837 Krieghoff and his brother Ernst arrived in New York. Here Cornelius enlisted in the army and was sent to Florida to fight against the Seminole Indians. His interest in painting Indians, which became a life-long occupation, seems to have begun at this time.

It was a meeting with Louise Gautier, a French-Canadian girl, that brought Krieghoff to Canada. Though the circumstances are not clear, it is known that he deserted from the American army and moved north. Eventually he arrived in Toronto with Louise and their little daughter. Shortly afterwards they moved to Longueuil, Louise's home town, and from there to Montreal.

This must have been a difficult time for Krieghoff, since Montreal was, for the most part, a commercial town. Its merchants, who were not yet secure financially, were unable and unwilling to invest in large works of art. Krieghoff made his living by selling small pieces to English visitors, instructing at a girls' school, and painting signs and other commercial material.

It was not until Krieghoff moved with his family to Quebec that his career really began to flourish. At about this time he and Louise spent a year in Europe, staying for a while in London and then returning to Düsseldorf. It was here that Krieghoff successfully renewed his acquaintance with European genre and landscape painting.

While he was in Quebec, Krieghoff painted literally hundreds of canvases. Though the majority are genre scenes, he also produced a number of landscapes. His style is dramatic and his landscapes often depict stormy scenes with strong contrasts of light and shade.

Krieghoff's great talent, though, lay in his handling of figures. Each one is distinct; to each he has given significant gestures and unique characteristics.

Krieghoff's art is, in many ways, a type of theatre. In *Merrymaking*, for example, his figures, like characters in a play, appear to be acting out a script he has written for them. Through posture and gesture, each character seems to be interpreting his role in his own individual way. Krieghoff exercises the control of a dramatist, supplying the script and arranging the scene. Unlike a narrator, he does not allow his own voice to interpret the events he portrays.

We, the audience, look in on the scene as if it were set on a proscenium stage, with an arch curving over the top. The landscape serves as a backdrop for the busy stage setting in front. It would not seem too surprising if, with a few grand musical chords, the whole company were to come to life, and the play begin.

Paul Kane

1810–1871

The Man That Always Rides, 1849–1855, oil on canvas
18-1/4" x 24" (46 cm x 61 cm)
Royal Ontario Museum, Toronto

Paul Kane is often associated with Cornelius Krieghoff, but in training and approach the two artists were quite different. While Krieghoff spent most of his professional life in Montreal and Quebec, Kane was based in Toronto. Both painters chose Indians as a main source of subject matter, but their aims and results differed widely.

Krieghoff painted lively genre scenes, showing both Indians and French-Canadian habitants, complete with their brightly coloured costumes. Kane, on the other hand, set himself a different sort of task. He dedicated his life to making a complete visual record of the life and culture of the Canadian Indians who, he feared, were rapidly disappearing.

Paul Kane was born in Ireland and around the age of nine came to Toronto with his family. His father was a wine merchant, but Paul was first apprenticed as a decorator to a furniture maker. He later received lessons in painting from Thomas Drury, the drawing master at Upper Canada College, and established himself as a coach and sign painter. In 1834 he moved to Cobourg, where he stayed for two years and began painting portraits. It was about this time that he decided to become a professional artist. In 1836 he left Canada for the United States, where he spent about five years studying and earning enough money to go to Europe. There he spent a further four years, travelling widely and copying the works of the Old Masters.

While he was in the United States, Kane probably saw the work of George Catlin and other American artists who were recording the lives and customs of the American Indians. Catlin wrote that he was determined to 'snatch from hasty oblivion...a truly lofty and noble race....' He added, 'I have flown to their rescue (so that) phoenix-like they may rise from the stain on the painter's canvas.'

Catlin shared with the French philosopher Rousseau the Romantic view that the truly noble man could only be found in his natural state, untouched and unspoiled by civilization. But Catlin seemed to accept that the destruction of the Indian life and culture was inevitable. He responded more by looking wistfully towards the past than by seeking some practical solution for the future.

He set about collecting a museum of Indian artifacts. To this he added many portraits, genre scenes, and landscapes that he painted in his studio from the quick sketches he made while travelling among the Indians. Catlin exhibited his Indian museum in the United States and Europe. During the time it was in London, Paul Kane would have had the opportunity to see it.

On his return to Toronto after an absence of nine years, Kane was determined to do for Canadian Indians what Catlin had done in the United States. On June 17, 1845, he set off on his first sketching trip, intending to record in his art the spirit of the Ojibway people. He painted a number of portrait-sketches and made many drawings of the Indians' surroundings and ceremonies.

Shortly afterwards he was put in contact with Sir George Simpson, governor of the Hudson's Bay Company. Since the company had trading posts throughout western Canada and the North, his association with it was valuable to say the least. In the winter of 1845 Kane completed his first Indian canvases. He also received the approval of Sir George Simpson to leave in the spring with the fleet of canoes bound for the West.

Late in the year of 1848 Kane returned to Toronto with hundreds of sketches he had made in preparation for oil paintings that he finished in his studio. Shortly after his return he held one of the first one-man public exhibitions in Canada.

In 1851 he again exhibited, this time in Brockville, and was highly praised. In his show he included some of the one hundred canvases that he intended to be a cycle recording 'the scenery and Indian life of the great North West'. When the hundred canvases were finally completed, they were bought by George Allan, a Toronto collector, and eventually donated to the Royal Ontario Museum.

In 1859 Kane published *Wanderings of an Artist Among the Indians of North America*, which was illustrated with prints from his sketches and oil paintings. Its descriptions, stories, and accounts of life in the Canadian wilds of the early nineteenth century have made it a popular book for over a hundred years.

As is often the case, Kane's sketches are more lively and forceful than some of his finished canvases. These tend to have a certain flatness, reflecting his careful European studies. But in other paintings, such as *The Man That Always Rides* (p. 62), he has allowed his romantic imagination to take control.

Kane has painted his Indian chieftain in the finest of regalia and mounted on a splendid rearing horse. It is obvious that he seeks a place for him in a long tradition of glorified mounted figures. This historical series, beginning with the Greek Parthenon riders (p. 4) and conquering Roman heroes, continues through the medieval knights of chivalry and the triumphant Napoleon. The very title of Kane's work, *The Man That Always Rides*, suggests his belief that the chieftain too deserves a place in this tradition.

We can sense that the feelings which inspired this painting were deep. Kane obviously felt great admiration for what he saw to be a fiery and undefeated spirit among the Indian people. But the fact remained that they were facing extinction, and so it is not too surprising that Kane should set his chieftain before a magnificent stormy sky and a burning sunset.

64

George Berthon

1806–1892

The Three Robinson Sisters, 1846, oil on canvas
44-1/8″ x 33″ (112 cm x 84 cm)
Art Gallery of Ontario, Toronto

George Berthon is one of the few Canadian artists whose father was also a painter of high repute. René Théodore Berthon (1777-1859) had trained in the studio of the great Neoclassical artist Jacques Louis David. Later he painted a portrait of Napoleon and became one of the Emperor's court painters.

As a result, his son George enjoyed fortunate connections and excellent training in Paris. This training, based on sound Neoclassical foundations, would have been similar to that which Antoine Plamondon received at approximately the same time.

In 1827, at the age of twenty-one, George Berthon emigrated from France to England. There he taught French and drawing to the daughters of the Tory statesman Sir Robert Peel.

While he was in England, Berthon would have seen the style of female portraiture that was popular at the time. Sweet, elegant, and charming though it was, it lacked depth of characterization. Berthon's *The Three Robinson Sisters* (p. 65), painted about two years after he settled in Canada, closely resembles the style of Alfred Chalon (1781-1866), Royal Painter to Queen Victoria.

Although exact information is incomplete, it appears that Berthon may have come to Canada in 1837. He seems, though, to have returned to England for several years and did not settle in Toronto until about 1844. There he established himself as a portrait painter, catering to the fashionable and wealthy people of Upper Canada, just as Plamondon was doing in Lower Canada.

In 1845 Berthon painted Chief Justice Sir John Beverley Robinson. This was the first in a series of portraits of members of the Law Society of Upper Canada. He also received commissions from military officers and important members of the government and church. In fact his portrait of Bishop Strachan is among his most well-known works.

Berthon did some teaching and painted a few landscapes and small genre works, but he made his name, and supported his twelve children, by portrait painting.

The Three Robinson Sisters is a group portrait of the daughters of Chief Justice Robinson. As such, it is a type of work that was still quite rare in Canada at this time. It shows Augusta on the left, who had previously married Bishop Strachan's son, and Louisa and Emily, who were both married on April 16, 1846. This was the day the portrait was presented to their mother by her three sons-in-law.

The figures in this painting, like those in Berczy's *The Woolsey Family* (p. 51), are set in a rather shallow space. The design is dependent on the rhythm of line and the arrangement of planes, as is evident, for example, in the angles of the heads and the set of the shoulders. Again, as in Berczy's *The Woolsey Family*, the artist has concentrated on a linear pattern within a limited depth.

The graceful lines of the design and the pastel colours of the painting are well-suited to the subject matter. They are also well-suited to the tastes of the time, and the result, though rather precious, has its own particular charm.

Robert Todd

1809–1865

The Ice Cone, Montmorency Falls, c. 1845
oil on canvas
13-1/2″ x 18″ (34 cm x 46 cm)
The National Gallery of Canada, Ottawa

In the early years of the nineteenth century it was not easy for an artist to make a living in Canada by painting pictures alone. Most artists had to be prepared to accept work in almost any related field.

When Robert Todd first arrived in Quebec in 1834, he advertised as a 'house, carriage, and ornamental painter'. In a later advertisement he expanded his talents to include figure-carving and gilding, both popular forms of decoration in Catholic Quebec.

This type of work was probably familiar to Todd, since, before he came to Canada, it seems he worked in London and Edinburgh as an ornamenter of carriages and a painter of coats-of-arms. There is no evidence that he was ever trained as a professional artist.

He must have become dissatisfied with his progress in Quebec, because he moved to Toronto about 1854. There he advertised again, this time as 'artist, herald, and ornamental painter'; later he reduced this to 'artist'. Todd's fortunes cannot have improved very much, since in 1861 he wrote that 'Toronto is too new and too poor to support an ornamental artist.'

We assume that his term 'ornamental artist' did not include portrait or descriptive painters, because George Berthon was already very successful by this time, and Paul Kane had also received much support for his Indian canvases. On the other hand, Cornelius Krieghoff had not stayed long in Toronto, while Robert Whale, who also worked in Upper Canada, was prepared to do any type of painting to make his living.

Although we do not have many of Todd's canvases, it is probable that others exist but have been bought and taken out of Canada. He is known to have done several sleighing scenes at Montmorency Falls outside Quebec.

Todd, though lacking a trained knowledge of art, has an appealing and decorative style. *The Ice Cone, Montmorency Falls* (p. 67) looks rather like a painting on porcelain: the surface of the canvas is smooth and clean, the lines graceful, and the colours sharply defined.

Perhaps this and his other similar paintings were intended as horse 'portraits', a type of work popular among the British military visitors. While in England, Todd would have seen the work of George Stubbs (1724-1806), the great animal painter, and also that of his followers.

Horses were Stubbs's particular interest. As well as painting them, he also wrote an important book called *The Anatomy of the Horse*. He is famous for his beautiful horse portraits and other animal paintings, but his graceful style was also suited for decorative work, and he received commissions from the Wedgwood china company.

It is unreasonable to compare Todd with Stubbs, because Stubbs was a great artist and far superior to the average horse painter. It is possible, though, to suggest that Todd had Stubbs, and his success, in mind when he directed his attention to sporting painting.

Not only would there have been a ready market among the officers for pictures of their favourite horses, but scenes of Montmorency would also have recalled many happy occasions to them and their ladies. In one account the following description appears:

Montmorency Falls has been a popular resort for Quebecers for ages. It was here that the Duke of Kent, father of Queen Victoria, passed the summer seasons for the most part while in Quebec with his regiment from 1791-1794. The Quebec Tandem Club, in the winter season at least, made Bureau's at the Falls, their rendezvous on a Saturday afternoon.... Viewing the Natural Steps as well as the falls in summer and sliding down the

huge ice cone or sugar loaf – one year being 126 ft. high –
which formed every winter at the foot of the falls were
among the attractions there at one time. The mountain or
cone formed by the spray from the great body of water
rushing over the falls in those days was as regular as if
formed by an architect. Refreshment booths or cabarets
were excavated from the body of the cone by enterprising
caterers and here beverages both hot and cold, as well as
strong, were obtainable. A popular drink in this unique
resort was the mulled, or hot, beer.

This was the background for the few paintings that
we have by Robert Todd. Graceful and decorative,
they are a delightful reminder of winter festivities in
Canada over a century ago.

Robert Whale

1805 – 1887

General View of Hamilton, 1853, oil on canvas
34-3/4" x 47-1/2"(88 cm x 121 cm)
The National Gallery of Canada, Ottawa

The Canada Southern Railway at Niagara, c. 1870
oil on canvas
23" x 40" (58 cm x 102 cm)
The National Gallery of Canada, Ottawa

Robert Whale was a professional artist in England before immigrating to Canada at the age of forty-seven. He was born in Cornwall and studied painting in London. There he saw the portraits of Sir Joshua Reynolds, a former president of the Royal Academy, and the landscapes of Richard Wilson, one of its founding members. These works obviously had an effect upon his artistic development.

Whale arrived in Burford, near Brantford, in 1852 and moved to Brantford twelve years later. With the exception of four years that he spent in England, he remained there for the rest of his life.

Whale produced many paintings during his stay in Canada, often doing several versions of the same subject. Robert Whale's nephew, John Hicks Whale, and his two sons, John Claude and Robert Heard, were also artists. The whole family exhibited widely at the provincial exhibitions. They entered as many categories as possible and submitted the maximum number of entries; invariably they would walk away with most of the prize money. This did not, of course, endear them to their fellow artists, but because the art market in Ontario was so small, they were greatly in need of the money.

Portraiture had been an important source of income for Robert Whale, but with the increase in photography even this field was undependable. As a result, he turned his attention to another type of art.

Panoramic views of important events were popular in travelling shows, where the public was admitted to see them for a small fee. To accompany one of these shows, Whale painted a vivid description of the Indian Mutiny of 1864, and his work was displayed throughout Ontario. Whale was not a fashionable artist, nor did he live in a fashionable centre, and so in order to make a living, he was forced to adapt his art to suit almost any field.

Whale's paintings reflect his English background and training. His landscapes in particular reveal a debt to Richard Wilson, whose works were gentle, classical, and inspired largely by the great French painter Claude Lorraine. In Wilson's landscapes, as in Claude's, nature is tamed, idealized, and bathed in soft light.

Whale's *General View of Hamilton* is similar in many ways to Wilson's work. The distant view of the town is painted in a smooth and careful fashion. As in Wilson's landscapes, and Claude's, the scene is framed by trees and stretches out into a distant horizon. The painting has the quiet, restful quality of classical art, yet it also shows a certain romantic dreaminess that was popular at this time.

Though Whale was obviously impressed by the width and grandeur of Canada, he often imposed an English atmosphere upon the Canadian landscapes he painted. In *The Canada Southern Railway at Niagara* he has applied his paint in minute brush strokes smoothly over the canvas. The effect is to tame, rather than capture, the wild magnificence of Niagara Falls.

Nevertheless, Whale has deliberately emphasized the feeling of space. There are no enclosing trees to accent depth, as there are in his view of Hamilton. Instead, Whale's composition is based on a series of horizontal planes that direct the viewer's eye back into the picture space. Whale also creates perspective by diminishing the size of objects and changing his lighting from foreground to background. But the absence of vertical elements and the emphasis on the horizontal lines lessen the effect of depth and give the painting its feeling of width and spaciousness.

This particular work is one of a series of train 'portraits', similar to the ship 'portraits' that were produced on the Atlantic coast. Again this suggests the interests and circumstances of the common man for whom these works were painted. The building of railways on the North American continent was one of the great achievements of the nineteenth century. The railways became a proud symbol of the power of man against nature.

By relating the train to Niagara Falls, Whale is drawing a rather obvious contrast between these two great sources of energy. But he is also reflecting the proud spirit of the time and its faith in the progress of civilization.

William Hind

1833 – 1889

At the Foot of the Rocky Mountains, watercolour
8-1/2″ x 12″ (22 cm x 30 cm)
McCord Museum, Montreal

William Hind appears to have been a quiet and retiring man. He might have remained almost unknown had it not been for his brother Henry Youle Hind, a well-known geologist. As a result of Henry's knowledge of the country, and based on his advice, William went on several expeditions through Canada. These journeys, which took place between the years 1861 and 1864, inspired a number of his sketches and watercolours. In fact, William's first experience with an expedition was as the official artist who made visual records for the expedition reports, just as the military topographers had done earlier.

On this first expedition to Labrador in 1861, William worked under Henry, who was the leader of the group. Engravings and lithographs that he made from his original sketches are part of the published record of the expedition. They show a variety of studies and views: canoeing and portaging, a forest fire, and many scenes of native life in Labrador.

Little is known of William Hind's early life. He was certainly born in England and may have had some artistic training there and on the Continent. His brother Henry immigrated to Canada in 1846 and soon made his name as a scientist. When he was about nineteen, William joined his brother in Toronto. There he opened his own studio and, at Henry's encouragement, exhibited a few paintings at the Upper Canada show of 1852. (The latter was no outstanding achievement because paintings were rated on the same level as wax flowers, false teeth, and other *objets d'art*.) Later Hind found employment at the Toronto Normal School as a professor of drawing.

Less than a decade later, the attention of the whole world was focused on western Canada, as adventurers from all countries flocked to the gold rush in British Columbia. At first the prospectors set out for the Fraser River, where findings were made in 1857. Four years later there were more discoveries at William's Creek in the Cariboo Mountains. Miners arrived by the thousands, twenty-five thousand mainly from California the first season, and then others in increasing numbers.

On April 23, 1862, William Hind left Toronto with forty-four other men to join the search for gold in the Cariboo. Other groups of mixed nationalities met them when they reached the Red River. This entire band later received the name the Overlanders of '62.

The travelling conditions were very difficult. Everything had to be carried by knapsack, oxen-carts, horses, or mules. One inventive prospector even bought some surplus camels from the United States Army, but they smelt so unpleasant and bit and kicked so viciously that the other packers revolted.

On the journey Hind kept a sketch-book that is filled with little studies of their adventures and experiences. He also painted extremely detailed watercolours in which every stick and stone is individually depicted in a style akin to engraving.

In 1863, after his expeditions, William settled for a while in Victoria. At that time there was a group of artists working there, and Hind himself opened a studio. He painted watercolours and oils, probably working from many of his earlier sketches.

His final days were spent in the Maritimes, where he worked for a local railway company. His paintings are of Nova Scotia, where his brother Henry had settled, and New Brunswick, where he himself lived. He spent the last nine years of his life in Sussex, New Brunswick, and died there at the age of fifty-six.

Years earlier, while Hind had been growing up in England, a group of painters had banded together under the name of the Pre-Raphaelite Brotherhood.

A Visit to Otelne in his Lodge, 1861-1862
watercolour
6-1/2" x 12-1/16" (17 cm x 30 cm)
The Agnes Etherington Art Centre
Queen's University, Kingston

Their principal aim was to convey symbolic moral messages, but they also stressed close attention to nature and detailed expression. This emphasis on detail, which so greatly affected Victorian painting, was also a result of the popularity of photography. The camera missed nothing, and so the artist attempted to match it. Perhaps it was from these ideas that Hind's own careful technique arose.

But there is also a rather naïve aspect in Hind's work that makes it particularly appealing. This aspect is a combined result of an observant eye, a talent for design, and a lack of formal training. Despite his normally careful method of recording what he saw, Hind seems to have had delightful and unexpected flashes of imagination that add spirit to his art. In *At the Foot of the Rocky Mountains* (p. 73), his minute attention to natural detail is obvious, yet his treatment of the mountains is imaginative and intensely personal. It seems as though he was overwhelmed by the mountains' grandeur and felt they could only properly be described as fairytale structures.

In his *Visit to Otelne in his Lodge* Hind has made clever use of a cross-section of an Indian dwelling to suggest the lunette form. This semi-circular architectural shape was often used in the past for decorative painting and sculpture. Hind has used it to arrange his group in a compact and interesting way, as well as to suggest the inside of the dwelling.

His technique is not nearly as detailed in this painting as it is in the other watercolour. In fact, his sketchy method has allowed him to catch strange and fleeting expressions on the faces of the Indians. He is obviously concerned with an imaginative rather than a realistic approach to his subject. Within this closely confined space the atmosphere seems almost menacing, though the artist himself looks relaxed and at ease.

75

John O'Brien

c. 1832–1891

British Naval Squadron off Nova Scotia, 1856
oil on canvas
25" x 35" (64 cm x 89 cm)
The National Gallery of Canada, Ottawa

John O'Brien was a painter of the sea. Born on a ship when his parents were emigrating from Ireland to Nova Scotia, he became one of the best-known artists in Halifax during the nineteenth century.

British Naval Squadron off Nova Scotia is one of O'Brien's finest works. Although painted in quiet greys, it conveys all the excitement of a stormy day at sea as the wind and waves batter the ships under an angry sky. Not all his work is of this quality. In many of his early paintings and in his late ones, the compositions tend to be stiff and the colours harsh.

When he was eighteen, O'Brien was sent to study in Europe. His expenses were paid by the merchants of Halifax who were impressed with his ability. *British Naval Squadron* was painted on his return and shows the influence of his European training.

In this particular seascape the artist has concentrated on capturing the atmosphere of a wild day at sea. But at the time, ship 'portraits' were one of the most popular subjects of painting on the East Coast. Artists from all over the world were commissioned by owners and captains to paint particular vessels.

Shipbuilding and cargo-carrying were major industries in Nova Scotia. According to official records nearly three thousand vessels were owned in Nova Scotia in 1873. This figure represents about three-quarters of all the ships registered that year in Canada and a large portion of the world's carrying vessels.

During the American Civil War there were no ships being used for this purpose. But events such as the Crimean War, the Indian Mutiny, and the discovery of gold in various parts of the world brought opportunities for the carrier trade. Shipping space was also needed to transport raw materials and finished products for international trading.

Because of its geographical position, Nova Scotia has always depended largely on the sea for food,

and before the 1830s small fishing boats were built. From 1840 until about the end of the century, when steamboats started to replace them, much larger wooden ships with three and four masts were constructed.

Unfortunately, very little remains of Nova Scotia's Golden Age of Sail. Ships that were not lost at sea were sold in foreign ports, some soon after they were built, while others ended their days as storage hulks. Even the original models of ships, which were used in British North America instead of naval architectural plans, are rare today.

As a result, most of the information we have comes from the numerous ship portraits. Many professional European artists painted vessels built in Nova Scotia, and many amateur artists, proud of their seagoing heritage, painted their own versions. These remain today as a visual record of a people for whom the sea was a way of life.

Adolphe Vogt

1842–1871

Approaching Storm, 1870, oil on canvas
49" x 88" (124 cm x 224 cm)
The Edmonton Art Gallery

Adolphe Vogt's *Approaching Storm*, painted in 1870, was one of his last works. It is a large canvas, over seven feet long and four feet wide. It is also highly dramatic and attracted much attention when it was shown in the second exhibition of the Society of Canadian Artists. This exhibition was held in Montreal the same year the canvas was painted.

Vogt was born in Germany but went to the United States when he was twelve. He studied painting there until he was nineteen, then returned to Europe for four years of further study in Germany and Switzerland. In 1865 he came to Montreal, where he remained until 1870. During this time he left Canada to visit Paris briefly, and, in the autumn of 1870, he moved to New York, where he died of smallpox soon afterwards.

Vogt's life was only twenty-nine years long. But he travelled a great deal and was exposed to a wide range of artistic styles. His own work is bold and dramatic, combining elements of both North American and European techniques.

As we have seen again and again, the handling of light is an important element in the language of painting. In fact, it is the primary element, since without light the artist could not show form, colour, or space.

Light, though, can also control the emotional tone of a painting. An artist who works in a classical manner keeps his light evenly distributed over his subject. Shapes are described by the light that flows gently around them, relating one to the next and binding everything together into one whole. The final effect is quiet and ordered (see Plamondon, p. 48).

The more emotional artists, who appeal to the imagination instead of the intellect, use light and shadow far more dramatically (see Légaré, p. 45). Strong contrasts add excitement to a painting and may often be combined with a sense of movement, as we see here.

In this painting Vogt has used the startling light of a thunderstorm very powerfully. The result is truly effective theatre. Like Cornelius Krieghoff, who was also of German origin, Vogt has chosen a genre subject to appeal to the taste of the general public.

Artistically, however, he has made his everyday subject dramatic and exciting. His contrasts of light and shade are strong. His composition is organized on a diagonal, an unstable angle compared with a horizontal or vertical, and he has introduced an abundance of movement into his painting.

Cattle and horses were favourite subjects of Vogt's. When he was studying in Switzerland, he worked under an artist who was specializing in this area. Vogt also copied the paintings of Rosa Bonheur (1822-1899), a French woman who was well known for her animal paintings, which are dramatic and full of movement.

Genre painting was popular in the United States while Vogt was studying there. The new democracy considered the everyday life of simple people to be a suitable subject for art; however, it was often portrayed in a romantic and sentimental way. Many of the American genre artists were trained in Germany, particularly in Düsseldorf. There emphasis was placed on painting peasant life not as it really was, but as something more quaint and theatrical (see Krieghoff, p. 59).

In Canada, Adolph Vogt's *Approaching Storm* was considered new and unusual, but it was actually painted in the tradition of the time. Vogt's training and experience in Europe and the United States had evidently impressed him deeply.

William Raphael

1833–1914

Behind Bonsecours Market, Montreal, 1866
oil on canvas
26-1/2″ x 43″ (67 cm x 109 cm)
The National Gallery of Canada, Ottawa

William Raphael, like Cornelius Krieghoff and Adolphe Vogt, was born in Germany and received his early training there. His choice of genre subject matter is therefore in the tradition of his native land, though stylistically his painting differs from the work of these other German artists.

Raphael was born in Prussia of German-Jewish descent. At the age of twenty-one he entered the Berlin Academy, where he studied art for a year before leaving for New York in 1856. There he became a portrait painter and continued this type of work in Quebec and Montreal after his arrival in Canada the following year. His genre paintings and some pure landscapes date from later in his career.

While he was in Berlin, William Raphael would have seen the work of some of the Biedermeier painters. Biedermeier was a title given to certain northern European artists of the early nineteenth century who stressed Naturalism as their principal aim, whether in portrait, landscape, or genre painting.

Their treatment of light played a particularly important role. Often it was bright and sunny, emphasizing the contrast of light and shadow and frequently highlighting the smallest of details. In fact, it was noted of one Biedermeier artist that his painting showed 'his love of detail and his simple joy in the visible world (which was) intentionally devoid of all mystery....'

The Berlin Biedermeier artists had studied the seventeenth-century Dutch views of towns. Eduard Gartner, a Biedermeier artist who would have been working in Berlin when Raphael was there, was noted for painting buildings in exact detail and mathematical perspective. There is no documentation to prove that William Raphael was actually influenced by the Biedermeier painters, but it seems quite reasonable to suppose that they had an effect on him.

Behind Bonsecours Market shows a strong sense of composition, both in its shaping elements and in its treatment of light. The solid masses and open spaces are logically balanced, and this balance is strengthened by the artist's use of light and shade. Details abound, and these too are emphasized by the brightness of the painting. The candelabra, which is carried by the man in the centre, sparkles in the sunlight. The tendrils of the vegetables in the wheel-barrow, the pattern of the basket on the left, the panes in the window high above, all stand out sharply and clearly.

The whole work is carefully thought out. It is lively in its subject matter and rich in genre details, but in construction it is classical and balanced. Even the little triangular group in the central foreground, composed of two boys and their pet, is a typically classical arrangement that adds order and balance to the painting.

Though this is a genre painting by an artist of German origin, it is unlike Krieghoff's *Merrymaking* or Vogt's *Approaching Storm*. Krieghoff was mainly concerned with presenting an appealing rustic comedy; Vogt, with the drama of light. But Raphael's painting, based on a carefully considered structure, was meant to be a truly realistic picture of daily life.

Lucius O'Brien

1832—1900

Sunrise on the Saguenay, 1880, oil on canvas
34-1/2" x 49-1/2" (88 cm x 126 cm)
The National Gallery of Canada, Ottawa

Lucius O'Brien became the first president of the Royal Canadian Academy of Arts in 1880. At that time the Marquis of Lorne was Governor General of Canada. Anxious to promote the arts in the new Dominion, Lorne suggested the foundation of an academy based upon the principles of the Royal Academy in London. He also proposed the opening of the National Gallery of Canada to house the works of those artists who received diplomas from the Academy. Lucius O'Brien's *Sunrise on the Saguenay,* painted in the year of the Academy's foundation, was the first of these diploma pieces.

O'Brien had been selected as president for a number of reasons. He was Canadian by birth, unlike many other important artists of the day. Born in a small town on Lake Simcoe, Lucius attended Upper Canada College, where he excelled in painting. On leaving school, he entered an architect's office, and later he trained and practised as a civil engineer.

It was not until 1872, at the age of forty, that he became a professional artist. He then joined the new Ontario Society of Artists and was vice-president from 1874 to 1880. It was at this time that he met the Marquis of Lorne.

The founding of the Academy took place amid much bickering and controversy, throughout which O'Brien acted as mediator. It cannot have been an easy task, because, as Lorne commented, 'There is a marvellous amount of bitterness and bad language. Half of the artists are ready just now to choke the other half with their paint brushes.'

Lucius O'Brien was chiefly a landscape artist who worked in oils and watercolours. Much of his painting was done in Ontario and the East, but he also visited western Canada on three separate occasions. There he painted in the Rocky Mountains and on the Pacific coast.

As editor of *Picturesque Canada* (1882), a two-volume publication of landscape views, he travelled across the country, making sketches and organizing the work of the other contributing artists. His own landscapes cover a wide range of scenery, from the thick growth of the British Columbian forests and mountain passes of the Rockies to the Saguenay River in Quebec.

Although O'Brien had had no European training, he had travelled in the United States. It is known that he was familiar with the work of the artists of the Hudson River School, a group of American landscape painters who worked mainly in the Catskill Mountains of the eastern United States. Some of them had received their early training in Europe at the time when Düsseldorf, Germany, was one of the main centres of Romantic landscape painting. The aims of the group were both patriotic and semi-religious. Nature, untouched and unspoiled as she was found in the new land, was, they believed, 'fraught with high and holy meaning, only

surpassed by the light of Revelation'. For the members of the Hudson River School, Nature was an expression of God's grace, and they felt compelled to paint her with reverence and truth.

Like many other Romantic artists, they wanted to escape from the pressures of competition, industrial growth, and all the other ills of a growing population. To do this, they sought peace of mind in the idea, if not the reality, of perfect Nature.

This perfection was not something that could be ordered and planned by the artist as rigorously as in a classical landscape. The individual parts of a natural landscape were not to be forced into a structure that expressed the artist's ideas about balance and order.

In these Romantic landscapes perfection is supposed to be natural, but, in fact, the result is as artificially planned and ideal as any classical work. Yet in contrast to classical art, these paintings attempt to create an ideal of feeling, rather than thought. The artist lulls the mind to dream and wonder; he does not alert it to reason.

Light becomes his medium. By diffusing it in a soft and misty way, sometimes called luminism, he creates an atmosphere of spiritual awe and mystery.

In *Sunrise on the Saguenay* Lucius O'Brien has created a world that exists half-way between dream and reality. The huge and rocky cliffs, which could seem menacing in other moods, are softened in the early morning light. On the calm water some fishing boats and a ship with unfurled sails prepare to leave their moorings. The mood is quiet and expectant, as if poised and waiting for the sun to bring the scene to life. It is a poetic painting that is an invitation to dream. It typifies the Romantic search for an escape into Nature.

Frederick Verner

1836—1928

Turned Out of the Herd, 1873, watercolour
20-3/4" x 29-1/4" (53 cm x 74 cm)
The Edmonton Art Gallery

Since his youth Frederick Verner had been an admirer of Paul Kane, and, like Kane, he travelled to western Canada, painting Indians in their native environment. Verner also frequently painted the great buffalo herds of the prairies, which he feared were slowly dying out.

Kane had concentrated chiefly on making accurate records of Indian life and culture, but some of his more imaginative works, such as *The Man That Always Rides* (p. 62), do show a certain Romantic spirit. Verner's buffalo paintings, however, are un-

ashamedly Romantic, and his animals are endowed with almost human qualities.

This practice was not uncommon among the animal painters of the middle and late nineteenth century, and Sir Edwin Landseer (1802—1873), a well-known English artist, was an expert at it. A favourite of Queen Victoria, he became extremely popular with a generation who enjoyed sentimental subjects and heart-rending scenes. Landseer painted his dogs, horses, deer, and other animals with semi-human expressions and in situations guaran-

The Upper Ottawa, 1882, oil on canvas
32-1/2" x 59-3/4" (83 cm x 152 cm)
The National Gallery of Canada, Ottawa

teed to move the hardest of hearts.

Verner's large canvases of buffalo herds tend to be rather artificial. The animals look like stuffed museum pieces posed in set scenery. But *Turned Out of the Herd,* a little watercolour with a soft and hazy atmosphere, has a poetic quality that is quite unlike the excesses in the large oils. The solitude of the lone buffalo is humanized and gives the painting a wistful emotional appeal. This feeling is increased by the artist's sensitive handling of colour. While his range of colour is limited, his effect is built up quietly tone by tone, and the whole scene is veiled in a misty light.

Frederick Verner was a Canadian by birth. His father was principal of the grammar school in Sheridan, Ontario. When he was twenty, Verner went to England to study art in London. At this time Landseer was at the height of his fame as a painter of animals and as the sculptor of the lions at the foot of the Nelson monument in Trafalgar Square. Verner would undoubtedly have been well acquainted with his work.

After finishing his training at art school, Verner, in true Romantic style, joined the British army and fought in Italy in support of Garibaldi's liberation campaign. At the age of twenty-six he returned to Canada to paint.

During the next few years he often travelled to western Canada, although he maintained a studio in Toronto. As a result of a meeting of Indian chieftains in Manitoba, he painted a series of twelve portraits. He also did many other works depicting Indian encampments, scenes from their daily life, and landscapes with buffaloes.

Later in his life Verner returned to live in England, though he came back to Canada on several visits. He died in London at the age of ninety-two.

The Upper Ottawa, painted in the latter part of his career, is a remarkable work. In spite of his English training, Verner has captured a sense of scale and atmosphere that is typically Canadian. The sparkling clarity of the light and the quiet early morning stillness belong to Canada and her lakes. So calm is the water that the smallest sound would echo across it; so vast are the dimensions that man seems almost an intruder.

We can see from this painting that Verner was one of those artists who recognized the immensity of Canada, not simply as a Romantic ideal, but as an actuality.

Allan Edson

1846–1888

Trout Stream in the Forest, 1880, oil on canvas
23-1/2″ x 18-1/4″ (60 cm x 46 cm)
The National Gallery of Canada, Ottawa

Allan Edson was born of American parents in the Eastern Townships of Quebec. At the age of fifteen he went to work in Montreal and there received his first art lessons. In 1864 he went to Europe to study, returning to Montreal when he was twenty-one.

On his return he became a member of the Society of Canadian Artists, which was formed to encourage the arts in Montreal. William Raphael and Adolphe Vogt were also among the founding members of this group.

As an artist, Edson's special skill lies in his own particular treatment of light. In *Trout Stream in the Forest* it is evident that his method of handling light differs from the various techniques of Raphael, Vogt, Verner, and Lucius O'Brien.

In *Behind Bonsecours Market* (p. 80) William Raphael has used light boldly and clearly, making it almost a part of the structure of his painting. Light areas are balanced against dark areas, and details are picked out and emphasized by light.

In *Approaching Storm* (p. 78) Vogt has also used light boldly, but he has used it to emphasize the drama of the scene. The viewer is made to feel the approach of the storm, and the urgency to escape it, because of the strong contrasts between the light and shadowy areas.

Verner, in his watercolour *Turned Out of the Herd* (p. 84), has used a misty effect that also adds to the meaning of the painting. The lone buffalo, isolated from the herd, is neither emphasized nor made to look dramatic. By distributing the light gently and evenly in quiet tones, the artist has related the buffalo to the loneliness of his open, empty scene.

In *Sunrise on the Saguenay* (p. 82) Lucius O'Brien has carried this misty effect even further with a technique called luminism. The solid forms of the mountains almost dissolve in the light of the rising sun, and nature is nearly a dream.

Edson's light flickers over surfaces, suggesting details rather than describing them. Some details are actually blurred together, but the radiance of the light gives the impression that every leaf and pebble has been clearly defined.

The sun filters down through the trees into this quiet and secret place where the boys are waiting for the trout to bite. It is a green place. The leaves, grass, and moss sparkle in the sun but look rich and cool in the shade.

Here nature seems very real and very private. Edson's *Trout Stream in the Forest* is not an escape into a dream world; rather, it is a place that all of us have known – if not in fact then in our imaginations. Nature for Edson is so lovely in itself that he feels no need to dramatize or create fantasies. The two boys fishing in the brook offer dreams enough.

Robert Harris

1849–1919

Harmony, 1886, oil on panel
12″ x 9-3/4″ (30 cm x 25 cm)
The National Gallery of Canada, Ottawa

Robert Harris was a very active artist. He is known to have painted nearly three hundred portraits, as well as other works on a wide range of subjects. In addition, about fifteen hundred of his drawings and sixty-six sketch-books have been found. Yet despite this enormous output, it was only after the first cross-country exhibition of his portraits in 1973 that he received much critical attention.

Certainly an artist cannot be judged on sheer quantity. Harris, though, was a conscientious man who was dedicated to art and deeply concerned about its quality. 'I don't want to do a parcel of trash,' he once said, when asked to submit sketches for a popular journal. Although he was a kind man with a delightful sense of humour, he could become quite outspoken on the subject of bad art or artists. He had no use for either.

Although some of Harris's paintings may seem rather safe and unimaginative, in fact many of his private works were quite experimental. These smaller canvases, many of them painted for his own enjoyment, show a wide range both of subject matter and style. While he specialized in portraiture, he also painted nudes and religious, historical, and genre subjects in an academic manner; in some of his landscapes he experimented with a lighter impressionistic style.

Robert Harris was born in Wales. When he was seven he came to Canada with his parents and six brothers and sisters. His father had suffered financial losses in Britain but looked forward to a successful life in Prince Edward Island. Sadly these hopes were not fulfilled, and Robert, determined to train as an artist, had to finance his own training in Boston with money that he had earned by painting portraits.

After leaving school, he paid a brief visit to England, where he spent as much time as possible in the art galleries. The paintings overwhelmed him.

'When you see them you forget everything but the pictures,' he wrote in a letter to his mother. It was then that he decided to become a professional artist.

Harris went to Boston when he was twenty-four, and he stayed there a year before returning to Charlottetown, where he again took up portrait painting. By doing so he planned to earn enough money for further study in Europe. Unfortunately his eyesight caused him a great deal of trouble, even at this early stage of his life, and it was always to be a source of pain and frustration.

Despite these difficulties Harris left for Europe in 1876. He stayed in London for a year, studying at University College and copying the works of the Old Masters in the galleries.

The following year he went to Paris to the studio of the French painter Léon Bonnat. He worked there with about fifty other students and enjoyed himself thoroughly. Harris admired Bonnat and wrote home saying, 'One of the critics said that his atelier (where I attend) was perhaps the best in Paris, *which means the world*.' He then added, 'Some kind of fun is always going on, notwithstanding that a good deal of good work is got through. Most of the students are about my age, many far older, but they are just as fond of play as a lot of little boys.'

While this visit to Paris lasted only one year, Harris returned to Europe on several later occasions to travel and study. In 1881 he worked again at the Atelier Bonnat and had a painting accepted at the Salon. He also studied at the Académie Julian, as did many other Canadian artists of the time.

What he learned abroad, both through studying the works of the great European artists and developing his technique, affected him throughout his life. But even more important was the artistic influence that he had in Canada. As George Reid, one of his pupils, commented, he 'almost at once introduced

Self Portrait, 1908, oil on pressed cardboard
10-1/2″ x 9-1/4″ (27 cm x 23 cm)
The Agnes Etherington Art Centre
Queen's University, Kingston

the French way of working, thereby considerably changing the teaching methods in the school.'

On Harris's return from Europe, Lucius O'Brien advised him to settle in Toronto, since he considered it 'the best art centre in Canada'. Here he quickly established himself as a successful portrait painter. Not only was he accepted as a member of the newly founded Royal Canadian Academy, but he was also appointed as one of the five members of the Committee of Management, whose task was to select the works to be accepted.

Harris received an extremely important commission at this time for a group portrait of the Fathers of Confederation. Naturally, this brought him a great deal of prestige. Unfortunately, the original painting was lost in the fire that destroyed the Parliament Buildings in 1916. All that remains are

the preparatory sketches and the cartoon, or final full-sized working drawing.

Harris was a popular and fashionable portrait painter both in Toronto and in Montreal, where he finally settled. His clients were wealthy, and he painted them as they wished to be seen. But, as one critic has said, 'He had no illusions about the pomp and circumstance of high society, but he realized that it was paintings for this class that would earn him his rent money.'

Even if some of these portraits appear to be a little dull and pompous to our eyes, there was nothing pompous about Harris himself. In his self portraits, such as the one shown here, we see a little man, with round glasses and a small neat beard, who frequently painted himself wearing a hat. Though his face is usually serious, he often appears to be on the verge of making a joke. With his lips pursed and the twinkle in his eye hidden in the shadows, it seems to be something of an effort for him to keep a straight face.

There is certainly nothing pompous either about his lovely painting of his wife Bessie playing the piano (p. 88). Entitled *Harmony,* it is just that. Bessie may or may not have been wearing a green dress that day, but Harris has used the colour most effectively to produce a soothing and restful atmosphere. And out of this simple subject he has created a quiet, harmonious mood.

By subtly introducing the element of music into his painting, Harris is drawing us gently into this quiet, untroubled scene through sound and sight. Even the misty outline of the glass vase on the piano adds to the effect. It seems so fragile that it would certainly shatter if the chords of music were too harsh.

George Reid

1860–1947

Mortgaging the Homestead, 1890, oil on canvas
50-1/2" x 83-1/2" (128 cm x 212 cm)
The National Gallery of Canada, Ottawa

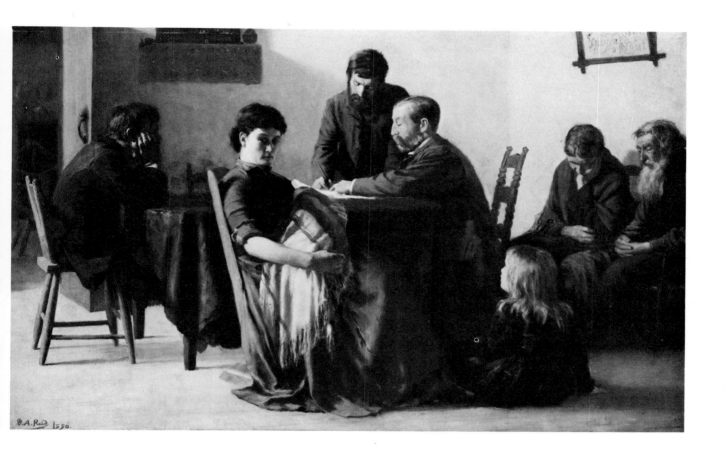

George Reid's *Mortgaging the Homestead* (p. 91) is a good example of the narrative type of subject matter that was highly approved by the French Academy. This style, popular during the latter half of the nineteenth century, was imported into Canada by artists trained in Paris.

Though it is a genre subject of farm life, this painting has none of the quaint, rustic quality of Krieghoff's work, for example. Instead, Reid has concentrated on arousing sympathetic feelings from the viewer and showing 'the trials and vicissitudes of Canadian agricultural life'.

The accepted academic style of painting supported these more serious aims. Careful modelling of the figures and graded tones of quiet colours emphasize the feeling of realism. Also in keeping with the Academy's standards, the composition is logical and balanced.

George Reid was born on a farm in western Ontario. His father, who was a pioneer, had planned that his sons would build homesteads and till the land. He strongly disapproved of George's interest in painting and at first made every attempt to discourage it. But eventually he relented, giving his son money to go to Toronto and enrol in the Ontario School of Art. There Reid worked for four years under Robert Harris, who had recently returned from Paris and was teaching according to French academic principles.

At the age of twenty-two Reid moved to Philadelphia to study at the Pennsylvania Academy of Fine Arts under Thomas Eakins. While he was there, he prepared several canvases for exhibition in Toronto and also became a demonstrator in anatomy. From Eakins he gained a solid background in realistic portraiture and figure painting.

In 1885 he left Philadelphia with his new wife, a fellow student, for a short visit to Europe. Afterwards they returned to Toronto to teach and earn money to study in Paris. On their arrival in Paris they met Paul Peel, William Brymner, and Maurice Cullen, and they worked with them at the Académies Julian and Colarossi.

The training and experience that Reid had gained in figure painting under Eakins served him well, and it was in this area that he excelled. While he was in Paris one of his paintings was accepted by the French Salon. On his return to Canada late in 1889, he became a full member of the Royal Canadian Academy. *Mortgaging the Homestead* was his diploma piece.

After returning to Toronto, Reid began teaching at the Central Ontario School of Art and Design and was principal from 1912 to 1918. He worked in oils, watercolours, and pastels and also did many murals for private and public commissions, including Toronto City Hall. Though he did paint some portraits, the majority of his work was of genre, historical, and landscape subjects. In 1944 Reid presented 459 paintings to the Ontario government.

Mortgaging the Homestead, in keeping with popular fashion, has a narrative theme. The artist appeals to the viewer to have sympathy with this poor family, now forced to give up ownership of the homestead they have built. Earlier Reid's own father had had to mortgage his home; his older brother John, probably reflected in the figure at the left of the painting, had been forced to work elsewhere to prevent the farm being lost to the creditors.

Independence, at that time, was a source of great pride, and to mortgage the family homestead was considered a terrible disgrace. To increase the sentimental effect of his story, Reid has included a weeping mother holding her baby, an innocent little girl with golden hair, and aged grandparents bowed over in dejection.

Often in this type of nineteenth-century narrative

painting there is an obvious moral message. This frequently took the form of a condemnation of laziness, drunkenness, or any other social vice that leads to bad ends. Here though there is no such moral.

The purpose of this narrative is to arouse feelings of pity for the poor family, and the sentiment is only surpassed by another painting of Reid's, *The Foreclosure of the Mortgage* (1934). Here a tearful family groups around a dying father, while the bailiff forecloses the loan on their home.

Reid's style of painting in *Mortgaging the Homestead* is as carefully studied as his subject. The composition is logical and balanced, and the figures are firmly drawn and modelled. Colours are subdued, and there is a harmony of light and shadow that assists the composition in binding all the parts of the painting together.

The signing of the mortgage is the major point of the narrative. Logically, Reid has placed it in the middle of the central triangle created by the main figures in the drama. Around them are the minor characters, but they too are held firmly into the picture by the angled chair backs, picture frames, and doorway. Each small group is complete in itself, but is also related to the whole.

In order to achieve the necessary realism and accuracy of lighting effects, Reid often set up a type of stage in his studio. After the painting was completed, he would display it privately before sending it off for exhibition. He was a popular artist who sold well, and he continued to be recognized in the French Salon and the Pennsylvania Academy, where he had trained as a young man.

Paul Peel

1860–1892

A Venetian Bather, 1889, oil on canvas
61-1/2" x 44-1/2" (156 cm x 113 cm)
The National Gallery of Canada, Ottawa

In 1890 Paul Peel won a gold medal at the Paris Salon with a painting of a nude entitled *After the Bath*. Sarah Bernhardt, the famous actress, was anxious to buy it, but its price was too high for her. Eventually it was purchased by a member of the Hungarian Royal Family, and at a later date it was returned to Canada. *After the Bath* and this painting, *A Venetian Bather*, were only two of several nudes painted by Peel in the late 1880s in Paris.

This was a bold step for the few Canadians painting nudes, since the strict morals of their nineteenth-century society forbade it. Nevertheless, owing to Peel's international reputation, and the fact that the model he chose was sufficiently young and innocent, *A Venetian Bather* was well received when it was shown in Toronto.

Paul Peel was born in London, Ontario. Encouraged by his father, he enrolled at the age of seventeen in the Pennsylvania Academy of Fine Arts in Philadelphia. Thomas Eakins (1844–1916), the great American figure and portrait painter, had recently returned there from Paris, where he had trained under the well-known French Academy painter Gérôme (1824–1904). As an accepted part of his studies Eakins had worked from the nude model. This, along with the study of anatomy, was considered essential for good figure painting.

In Philadelphia Peel received similar training, and for a while he was an instructor of anatomy at the Academy. In 1880, after three years in Philadelphia, he went to Europe, where he studied briefly at the Royal Academy in London. He then moved to Paris and for five years worked under Gérôme, Constant, and other academic painters. Peel never returned to live in Canada, but he paid several visits home, holding exhibitions and selling his paintings. In 1882 Peel married a Danish art student. He was only thirty-two when he died in Paris.

A Venetian Bather is a painting that makes a strong appeal to the senses. Carefully posed and subtly lit, it shows the artist's skilful use of colour and texture. The young girl's skin is warm and soft against the gleaming surface of the glass. The hot reds and cool greens of the furnishings are held in balance by the glow of the golden mirror. The velvet chair, damask curtain, and crisp cotton petticoat all tempt the sense of touch, while the eye is seduced by colour and line. Curves and counter-curves ripple and flow.

It is an elegant painting in keeping with the increasingly refined tastes of late nineteenth-century France. But undisguised and with no diversions, it would probably have outraged the Canadian public. Skilfully, the artist has protected himself by choosing a child model who plays innocently with a pretty kitten. Victorian morals could thus be satisfied, and the painting enjoyed without guilt.

Peel was not alone in his approach to the painting of the nude. It was, in fact, an almost inevitable result of the moral restrictions of the time. With the exception of a few artists who were breaking away from tradition, the academic painters of the later nineteenth century 'disguised' their nudes. To do this they depicted them as figures in so-called mythological stories or in coy and artificial situations. For example, Cabanel and Bouguereau, who were working in Paris when Peel was there, painted the female figure with sugary sentimentality.

The nineteenth-century artists who painted nudes extracted from the art of the past both the spiritual goddess and the worldly flesh-and-blood woman. They then combined them into a single figure who was neither pure nor earthy. *The Venetian Bather* belongs to the same tradition, and, as a result, it seems to lack an honest expression of sheer delight in the beauty of the female form.

William Brymner

1855–1925

A Wreath of Flowers, 1884, oil on canvas
47-1/4″ x 55″ (120 cm x 140 cm)
The National Gallery of Canada, Ottawa

Although William Brymner was born in Scotland, he came to Canada as an infant. His father became Dominion Archivist in Ottawa and later was able to arrange for William to study architecture there under the Chief Dominion Architect. Throughout Brymner's career as an artist, his father remained his firm supporter and adviser.

At the age of twenty-three William was sent to Paris to assist with the Canadian exhibition at the Universal Exposition of 1878. He remained there until 1886, at first planning to study architecture but later deciding to become an artist.

In the autumn of that year he entered Julian's, where A.W. Bouguereau and several other noted French artists were the official instructors. In actual fact, most students at the large private academies and at the Ecole des Beaux-Arts received little personal attention from major artists. Instead, they learned from constant practice and repetition and from observing the work of others.

The style that Brymner absorbed was a form of Naturalism. At this time, simple scenes of ordinary life were popular as subject matter, but they were portrayed on large canvases as if to emphasize their importance and make them grand. Subjects that suggested a story, even a simple one, were the most popular. Brymner's father wrote the following advice to his son: 'Some little domestic genre pieces, or some touch of humour, with a taking title... anything that people can fix a story on would be good policy.... There must be some *human interest* to attract those who know little about technique.'

Styles and techniques were changing greatly in France during the 1880s. The old academic methods were still being taught in the schools, but younger artists were experimenting with newer ideas and approaches.

By this time Impressionism was a generally accepted style of painting outside the official academic circles and was even affecting the more traditional artists. The aim of the Impressionists was to capture the effects of light as it played off the surface of objects. Their palettes became lighter; their canvases, airier. Solid forms became less important in the search for general effects and impressions. Although Brymner and many other artists in this transitional period never became Impressionists in the full sense of the word, their work did become more impressionistic.

Brymner was still influenced by the academic approach to painting and by the work of particular artists. Ernest Meissonier (1815—1890), for instance, impressed him greatly with his close attention to every tiny detail in his large canvases.

This influence and others are apparent in Brymner's *Wreath of Flowers*. The subject matter, children making daisy chains on a warm summer day, is simple and natural and lends itself to a mild little story. But despite the simplicity of the subject, the scene is made important by the artist's treatment of it and by the large size of the canvas. The composition, in fact, is quite daring. Organized on a strong diagonal, it is kept stable by the placement of the figures on a horizontal line and the path on an almost vertical one.

As if caught by the camera, the foreground details are clearly defined in a way that Meissonier might have painted them. But the middle distance and background are suggested in a more impressionistic way.

Colour is not used in clearly defined areas, as it had been in the classical academic tradition. Instead, there is a general blending of tones of green and brown, giving a broad effect of light and space. The painting, though neither intellectually nor emotionally stirring, is pleasing in its quiet naturalism.

In 1886 *Wreath of Flowers* was exhibited in

London, where is was praised by the critics. It was then sent to Ottawa as Brymner's diploma piece for membership in the Royal Canadian Academy.

On his return home that year, William Brymner replaced Robert Harris as head instructor at the Art Association of Montreal, a post he held for thirty-five years.

He was greatly respected as a teacher and was a friend of many artists, including Homer Watson, Horatio Walker, and Maurice Cullen, with whom he travelled and sketched. In the later years of his life, his style became looser and he became increasingly concerned with effects of light and atmosphere. Although never a modern artist himself, Brymner was one of the first Canadians to lay the foundations of a bridge between the old artistic world and the new one.

Blair Bruce

1859—1906

The Phantom Hunter, 1888, oil on canvas
59-1/2″ x 75-1/4″ (151 cm x 191 cm)
The Art Gallery of Hamilton

Blair Bruce was born in Hamilton. His father William was a well-known astronomer and amateur artist, who took an active interest in his son's career. At the age of eighteen Bruce entered the Hamilton Art School and then worked for three years in an architect's office.

In many ways Bruce's early career is curiously like that of William Brymner. Both young men gave up architecture to study art in Paris in the Académie Julian. (Bruce enrolled there in 1881.) Both worked under Professor T. Robert-Fleury, who taught design, and under A.W. Bouguereau, the Salon painter. But while Brymner returned to Canada to live, Bruce only came back on visits. On one disastrous occasion in 1885 Bruce was shipwrecked in the St. Lawrence at Anticosti. Much of his work was lost in the accident, and as a result he suffered a collapse.

In 1888 he married Caroline Benedicks, a Swedish sculptress, and together they travelled widely. Finally they settled in Visby on the Swedish island of Gotland. Bruce live there until he died at the age of forty-seven.

Bruce was an eclectic artist. He was easily influenced by many different styles of painting, and, as a result, he produced a wide range of works during his lifetime.

At the Académie Julian he was taught in the traditional manner with its emphasis on figure painting, studied from plaster casts and nude models. Here he was also taught to aim for realism in his art and to pay strict attention to exact detail. He learned too that sentiment in subject matter was another desirable quality. In 1884 one of his paintings was accepted and hung in the French Salon, making him feel that he could now 'take his place in the world of Art with a solid, solid footing'.

After his first year at the Academy, Bruce began to work outdoors more often. He lived for a while with several English and American artists in Théodore Rousseau's house in the village of Barbizon. Rousseau (1812–1867) had been one of the principal painters of the mid-nineteenth-century group known as the Barbizon School. Their aim had been to work directly from nature, depicting exactly what they saw. They carefully avoided the composed and studied style of academic landscape painters. Even fifteen years after the death of Rousseau, the influence of the Barbizon School was still strong.

Bruce was also becoming interested in experimenting with Impressionism, a style that was firmly established by the time he arrived in Paris. The first Impressionist exhibition was held in 1874 and was followed by seven others, the last in 1886.

Despite these influences on his work, Bruce never ignored his original academic training. As a result, his paintings vary considerably in style and lack any one definite direction.

Bruce never returned to live in Canada, but it seems from his letters that he often felt homesick and frequently chose Canadian subject matter to express his sense of nationalism. For *The Phantom Hunter* (p. 99) his father sent him authentic trapper's clothing and snowshoes.

The story for the painting comes from what he thought to be an old Canadian legend of the Walker of the Snow. In a letter to his father he spoke of having read a poem on the subject. He believed that the 'walker' was the ghostly old Jack Frost, who pursued trappers through the snow and froze them to death.

Both in style and subject matter Bruce's painting is in keeping with the current tastes. The Romantic subject of the hunter, alone against the harshness of Nature, is another expression of the fear and loneliness often seen in nineteenth-century art. Nature made sweet and sentimental or sublimely moving was one source of escape from the pressures of life. Otherwise she was portrayed as she is here: cruel, impersonal, an enemy to man in his solitude.

In painting style Bruce followed the newer academic trend towards a more open composition and a sense of light and space. The relationship of muted tones, here limited to shades of grey and ochre, has an atmospheric quality that tends to blur rigid shapes and give a more generalized effect.

Referring to *The Phantom Hunter* in a letter to his mother of March 24, 1888, Bruce said that this was the first time he had 'attempted to show anything of our national works in France'. Yet it is interesting to note that this was still a studio painting, Canadian in content only, and even that acquired from a hazy myth in a literary source.

Homer Watson

1855–1936

The Stone Road, 1881, oil on canvas
36" x 51-1/4" (91 cm x 130 cm)
The National Gallery of Canada, Ottawa

In comparing two of Homer Watson's paintings, *The Stone Road* (p. 102) and *The Flood Gate* (p. 104), we are able to see just how much an artist's style can change during his lifetime. But his paintings also give us the opportunity of looking at two interesting and very important aspects of art – aspects that we have touched upon when considering the work of Thomas Davies.

Obviously, all artists change. The more they paint, the more they become aware of their own weaknesses and the more they strive for new goals. But often the greatest changes of style take place when artists look carefully at the work of other artists. Art tends to grow out of art more than it does out of looking at the real world. This is because art is not a copy of nature; it is a world of its own with its own rules.

But every artist uses his own personal experiences as a kind of base from which he works. Many of the painters we have already considered were born in Europe; others were greatly influenced early in their careers by the training they received in other countries. A few, like Homer Watson, lived most of their lives in one place and felt deeply attached to their homes. Although Watson did go to Europe for a while, it was not until he was in his thirties and had already painted for some years.

Watson, though, was so influenced by what he saw abroad that it seems he altered his vision to make it suit the painting styles he admired. As one critic so well expressed it, in Watson's later painting he lost 'the magic of place. Though probably better painting, it is poorer art.'

The Stone Road was painted in 1881. Watson at this time was living in Doon, a small village near Kitchener, Ontario. It was here that he had been born and brought up, and his deep feelings for the place of his youth remained with him throughout his life.

As a child, Watson had shown interest in the illustrations that he saw in books and magazines. When he was nineteen he moved to Toronto, where he saw real paintings for the first time. In fact, the paintings that he saw at the Toronto Normal School were only copies of the Old Masters, but with his lack of art education, he felt that they were all he needed and set about copying them.

Watson stayed in Toronto for about a year, working in a photographic studio. There he met John Fraser, a partner in the firm and one of the leading landscape painters in Toronto, who encouraged him and gave him some lessons.

Later, journeying to the United States, he met George Inness, a member of the Hudson River School of landscape painters, and did some sketching himself in the Adirondacks. After one year he returned to Doon and opened a small studio.

Watson's lack of formal training did not seem to hamper his general acceptance as an artist. In fact, one painting, *The Pioneer Mill,* was purchased as a gift for Queen Victoria when it was exhibited at the Royal Canadian Academy in 1880. Despite the fame and publicity that this event brought him, Watson continued to live quietly in Doon, painting some of his most personal and sincere works. *The Stone Road* is one of these.

When viewing the paintings of Thomas Davies (pp. 33, 34), we considered his vision and the way in which he looked at the world with intense concentration. Homer Watson's *Stone Road* conveys much the same feeling. The little buggy travelling down the road seems immensely important. It is small, actually out of proportion with the rest of the picture, yet it attracts the eye with an almost magnetic force. This is partly because of the position that it occupies in the artist's overall design.

We are led into the picture by the road, which curves around and disappears, bringing our view

The Flood Gate, 1900, oil on canvas
32-1/2″ x 46-3/4″ (83 cm x 119 cm)
The National Gallery of Canada, Ottawa

into the centre of the painting. The high mass of trees on the left prevents the eye travelling on, while the blocks on the right again hold us back. The buggy, a dark spot on the light road, is placed on the same horizontal line as the small light tree on the left and the dark trees on the right.

Throughout the painting there are other small details that later catch the eye and hold it: the little cottage at the end of the road, the sheep in the field to the left, the glorious blue-green of the river, and the branches of the trees sharply outlined against the sky. Every detail has its own importance. Each one is a particular object, painted with intense concentration and concern. Like Davies's work it gives the impression of an amateur, or naïve, artist painting with love, rather than a professional artist painting with technical knowledge and skill.

The Flood Gate was painted nearly twenty years later. By this time Watson had been to London, where he had had a very successful exhibition. He had been most impressed by the work of John Constable (1776–1837), the great English landscape painter, and also by the work of the French Barbizon painters (p. 100). In fact, *The Flood Gate* depicts the same sort of subject that was often chosen by Constable, and Watson's style is modelled on his.

It is a far more accomplished and finished work than *The Stone Road*. In it we can sense that all the separate parts have been consciously woven into one strong overall design. The curving sweep of the road holds the foreground and the middle ground together. The shapes of the trees are repeated in the shapes of the clouds.

Yet, in relating each part to the next, and in building up a consistent pattern, the artist has lessened his intense concentration on each little detail. He has had to sacrifice the individual parts of his painting for the sake of creating a general impression. In some ways the painting becomes less interesting and less magical, though in others it is stronger and more complete.

Nevertheless, *The Flood Gate* is a fine painting. Watson's concern for capturing the effects of light is similar to Constable's. The painting was widely admired in England, and Watson was almost tempted to settle there. He decided against it, though, and remained in Doon, the village he had always loved so much.

Ozias Leduc

1864–1955

L'Enfant au Pain, c. 1892–1899, oil on canvas
19-7/8" x 22" (50 cm x 56 cm)
The National Gallery of Canada, Ottawa

Ozias Leduc's paintings of everyday objects and simple scenes have a spirit that is unique in Canadian art. They communicate feelings that cannot be expressed in words. Though his subjects are chosen from daily life, they seem to exist in a quiet and lovely world of their own. Simple and honest, they have a quality that reflects Leduc's sincere religious faith and suggests a state of being that is wholly good.

Les Trois Pommes (p. 108) is a tiny canvas, and the three apples in the wooden bowl are as straightforward a subject as an artist could choose. Yet Leduc has painted the apples with such love for their shape and colour that they seem to become objects of infinite importance and almost unearthly beauty. In the soft candlelight the apples glow with the warm colours the artist has applied brush stroke by tiny brush stroke.

Leduc's art is close in spirit to that of the French artist Chardin (1699–1779), one of the finest painters of still lifes and simple genre scenes. Like Leduc, Chardin painted objects of everyday life, such as jugs and bowls and copper urns. He also chose scenes from the daily lives of ordinary people. The aim of his art was to show the reality of his subject matter by concentrating on its form and texture and on the relationships between one object and another. But though Chardin painted his simple subjects with all the deep respect that he held for them, his approach was basically a worldly one. Leduc's idea was different: he seemed to be searching for the inner, spiritual meaning of all created things.

In *L'Enfant au Pain* there is the same sense of deep respect for ordinary objects and daily life. The form of the painting is not complicated, and throughout there is a sense of harmony of shapes and colours. The curves of the small bowl contrast with the straight lines of the table, but the shape of the bowl is echoed in the circular form of the hat. The angular position of the right arm is balanced by that of the left leg. The curve of the boy's back guides the eye and helps it travel easily within the composition. Just as gradually, but with enough contrast to keep the painting interesting, the colours move through a range of browns, golds, and oranges.

The boy seems completely absorbed in his own world, and his sense of concentration seems to penetrate the whole painting. It is as if this particular moment would last forever. The notes he plays on his harmonica hang in the air and time stands still. Leduc had that rare gift of being able to lift up the commonplace things of the world and give them perpetual life.

The poet William Blake put these feelings into words when he said that in our imagination it is possible

To see a World in a Grain of Sand
And a Heaven in a Wild Flower,
Hold Infinity in the palm of your hand
And Eternity in an hour.

It is in this sense that Ozias Leduc's paintings display a state of being that is wholly good. Such goodness has nothing to do with the solid moral virtues that the academic painters tried to show in their narrative pictures. Nor does it reflect the same spirit that Plamondon was suggesting in *Soeur Saint-Alphonse* and the *Still Life* (pp. 48, 49). There, a balanced and controlled style has been used to express the artist's sense of purpose and order in the world.

Ozias Leduc was a religious man who believed in God and the goodness and beauty of His creations. In his painting he attempted to show more than the everyday reality of the objects he saw. He wanted to

Les Trois Pommes, 1887, oil on canvas
8-7/8″ x 12-1/8″ (22 cm x 31 cm)
Private Collection

express his own inner feelings about the spiritual mystery of creation.

Leduc was born in the village of St-Hilaire, which lies at the foot of two curiously shaped mountains southeast of Montreal. Here he spent all of his ninety-one years, except for a short trip that he took to Europe when he was thirty-three. Leduc received no formal training in art, but he had a natural talent and found employment as a church decorator.

When he was young, the people of St-Hilaire were very poor. But Leduc, a shy and retiring man, was happy in their company and made little attempt to associate with the fashionable artists of Montreal. He felt a great sense of loyalty to St-Hilaire and to its people. He decorated the church there and painted portraits of his friends and relatives. Little canvases, like the two here, he produced for his own pleasure.

For money he depended on his commissions for church decoration. During his lifetime he painted about one hundred and fifty large paintings and additional decorations for twenty-seven cathedrals, churches, and chapels. The art of church ornamentation had declined badly in the late nineteenth century, owing to the efforts of uncreative decorators. But because of his dedication, Leduc was largely responsible for restoring dignity to this art.

On his visit to Europe in 1897, Leduc saw the work of the Pre-Raphaelite artists in England. In Paris he was also impressed by some of the Symbolist painters. Both groups were searching for new expressions and meaning in art. Through imagination, dreams, and legend they hoped to reach a more spiritual understanding of life, and their approach appealed to Leduc.

Not only did he become interested in the work of the French Symbolist movement in art and literature; he also started a subscription to a French art magazine that he kept for many years. So in spite of his continued isolation in St-Hilaire, he was familiar with the movement in Paris for most of his working life.

In his later years his work became more and more symbolic. Landscapes that he painted on Mont St-Hilaire took on a strange and mysterious quality. As one critic has said, Ozias Leduc 'saw nature in the light of his dreams.'

Horatio Walker

1858 – 1938

Ave Maria, undated, oil on canvas
46″ x 34″ (117 cm x 86 cm)
The Art Gallery of Hamilton

Of the many artists we have considered who were interested in genre painting, each has revealed his own particular attitude towards his subject. Krieghoff (p. 59) usually chose to show the fun and jolly times that the French-Canadian habitants enjoyed. He avoided looking at the hardships of farming life and concentrated on the quaint scenes he believed people would rather remember. Vogt (p. 78) and Raphael (p. 80) depicted some of the daily activities of peasant life, yet both artists used their subject matter as suitable material for their own particular artistic styles. Reid emphasized the narrative story of *Mortgaging the Homestead* (p. 91) in order to make the viewer feel pity for the characters involved. Ozias Leduc (p. 106), however, took a completely different approach. He used the language of painting itself – forms, composition, colour – to emphasize the simplicity of his subject and his respect for that way of life.

Horatio Walker was also a genre painter who had great respect for farming people and for the dignity of life spent close to the soil. But his approach differed yet again. As usually happens, the circumstances of his early life and training influenced, indeed formed, his style and opinions about art.

Walker was born at Listowel, Ontario, but went to Toronto when he was fifteen. There he met Homer Watson, and the two young men began a friendship that lasted the rest of their lives. They both worked at William Notman's photographic studio, where they received encouragement and help from the landscape painter John Fraser, a partner in the firm.

Three years later Horatio Walker went to the United States. Unlike his friend Watson, who returned after a year, Walker settled in New York City in 1878 at the age of twenty and kept a studio there for most of his life. Later he built a house on Ile d'Orléans, near Quebec City, where he spent his summers and retired in his old age.

In 1881 Walker went to Europe for the visit that was to become the vital shaping force of his artistic life. While he was there, he became deeply impressed by the work of the famous French artist Jean François Millet (1814–1875), who had died six years earlier.

Millet had been one of the most renowned members of the Barbizon School, a group of artists who had painted around the village of Barbizon in the Forest of Fontainebleau. Though it is called a forest, the scenery is actually quite tame, consisting of fields, woods, farms, and cottages. But for the Barbizon painters it possessed the peace and tranquility of natural beauty. The life of the peasants who lived there also seemed to be ideally good and innocent.

The aim of the artists was to capture nature as it actually was. To do this they painted outdoors, directly onto their canvases. Today this does not seem extraordinary, yet until the Barbizon painters introduced the method, nearly all landscapes were painted indoors from memory, imagination, or from small sketches. These artists wanted to paint nature directly, but more than this, they wanted to catch its moods and spirit.

Horatio Walker was impressed by what he felt to be the simple honesty of the Barbizon group. Much of the work he did after his return to this continent was based on their approach. Oxen ploughing fields, woodcutters at work, and cows drinking in a stream are typical of the subjects he painted.

But Walker's particular hero was Millet, whose art captured what he felt to be the natural goodness and nobility of peasant life. Today it is sometimes thought that Millet's interpretations went too far, that his peasants seem a bit too good and too symbolic – in fact, that his subjects are too sentimental.

111

Horatio Walker's *Ave Maria* (p. 110) shows an obvious resemblance to Millet's famous painting *The Angelus,* a work that hung in almost every Victorian household as a symbol of the noble poor. In it two peasants are seen pausing from their labour in the fields, with heads bowed in prayer, while the church bells chime the evening blessing. In his *Ave Maria* Walker has used the same theme, showing a farmer praying at a roadside shrine against the glow of the setting sun.

In the nineteenth century there was a tendency to preach, particularly to the poor, about proper feelings and behaviour, and in both these works there is a certain sense of moralizing. But Millet, born a peasant himself, was a sincere artist who had shared the life of the working man.

His work caused considerable controversy, and he was accused of being a radical socialist. One French critic of the time said, 'This is the painting of men who don't change their linen, who want to intrude themselves upon gentlemen; this art offends and disgusts me.' But in England and the United States Millet's work was greatly admired, and it influenced the Hudson River School and many of the American genre painters.

Horatio Walker followed in Millet's footsteps and became immensely popular with the American public on his return from Europe. But while Millet had been a peasant and, even after becoming successful, had lived quietly in the village of Barbizon, Walker became a wealthy painter who divided his time between New York and Ile d'Orléans. His paintings sold in the United States and Canada at very high prices.

In keeping with this transitional period of painting styles, Walker's work shows various influences. His choice of rural subject matter remained close to that of the Barbizon painters, but his rich treatment of colour and light became far more dramatic.

He himself saw his work as a tribute to rural life and simple country people. He expressed his thoughts in the following words that are typical of the sentiment of the time:

The pastoral life of the people of our countryside, the noble work of the Habitant, the magnificent panoramas which surround him, the different aspects of our seasons, the calm of our mornings and the serenity of our evenings, the movement of ebb and flow of our tides which I have observed on the shores of my island which truly is the sacred temple of the muses and a gift of the gods to men: such are the preferred subjects of my painting.

PART V

THE EARLY YEARS OF THE
TWENTIETH CENTURY

circa 1910 to 1940

As in earlier years, painting in Canada during the first part of the twentieth century was heavily influenced by European styles. In increasing numbers, artists were training abroad, both in Europe and the United States. It was also becoming easier for artists to make short visits to other countries in order to see styles or particular paintings that had been made popular through photographs and magazines. The First World War also brought many Canadians across the Atlantic, where they too were able to see original European works of art.

The first real Canadian school of painting, the Group of Seven, emerged during this period. At first the Group encountered strong criticism and even insults, but by the 1930s they were so well accepted that they had become almost a national symbol. Despite the advantages of achieving an art form that had wide popular appeal, this patriotic attitude was also, unfortunately, largely responsible for the rejection of many newer forms of art that had been recognized in Europe thirty years earlier.

In the last years of the nineteenth century and the early years of the twentieth, there were tremendous changes in the artistic ideas and styles of Europe. In fact, the changes were so great that the main aims and directions of art in the Western world shifted for the first time since the Renaissance.

The Renaissance of the fifteenth century had restored an intense interest in the visible world – an interest that had been almost dead during the previous era, dominated by the developing Christian church. During the Middle Ages, the church had emphasized the importance of man's soul over his body. It taught that this world was only a passing phase in man's existence and that life on earth should be spent preparing for the life hereafter. For this reason, artists made little attempt to create realistic descriptions of the world around them.

This period of the Middle Ages came to an end when philosophers, artists, and writers began to look back with admiration to the Classical era of Greece and Rome. At that time, man and his personal achievements in the real world had been considered to be of supreme importance. Thus, artists had been more concerned with depicting man in his physical form than in preparing him for a life after death.

The Renaissance was literally a rebirth of an interest in man and his world. But Christianity was still strong, and so the Renaissance combined the Classical belief in the importance of man with the Christian belief in God. Now mankind was seen as the greatest of God's creations, made in His image in the world of nature.

Physical and natural sciences were eagerly studied, and the arts reflected a new interest in the visible world. Artists and sculptors studied anatomy, devised perspective as a method of representing three-dimensional space, and used effects of light to give a sense of realism; they sought every possible way to create an illusion of the real world.

Until the end of the nineteenth century, these ideas were still the basis of all Western art. Certainly there were different styles and aims, but basically the artist sought to transform a flat canvas into a window on the world.

The confidence in man and God that had brought this style into existence, and maintained it for so long, was already being questioned during the nineteenth century. The Romantic artist was looking inwards, exploring his feelings and imagination, instead of expressing a belief in the order and purpose of nature, as the Classical artist had done.

The French and American Revolutions, the Industrial Revolution, and new scientific discoveries were turning all accepted traditions upside down. Machines were replacing man, and the old social patterns were being overthrown.

Religion, too, was questioned. Theories stating that man was descended from a monkey, instead of from Adam, and that nature had evolved over millions of years, instead of being created in seven days, caused people to question the existence of God.

Increasing populations and devastating wars made human beings feel less and less significant. And at the same time, psychological studies by men like Freud and Jung were encouraging people to look inwards, instead of outwards.

By the end of the nineteenth century in Europe, artistic expression began to change violently. Instead of painting realistic scenes of the visible world, artists were becoming increasingly concerned with themselves and their reactions to life around them.

Feelings took a wide variety of forms, and as a result this period of art became a period of 'isms': Impressionism, Fauvism, Expressionism, Cubism, Surrealism. The movements followed each other in rapid succession.

In Canada the pace was slower and the range of styles more limited, since the population was smaller and art in those years was not of great general interest. Nevertheless, painting in this country was strongly influenced by the European developments. Though their full effect became more evident from the 1940s onward, the foundation was clearly laid in the early part of the century.

James Morrice

1865–1924

The Ferry, Quebec, 1909, oil on canvas
24″ x 32″ (61 cm x 81 cm)
The National Gallery of Canada, Ottawa

James Morrice was one of the most important Canadian artists to bridge the gap between the art of the nineteenth and twentieth centuries. He was also one of the first to understand that the changes taking place in art were of great significance and that, in fact, a new era was beginning.

Morrice was born into a wealthy family in Montreal. He began his career in law, but at the age of twenty-four he decided to go to Paris to train as an artist. Like so many Canadians before him, he enrolled in the Académie Julian, but his training there did not have the strong influence upon him that it had had upon other students. Instead, the ideas of Morrice's wide circle of scholarly and artistic friends proved far more influential to his developing style. With his friends, among whom were Maurice Cullen and William Brymner, he painted in the French countryside and by the sea. While Morrice exhibited regularly in Montreal and remained a Canadian citizen, Paris became his home.

During the later years of the nineteenth century, the most popular types of painting in Canada were those based on academic subject matter and style. Many people, particularly in Montreal and Toronto, were now wealthy enough to buy works of art and were guided in their taste by what was fashionable among the 'experts'.

Portraits were popular, as were genre scenes based on sad, sentimental little stories, such as Reid's *Mortgaging the Homestead,* and landscapes of mood and atmosphere, such as Lucius O'Brien's *Sunrise on the Saguenay.* Some of the best of these are fine works of art, but many are dry and dull.

Canadian collectors of the late nineteenth century were also fond of the mood landscapes of a group of Dutch artists known as the Hague School. Their works were related in style to the works of the Barbizon painters but often tended to be rather dark and gloomy. Large numbers of these paintings were imported into Canada to meet the demands of the buying public.

In reaction to the tired repetition of style and uninspired approach to subject matter, drastic changes began to occur in European art in the 1870s. In Canada, though, it was another thirty years before these changes had much effect. Basically, the reaction against the academic tradition came from two directions and was founded on two different artistic theories: one was English and was founded on the idea that art is art and should be enjoyed for itself alone – art for art's sake, as the theory was called; the other source was French and was largely a result of new scientific experiments with light and colour.

The chief promoter of the English theory was James Whistler (1834–1903), who later became James Morrice's greatest inspiration. Briefly, Whistler's theory stated that a painting exists in its own right; it should be enjoyed for itself and does not have to have any particular story or dominant subject. Although after 1910 Morrice was influenced by other artists, particularly the French painter Matisse, his style was largely based on Whistler's convictions.

Morrice's *The Ferry, Quebec* (p. 115) is quite clearly a landscape in which each object is recognizable, and it is so closely related to nature that we can almost feel the cold winter air. But the scene is not carefully or realistically described. Instead, it is the artist's impression of his subject, which he has translated into a formal work of art.

Neither the figures on the wharf, nor the horses and carts, nor even the ferry boat has a strong individual identity. The artist has merely provided clues for his viewers to recognize some of the factual details of the scene. Instead of concentrating on these, he has given only a general impression of the view in order to keep the subject in balance with its artistic qualities.

Morrice has applied his paint in a fine, silky sheen, through which the underlying canvas can be seen in places. The white-caps on the water and the flecks of deeper colour that highlight the blue river also give interesting effects of texture.

Colour too contributes to the overall impression of the scene and its aesthetic effect. The clear cold blue of the water, the grey sky, and white snow suggest a winter theme. But the warm red roof on the yellow house and the echoing gleams of yellow on the snow make a lively artistic contrast.

The composition is subtle and interesting. The canvas is divided into three main horizontal bands. The river crosses the whole surface, while the wharf and the far shore each project three-quarters of the distance from the left and the right. Like the diagonal in the letter Z, the angle of the house carries through to the ferry, whose funnel and curling smoke complete the link. But to tie the parts more firmly together and prevent too obvious a Z-shaped composition, Morrice has quite casually introduced the dark shapes of the horses and figures on the wharf.

Despite its skilful composition, nothing in the painting looks forced or studied; its beauty is subtle and understated. *The Ferry, Quebec* has a cool detachment and harmony of design and colour that give the painting its own identity. Its meaning lies principally in its aesthetic effect.

Maurice Cullen

1866–1934

Lévis from Quebec, 1906, oil on canvas
30-5/16″ x 40-3/16″ (77 cm x 102 cm)
Art Gallery of Ontario, Toronto

Maurice Cullen, like his friend James Morrice, was an artist of major importance in the development of twentieth-century Canadian painting. In fact, there are some artists and scholars who think that Cullen's work had even more influence in Canada than Morrice's. A.Y. Jackson, for instance, said, 'to us he was a hero'.

Certainly his painting technique, which was based on French Impressionism, differed from anything that had been seen before in this country, and it did have considerable influence on the generation of artists that followed him. But eventually the theory behind James Morrice's work, that a painting has its own rules and is independent of any definite subject, led more directly to twentieth-century abstract art.

Maurice Cullen was born in St. John's, Newfoundland, but moved with his family to Montreal when he was four. He started his art career as a sculptor and enrolled in 1889 at the official school of the French Academy in Paris. His major interest, though, changed from sculpture to painting, and it was in this area that he later studied for three years at the Ecole des Beaux-Arts.

Cullen then spent three more years painting landscapes in several regions of France. During this time he began painting in a style similar to that of the French Impressionists, though he never strictly followed their techniques.

In 1895 Cullen returned to Montreal and painted one of the first canvases in Canada that was based on Impressionistic ideas. Though his style was moderate and traditional compared with the work of the Impressionists in France, the Canadian public rejected it violently at first. But Cullen became increasingly popular, and by the 1920s he was earning a great deal of money as a painter. By that time the style had been established for fifty years and, even in Canada, was considered traditional compared with the work of the Group of Seven.

In many ways French Impressionism was a revolt against academic art, but, perhaps even more important, it was based on new scientific discoveries. In the latter half of the nineteenth century, a number of scientists had been studying the physics of light and colour. They found that our perception of colour is a result of the reflection of light off different surfaces. By shining light through a prism, the scientists proved that light is made up of the six colours of the spectrum: red, orange, yellow, green, blue, and violet. Thus, the objects we see in nature are actually blends of colours. The human eye mixes these so that surfaces appear to be made up of single hues, though, in fact, they are not.

Based on these theories, the Impressionists attempted to paint exactly what we see. As a result, no object is painted one single colour in Impressionist art; rather, it is composed of small flecks of many colours. These are the different hues in light itself, and they change as light is reflected off other objects.

It was also discovered that the shadow of an object contains the complementary colour of that object. (By arranging the colours of the spectrum in a circle, red is complementary to green, blue to orange, and yellow to violet.) This scientific information gave the Impressionists even more opportunity to brighten their canvases.

The other important idea that emerged from the Impressionist's theory of colour was that we do not actually see solid forms, but only the light that is reflected off them. As a result, Impressionist painters tended to break down the outlines of objects, because, they said, the eye only sees blurred forms made up of many coloured spots.

These theories were completely opposed to the traditional artistic methods of setting clear, solid shapes in a believable space and painting them in definite colours. So it was not too surprising that they caused a public outcry.

Nevertheless, the new style resulted in paintings that were light and lively. The sombre colours of many of the academic works and the dark, moody landscapes of the Hague School gave way to the new clear colours, based on white.

Cullen introduced many of the ideas of the Impressionists into Canada. But, as we can see in *Lévis from Quebec* (p. 118), he did not use the small, bright brush strokes of pure colour that were so popular among the French artists. Instead, he blended the colours that he used into harmonies and contrasts.

He was a master at painting snow in sunlight and in shadow. Understanding Impressionist theory, he knew that snow is not pure white and often reflects the blue of the sky. But in this painting, the near shore of the St. Lawrence, which reflects blue, is contrasted with the far shore, which is bathed in golden sunlight. This contrast of violet-blue and yellow-orange is often seen in Cullen's work.

His careful positioning of complementary colours is what gives a sense of unity to the whole work and relates each of its parts to the next: sky to snow to water, sunlit shore to smoke to cloud, houses to water to smoke to cloud. Everything is held together by the relationship of these colours that originate in light, shadow, and reflection.

It is interesting to compare the two paintings of *Lévis from Quebec,* the one by James Morrice (p. 115) and this one by Maurice Cullen. Although they were painted only three years apart by two friends whose training was similar, the individual aims of the artists were completely different.

Morrice was interested in a total, overall design that could be abstracted, or taken out of, his impression of a scene. As a result, he simplified his subject and concentrated on general effect, rather than on particular details. Morrice believed that a painting is a work of art that has a life of its own and is not meant to be a careful description of the real world. This is a basis for the idea that art is created solely for the purpose of giving us pleasure and adding something extra to our lives.

But Cullen, following the theories of the French Impressionists, which were based on scientific knowledge, was giving an even more accurate picture of the real world than earlier artists had done. His impressions, based entirely on light, portray the instant effects that our eyes actually perceive.

Marc-Aurèle de Foy Suzor-Coté

1869–1937

Passing Shadows, 1918, oil on canvas
40" x 54-1/8" (102 cm x 137 cm)
The Edmonton Art Gallery

The sparkle of sunlight on snow, chunks of ice floating on a thawing river, branches brittle with winter frost, all these are a part of early spring in Canada. It is an in-between time. The air is cold, but the sun is warm. The water has started to flow, and soon the snow will break away from the banks and be carried down the stream.

Passing Shadows is a winter scene that was painted outdoors. An example of what the French Impressionists called *plein air* painting, it was not composed from memory in a studio. The artist has caught the effect of sunlight and shadow on the snow and water. The deep blue of the stream is brought to life with touches of pink that reflect the overhanging branches, the trees, and the hills. Similarly, the snow catches the blue of the sky and the water, and it too shimmers with pinkish flecks. The whole painting, much like Cullen's *Lévis from Quebec* (p. 118), is woven together by this interplay of colour.

Suzor-Coté has created a bright and appealing atmosphere where light is the key element. There is no sense of moodiness, no suggestion of a mysterious spirit of Nature, and no questioning of man's place in the world of Nature. While these were all factors that influenced earlier nineteenth-century landscape painters, here it is the scene itself that interests the artist. What he seeks to describe is the impression that his eye receives when he views the effects of light and colour.

In *Passing Shadows* Suzor-Coté's style is closer to that of the French Impressionists than Maurice Cullen's was in *Lévis from Quebec*. Suzor-Coté has used small, individual brush strokes of separate colours and has applied them in thick layers of tiny flecks. From a distance, the eye mixes and melts these flecks into broader areas of sun and shadow, as it does when viewing nature. This technique, which represented the ideas of French Impressionism in their most basic form, was carried to its farthest extreme by Claude Monet, the greatest Impressionist of them all.

It is interesting that Morrice, Cullen, Gagnon, and Suzor-Coté all began their training in the academic schools of Paris, but eventually were drawn away to the countryside to sketch and paint. Early in their careers they were encouraged by younger artists who were tired of the older styles and theories, and finally all these Canadians became Impressionists. In fact, even some of the older artists, such as William Brymner, Robert Harris, Blair Bruce, and Horatio Walker, were affected to some degree by the new style.

Suzor-Coté was born in the little village of Arthabaska in Quebec. He first began to paint in the village church as assistant to the church decorator. His introduction to art was therefore much the same as Ozias Leduc's.

When he was twenty-one, he left for Paris and enrolled at the Académie Julian in 1890, the same year that Morrice enrolled there. But while Morrice remained only a short time, Suzor-Coté stayed for several years and then continued his academic training at the Académie Colarossi. He finally finished his studies at the Ecole des Beaux-Arts, the French Academy's official school. Suzor-Coté's early historical and figure paintings reveal all the characteristics of the formal methods he had learned

Altogether he spent eighteen years working in France and so had ample opportunity to observe all the new painting styles. Soon he began experimenting with Impressionist techniques. Since the first Impressionist exhibition was held in 1874, sixteen years before his arrival in Paris, and the final exhibition in 1886, four years before his arrival, Suzor-Coté was able to see the style in its fully developed state.

It was the style of the Impressionists that he brought back with him to Canada. Many of the paintings he did after his return were variations on one subject. *Passing Shadows* is one of several canvases that depict streams in early spring; another series is of winter landscapes. Later in his life Suzor-Coté explored the style even further, so that in scenes of snowstorms or cityscapes shrouded in smoke, solid forms began to melt completely into effects of light and haze.

Clarence Gagnon

1881–1942

Lonely Village on the St. Lawrence, c. 1922–1923
oil on canvas
20-1/8″ x 26-1/4″ (51 cm x 67 cm)
Art Gallery of Ontario, Toronto

Although Clarence Gagnon received most of his training in Paris, where he came into contact with academic and impressionistic styles, he is best remembered for his paintings of life in the Quebec countryside. In fact, his illustrations for the novel *Maria Chapdelaine* are among the most famous in French Canada. Basically Gagnon was a genre painter, and his style reflected his knowledge and love of the regions he painted.

Gagnon was born in Montreal and, like so many of his fellow artists, studied under William Brymner. He was sixteen when he began his studies at the Art Association of Montreal, and he stayed there for three years. In 1904 he was sent to the Académie Julian by a wealthy collector who was impressed with his work. Like other Canadian artists working in France at this time, Gagnon spent much of his spare time sketching and painting in the countryside.

In 1909 Gagnon returned to Montreal and worked in the Baie St-Paul area of Quebec, north of the St. Lawrence. This region, where Gagnon had often painted in his youth, was also the home of Simone Mary Bouchard and a favourite haunt of A.Y. Jackson.

At this stage of his career Gagnon was following the style of later French Impressionism, where forms dissolve into mists of colour and light. But afterwards he abandoned this more extreme form of Impressionism and concentrated on his genre subject matter. Although his work did not always contain figures, it did suggest the lives of the peasants and their surroundings.

After the First World War Gagnon returned to France, where he lived for several years and became a well-known illustrator. Having abandoned the misty effects of his first Impressionist paintings, his forms became more solid and easier to read. Though Gagnon was not an experimental artist, his work is pleasing and his impressionistic technique adds sparkle and life to his canvases.

Lonely Village on the St. Lawrence (p. 123) is typical of the scenes he painted on his visits to the Baie St-Paul area. Although he has used much brighter colours than the pastel hues of earlier Impressionism, his technique of applying paint is the same. Each small brush stroke is fully charged with colour and laid side by side with the next. Gradually the surface is built up, colour by colour, so that the whole scene shimmers with liveliness.

By the 1920s, when this work was painted, these brighter colours were characteristic of newer styles in Europe and were also being used in Canada by the Group of Seven. In fact, Tom Thomson, who was known for his remarkable brilliance of colour and skill in using it, was already dead.

Clarence Gagnon's work serves as a reminder that in art one style does not end abruptly when another begins. In fact, his later paintings show a combination of several styles and periods. Although he remained faithful to the basic technique of the earlier Impressionists, he used the newer, brighter colours to depict traditional genre subjects.

Tom Thomson

1877–1917

The Pool, c. 1915, oil on canvas
30" x 32-1/4" (76 cm x 82 cm)
The National Gallery of Canada, Ottawa

Tom Thomson has become an almost legendary figure in Canada. Many stories have been told about how he hated towns and spent his life in remote parts of the bush, camping, fishing, and painting. Because he was an expert canoeist, the story of his drowning is surrounded in mystery and even suggestions of murder. He has been thought of as the ideal Canadian artist, a rugged individual who had no formal art training, but who painted Canada as it really is.

The difficulty in presenting a fair account of the life and work of any legendary hero lies in distinguishing fact from fiction. Tom Thomson certainly had a great natural talent, but he also knew a good deal about current European styles, and these obviously affected his work. He was deeply concerned with painting the Canadian landscape as he saw it, but his training as a commercial designer and his knowledge of artistic techniques resulted in canvases no more real than most other paintings. He did spend much of his time alone in the bush, but he also earned his living working in the city and learning from his colleagues.

Tom Thomson was born and brought up in Ontario. In 1901 he went to Seattle and began his career in commercial art. By the time he was twenty-eight, Thomson was back in Toronto, working in a photo-engraving firm, sketching in his spare time, and taking some formal lessons in painting. Over the next few years he met the other artists who eventually formed the Group of Seven.

It was from A.Y. Jackson that Thomson probably learned the most about painting. The two men became close friends, and Jackson introduced him to the European styles and techniques that he himself had recently observed in Paris. They also shared a studio in Toronto and sketched together regularly in Algonquin Park.

When looking at Thomson's paintings of the Canadian landscape three things should be remembered: Thomson was trained in the current fashion of commercial design; he had been exposed to the new styles of European Post-Impressionist painting through his artist friends and various art magazines; he and the other members of the Group of Seven recognized the country's unique qualities and sincerely wanted to paint Canada in a realistic way.

All the artists of the Group except Lismer were trained in commercial art. Among other skills, they had learned to make clear, bold, eye-catching designs and to concentrate on general effects rather than on details. In additon, they had learned rules for handling colour and had explored techniques of decoration. As to the relationship between decoration and art, J.E.H. MacDonald commented, 'The Decorative Element is perhaps not so much a component part, as the element in which art lives, moves and has its being.'

Around the turn of the century a certain style of decoration called Art Nouveau became very popular. It consisted of flat, linear patterns that curled and twisted like tendrils or branches on a vine, and it was used on everything: architecture, iron railings, furniture, and dress material. Tom Thomson's *Decorative Panel* is a typical example.

In *The Pool* (p. 125) there is also a strong suggestion of Art Nouveau design. The surface of the canvas has a flat effect, and the branches of the trees curl and twist upon it in decorative patterns. A comparison of the painting and the *Decorative Panel* reveals an interesting relationship between the two styles. In fact, the one style has contributed to the other.

The flatness of the composition, however, is not only a result of Art Nouveau; it was also influenced by Post-Impressionist art. Post-Impressionism is a general term that is used to describe the many different styles that arose from Impressionism. As

Decorative Panel, Forest Undergrowth III
oil on beaverboard
47-3/4″ x 36-3/8″ (121 cm x 92 cm)
The National Gallery of Canada, Ottawa

we saw in the work of Morrice, one aspect of Impressionism was to stress that a painting is a work of art and does not have to look like nature. Therefore, said the Post-Impressionists, it is not necessary to create a sense of depth or real space. A canvas is flat, and so flatness is quite acceptable.

The composition of *The Pool* is basically flat. There is some suggestion of depth as we look through the trees at the water beyond. But the bright flecks of pink on the surface of the pool leap forward towards us, instead of allowing our eye to travel into the distance. The thick strokes of blue and green paint that are used for the background also tend to blend into the foreground, instead of tempting us far beyond.

What immediately impresses us about *The Pool* is, of course, the colour. Yellows, oranges, reds, greens, blues, and purples are built up into a brilliant mosaic, and the whole canvas vibrates before our eyes. As colour crashes against colour, the painting becomes a moving, living thing.

Nothing like this had ever been painted before in Canada. Critics who were used to mood landscapes, based on quiet European scenes, or softly Romantic paintings, like O'Brien's *Sunrise on the Saguenay* (p. 82), found the colours crude and violent. Yet they could not deny that the colours used to depict the Canadian autumn were realistic.

It is interesting, though, that at this time in Europe violent colours were also being used in landscape painting, not to describe a scene realistically, but to express feelings of excitement and joy in pure colour and design. A group of Post-Impressionist painters, one of whom was the well-known Matisse, used the basic Impressionistic technique of applying their paint in brush strokes of pure but varied colours. But unlike the light pastel effects the Impressionists created, these artists used brilliant colours in thick strokes that clashed and vibrated with energy.

European critics were shocked and named them *Les Fauves,* or 'the wild beasts'. In Canada too the argument raged. The critics condemned the Group of Seven, calling them the Hot Mush School whose paintings 'look pretty much alike, the net result being more like a gargle or gob of porridge than a work of art'.

The Group replied that they were painting Canada as it really was and that their aim was to produce 'an art of the soil and woods and waters and rocks and sky'. Undoubtedly the members of The Group were influenced by the European Post-Impressionists, yet their stated intention was to produce a truly Canadian art for Canadian people.

James E.H. MacDonald

1873–1932

The Solemn Land, 1921, oil on canvas
48″ x 60″ (122 cm x 152 cm)
The National Gallery of Canada, Ottawa

The beginning of the Group of Seven movement may be traced to an exhibition of J.E.H. Mac-Donald's sketches that he held in Toronto in 1911.

Born in Durham, England, MacDonald had come to Hamilton with his Canadian father when he was fourteen. He received his early training at the Hamilton Art School and later at the Central Ontario School of Art in Toronto, where George Reid was one of his instructors.

From the time he left college until 1911, MacDonald worked as a commercial artist in Toronto and for three years in England, where he was joined by his wife and son. Although he was employed as a graphic designer, he continued to take courses in painting. The sketching trips and life-drawing classes that he took regularly with several art clubs were a very important part of his career. In his personal opinion these informal sessions, based on the sharing of mutual interests and an unacademic approach to painting, formed the basis for the Group of Seven's methods.

MacDonald's exhibition of 1911 was held at the Arts and Letters Club, where Lawren Harris was a member. Harris was so impressed by MacDonald's work that he convinced him to give up his commercial career and become a professional painter.

At that time MacDonald was working for Grip Limited Studios, a firm of graphic designers, where Tom Thomson, Arthur Lismer, Frank Carmichael, and Frank Johnston (all members of the Group of Seven) were also employed. A.Y. Jackson was working in Montreal as a commercial artist, but in 1913 he was persuaded to come to Toronto and join the others.

While it was through the Arts and Letters Club that the painters really came together, all of them except Lawren Harris had known of each other's work. Their long association, which started with the 1911 exhibition, continued until 1931 when the members of the Group each went their separate ways.

At first the movement was made up of a group of friends: MacDonald, Harris, Thomson, Lismer, Varley, Jackson, and Carmichael. After Thomson's death in 1917, Frank Johnston joined them. But it was not until their first formal exhibition in May, 1921, that they took the Group of Seven as their official name.

From then until 1931 the Group, particularly MacDonald, fought a fierce battle for acceptance by the Canadian public and critics. In opposing the Group, one critic wrote,

To sensitive eyes (the exhibition) is like a chamber of horrors: a vision of things hard, glaring, repellent.... And as for poetic feeling and gentle emotion, these are dismissed as sentimental heresies.

The first work to receive violent criticism was MacDonald's *The Tangled Garden,* which was exhibited in Toronto in 1916. The same critic wrote, 'The chief offender seems to be J.E.H. MacDonald, who certainly does throw his paint pots in the face of the public.' It is true that the colours and design of *The Tangled Garden* were stronger and more emotional than the Canadian public had seen before. The work of the Fauves and the other European Expressionists was still unknown in Canada.

Nevertheless, in *The Tangled Garden* the first signs of MacDonald's particular talent are evident. More than any other member of the Group, he had the gift of making the smallest objects important and even monumental. Flowers in a garden or leaves in a stream became big, bold statements of the power of nature. And yet the critics continued to protest.

In the first place the size of the canvas is much too large

for the relative importance of the subject, and the crudity of the colours, rather than the delicate tracery of all vegetation, seems to have appealed to the painter: but it is a masterpiece compared with *The Elements* or *Rock and Maple* which for all they really convey might just as well have been called *Hungarian Goulash* and *Drunkard's Stomach*.

The members of the Group of Seven were not overly discouraged by the criticism they received; instead, it seemed to spur them on even more, and, as their skills developed, they continued to produce some of their finest paintings.

The Solemn Land (p. 128), perhaps more than any work of art up to this time, captures the immensity and grandeur of the Canadian northland. The painting has the slow, measured rhythm of a grand piece of music. The strong, rich colours and heavy forms seem to be composed in the musical sense of the word. Each element of the painting, like the individual instruments in a symphony, contributes to the overall harmony. Small accents of brilliant reds or yellows, like the occasional high note or trill, add a sense of life and variety but never disrupt the total pattern.

By taking up a position high over the water, the artist had the advantage of being able to look across the scene and down on it at the same time. His technique of combining the two views into one composition has allowed him the opportunity of achieving a great sense of space.

The Solemn Land is a fine painting, showing everything that the Group of Seven aimed for. There is nothing here that is gentle, pretty, or picturesque. With its sense of immense distances, massive forms, and rich colours, it is a dramatic statement about Canada's northland.

Arthur Lismer

1885–1969

September Gale, Georgian Bay, 1921, oil on canvas
48" x 64" (122 cm x 163 cm)
The National Gallery of Canada, Ottawa

Arthur Lismer's *September Gale, Georgian Bay* is one of the best-known works of the Group of Seven. It climaxes a series of paintings in which various members of the Group have explored the theme of a lone tree standing in front of a lake. The two earliest paintings in this series are by Tom Thomson and show the decorative qualities of Art Nouveau. But by the time that Lismer painted *September Gale, Georgian Bay*, the tree, though still decorative, had become something far more symbolic of hardship and endurance in the rugged landscape.

The series began with Tom Thomson's *The West Wind,* which was painted in 1917. In it the pine stands alone, bending before the wind. But the curves of the trunk and branches and the flat treatment of the foliage and rocks emphasize the surface of the canvas and the general overall pattern.

Sketch for September Gale, oil on panel
12" x 15-3/4" (30 cm x 40 cm)
Collection of Dr. John L. Parnell

In *The Jack Pine* (1917) the tree stands upright, its drooping branches making lacy patterns against the sky in the serene atmosphere of a calm, still evening. Again, Thomson's arrangement of forms is flat and his composition two-dimensional.

Of all the paintings in the series Varley's *Stormy Weather, Georgian Bay* (c. 1921), which was painted in the same area, is closest in approach to Lismer's *September Gale, Georgian Bay*. It particularly resembles the first preparatory sketch. The lone pine, buffeted by the wind, looks quite tiny against the huge expanse of Georgian Bay and seems to cling to the rocky ground from which it grows. Though more realistic than Thomson's trees, it does not have the symbolic strength that Lismer's has.

In *September Gale, Georgian Bay* the artist seems to have directed all his efforts towards condensing the scene into one strong statement about endurance. The development of the painting, from the early preparatory sketch through the oil study to the finished work, reveals a great deal about Lismer's intentions.

In the first sketch he has included the whole tree. But though we can sense the strength of the wind and waves, the pine itself has no special significance.

In the oil study the top of the tree has been cut off, and some of the undergrowth and reeds have been added below. But because the design is rather confused, the impact of the painting is weakened. There are too many small parts; the waves are too choppy; the distant shore line is tiny; the clouds have no particular pattern or rhythm.

In the final painting the confusion has been eliminated. The whole design is simpler, bolder, and stronger. Now the tree, the undergrowth, and the reeds, though twisted and torn by the raging wind, somehow remain strong and stable. The waves, the clouds, and the patterns of the rocks all have a consistent rhythm.

Yet there is also a pronounced feeling of tension between the tearing wind that bears down from the right and the thrust of the forms that push outwards from the left. By means of this tension Lismer describes the eternal battle in nature of assault and resistance, of water against land, of the elements against all living things.

By the time Lismer painted *September Gale, Georgian Bay,* there had been many changes in European styles and opinions. The Impressionists had broken away from the rules and systems of the Academy, and the Fauves had then adapted the methods of the Impressionists. Another movement of the Post-Impressionist period was called Expressionism and was closely related to Fauvism. The most famous artist in this movement was Vincent van Gogh (1853–1890), a painter who used a highly emotional manner of expression. It seems that his paintings are almost the result of an explosion of the powerful and innermost feelings that he had for his subject. With strong colours, thick brush strokes, and sweeping lines he painted

September Gale, Georgian Bay (Study), 1920
oil on canvas
20-1/8" x 24" (51 cm x 61 cm)
The National Gallery of Canada, Ottawa

according to his deepest emotions.

Lismer's *September Gale, Georgian Bay* is also an Expressionistic work. This does not mean that he deliberately copied van Gogh, nor that he was necessarily influenced by him directly. But he does share with van Gogh a strongly emotional approach to his subject. Lismer, like other members of the Group of Seven, was determined to express the feelings that he had for the Canadian landscape. Certainly he saw a stormy day with wild waves and sweeping clouds, but he felt the storm as well, and the combination of these two states of mind produced *September Gale, Georgian Bay*.

Lismer had been in Canada for ten years when he painted *September Gale, Georgian Bay*. Born in Sheffield, England, he attended the art school there for seven years as an illustrator and printing apprentice. At the age of twenty-one he enrolled in the Académie Royale des Beaux-Arts in Belgium, where van Gogh himself had studied for a short time. Lismer stayed there for a year and a half.

On his return to Sheffield he set up his own business as a 'specialist in pictorial publicity'. But when two Canadian firms of engravers approached him with offers of employment, he decided to immigrate to Canada in 1911. In Toronto he met four of the other artists who formed the original Group of Seven; Varley and Jackson had not yet arrived. From 1913 onward, Lismer began to take sketching trips with them, and these trips eventually led to the painting of *September Gale, Georgian Bay* in 1921.

It was in the field of art education, though, that Lismer made his greatest contribution. Even in his Sheffield days he had been interested in the idea of presenting art as an important part of ordinary life. Two years after he arrived in Canada, he began teaching as a part-time instructor at the Ontario College of Art. In 1916 he was made principal of the Victoria School of Art in Halifax. Three years later he became vice-principal of the Ontario College of Art under George Reid. Lismer kept this post until 1927, when he resigned over differences of opinion about the teaching of art.

Lismer strongly believed in the encouragement of free artistic expression, as opposed to a traditional, more structured approach. For the rest of his life he devoted himself to writing, lecturing, and teaching this system. The influence of his methods is still felt in Canada today.

Frederick Varley

1881–1969

Portrait of Janet, 1919, oil on canvas
24" x 20" (61 cm x 51 cm)
Beaverbrook Art Gallery, Fredericton

Of all the artists in the Group of Seven, Frederick Varley was the only one who was seriously interested in painting portraits. In the early years of their association, he joined the other members of the Group on their sketching expeditions and produced some fine paintings. One of his most interesting canvases from this period is *Stormy Weather, Georgian Bay*, which was painted in about 1920.

His most outstanding works, however, are his later landscapes and his portraits. In fact, some of his portraits, particularly those of women, are among the finest in the history of Canadian art. Not only are they beautiful paintings in themselves; they also show a sensitive understanding of the human mind and emotions.

Varley, like Lismer, who was four years younger, was born in Sheffield, and the two men led strangely similar lives for many years. At the age of twelve Varley enrolled in the Sheffield School of Art, where as a part of his course he served for seven years as an apprentice to an industrial designer.

After completing his early training, he was so determined to become a professional artist that his father allowed him to study at the Académie Royale des Beaux-Arts in Belgium. On Varley's advice, Lismer undertook the same training seven years later. While Varley was at the Académie, he showed a particular interest in the life-drawing classes, and this training helped him later with his portraiture.

On his return to England he found work as a commercial designer and magazine illustrator. At this time he married and became the father of two children. In 1912 Varley again met Lismer, who had returned from Canada to Sheffield in order to be married. From Lismer he heard about the good prospects in Canada and decided to immigrate there also.

Thus began his long association with the members of the Group of Seven. It was Varley, in fact, who became a spokesman for their common aim. 'We are endeavouring,' he said, 'to knock out of us all the preconceived ideas, emptying ourselves of everything except that nature is here in all its greatness.'

Yet styles of painting, acquired by looking and learning, become deeply fixed in an artist's mind. While the Group of Seven produced work that was new in Canada and explored areas never painted before, their techniques were closely related to the work of the European artists.

From early in 1918 until 1920, Varley, like Jackson, served overseas as a war artist. His experiences depressed him, and he became particularly alarmed by the contrast between the violence of war and the wild excitement of final victory. Some of his paintings from this period of his life are moving, though horrifying.

Fred Varley had always been a religious man. In his later years his religion played a major role in his attitude and approach to art. In 1924 he saw the Rockies for the first time. They inspired him deeply, and some of his finest landscapes were painted there. Moving to Vancouver at the age of forty-five, he became friendly with a group of artists, musicians, and philosophers whose particular interest lay in mystical and spiritual ideas.

At this time he painted *Vera,* his most famous and beautiful portrait, in which the colour green predominates. It is an Expressionistic statement of what he felt for his subject, not a description of what he saw. Varley was not the first artist to introduce unusual colours into portraiture. Van Gogh, Cézanne, and Matisse, among many others, had used colour as a purely artistic element. They would use any colour, by itself or in relation to others, providing that it expressed a form or a feeling they wanted to express. Whether or not it actually existed in real life was irrelevant.

In Vancouver Varley became head of drawing, painting, and composition in the School of Design and Applied Arts. Later, in 1933, he and Jock Macdonald founded their own school, the British Columbia College of Art. Unfortunately, this venture was not financially successful, and the college had to close. Varley later returned to Toronto, but his influence as a teacher had already made a deep impression on the art community of Vancouver.

Although his portrait of the young Janet Beaverbrook (p. 134) is an early work, it is characteristic of Varley's sensitive use of colour and light. It also demonstrates his skill in capturing the inner nature of the person he is painting.

Soft blue and mauve shadows are folded into the fine white material of the girl's dress, associating her with the sky and clouds behind. Varley's use of paint is rich and creamy in its thick impasto treatment, where each stroke of the brush adds greater subtlety to the colour. The cool blues and whites provide a glowing yet airy background for the young girl's fresh skin and dark hair. These are also complemented by the deeper, richer colours of the leaves above her.

Although Janet looks straight outwards from where she stands, she is quiet and reserved. The shadow that falls across her face partially shades her thoughts. While the portrait has a feeling of freshness and youth, there is a serious element in it as well. And this impression is emphasized by the light and colour, the subtle contrast between sun and shade, and between the blues and whites of spring and the browns and golds of autumn.

This is one of Varley's early portraits, and, because it is a study of a young girl, it does not show the deep exploration into character that is evident in *Vera,* for example. Nevertheless, it is a sensitive presentation of a child who will soon become a woman.

Alexander Y. Jackson

1882–1974

Grey Day, Laurentians, 1931, oil on canvas
25″ x 32″ (64 cm x 81 cm)
The Montreal Museum of Fine Arts

By the 1930s, when A.Y. Jackson painted *Grey Day, Laurentians* (p. 137) and *Winter, Charlevoix County* (p. 139), his style had matured and he was producing some of his finest work. In both paintings we can sense Jackson's strong feeling for rhythm and movement. But we can also see that he was working these elements into a composition where surface patterns are balanced with effects of depth and space. In comparing the two landscapes, which were painted a year or two apart, we can also trace Jackson's attempts at resolving certain artistic problems.

In the late 1920s Jackson was spending a great deal of time painting along the north and south shores of the St. Lawrence. In these Quebec landscapes his style is far less dramatic than it was in some of his well-known earlier paintings, such as *Terre Sauvage* (1913) and *The Red Maple* (1914). While Jackson's early work shows the strong influence of styles he had seen in Europe, by the time he painted *Grey Day, Laurentians* and *Winter, Charlevoix County*, he was developing an individual style that presented his own particular vision.

In painting his Quebec landscapes, Jackson was concerned that his snow scenes could become too pretty and quaint. In a letter to MacDonald he wrote, 'Here we are in the Christmas card country, at least it often looks that way, while what I want to see are big bold compositions that will enrage the critics.' Whether or not this was what prompted him to re-work this particular landscape, we do not know. Nevertheless, it is interesting to compare the two paintings to see exactly what he did achieve.

Grey Day, Laurentians has an open, loose composition. Unlike the method used by the Group in many of their earlier works, Jackson has not placed a tree or another large object in the foreground of his painting to emphasize the surface of his canvas. Instead, he leads us back into his picture space by means of a road that curls around to the right, at the end of which is a fairly prominent farmhouse. The eye, accompanying the sleigh, travels down the road and is tempted to continue around the bend and pause at this farm. Yet in the centre of the painting, there is a hill with dark trees on it. This too attracts the eye, which has also been led towards it by the repeated horizontal folds of snow. The hill pulls the eye towards the centre, then continues down the slope to the left, creating a tension between two strong centres of interest. This tension, which first draws us into the picture and then directs us from right to left, is one of Jackson's principal methods of conveying the breadth of the scene.

In *Winter, Charlevoix County* the field of vision is narrowed. Rather than presenting a great width of landscape into which the eye moves, Jackson has compressed the view into a smaller area. Yet the surface pattern is much richer, and there is more emphasis on texture. The snow has deeper furrows; its surface has been scarred by the wind and rain. The telegraph poles are bent and irregular, and snow banks are piled unevenly. The sleigh is no longer prominent, and the farmhouse is smaller. The hill in the centre is not as large, but the ridge on the left has been given more emphasis. The whole painting now is dense with pattern and texture.

In gaining this richer quality, though, has Jackson lost some of that original sense of size and depth? Is there still the same feeling of Canada's vast and lonely space?

At first, the aim of the Group of Seven was to capture this very feeling, and in doing so to describe the unique atmosphere of the Canadian landscape. But by the 1930s each artist had developed a style of his own and had set off in different artistic directions.

Sketching and painting all the while, Jackson had travelled across the country more than any of his

Winter, Charlevoix County, c. 1932–1933
oil on canvas
25″ x 32″ (64 cm x 81 cm)
Art Gallery of Ontario, Toronto

colleagues had at this time. With the exception of Lawren Harris, he had also received the most thorough European training in art.

Born in Montreal, Jackson had studied there under William Brymner. Between 1905 and 1913 he spent intervals of time in Europe, travelling and studying. In total, he was there for about three years, six months of which were spent at the Académie Julian, where he learned the academic techniques. During this period of his life he also worked as a commercial artist and learned the basic principles of design.

But the new ideas and methods of Impressionism and Expressionism had particularly affected him. In his early European and Canadian canvases and the work he produced as a war artist, these influences were especially strong. Before he joined the original members of the Group in 1913, Jackson's paintings were quiet in mood. He was concerned with capturing the atmosphere of the landscape, but he did this with a light touch, using the Impressionistic effects of sun and shade.

After 1913 many of his paintings became more emotional. In them he combined his own feelings for the Canadian landscape and his efforts to discover its particular qualities. From that time on he painted with the flowing, rhythmic line that is so typical of his work. Sometimes, as in these two landscapes, it remained controlled and gentle; at other times, particularly in some of his Arctic paintings of the 1920s, the emotional force of the line seemed almost to take control.

Lawren Harris

1885 – 1970

Maligne Lake, Jasper Park, 1924, oil on canvas
48″ x 60″ (122 cm x 152 cm)
The National Gallery of Canada, Ottawa

Lawren Harris was one of the founders and leaders of the Group of Seven. Unlike the other members, Harris had come from a wealthy family and had never needed to earn his living as a commercial designer. For this reason he had had the money, the time, and the training to devote himself to encouraging the arts.

Harris was born in Brantford, Ontario. He had a good education, including a year at the University of Toronto, before deciding that painting was his great interest. At the age of nineteen, Harris left for Europe to stay with relatives in Berlin and to study art.

On his return to Canada four years later, he became one of the first members of the Arts and Letters Club, a group of people interested in encouraging the arts in Toronto. Here Lawren Harris met J.E.H. MacDonald when he exhibited some sketches at the Club in 1911. The two artists became friends and began sketching together; eventually they founded the Group of Seven movement.

In his early work Harris experimented with the bright colours of the Fauves, but for the most part he painted city and street scenes. His landscapes, often depicting snow subjects, were basically decorative. It was not until he visited Nova Scotia and Newfoundland in 1921 that his style really began to change. From the flat two-dimensional compositions of his earlier canvases, he started to work in a more solid three-dimensional style. His paintings also began to show more of his feeling for his subject. In fact, these Maritime canvases clearly describe Harris's outrage and concern for the extreme poverty and crude living conditions that he found there. In the autumn of that year, Harris also visited the north shore of Lake Superior for the first time. The vast open spaces of the landscape inspired in him an almost religious feeling for its grandeur.

From his student days in Berlin, Harris had been interested in religious and spiritual ideas. Later he became involved in theosophy, an ancient philosophy based on Eastern religious beliefs. One of the main ideas in theosophy is that the Creator of the world can be seen in his creations. This belief is the basis of most of Harris's work after 1921.

From that time until 1928, Harris visited the north shore of Lake Superior each autumn; in 1924 he began similar journeys in the summer to the Rockies. Here he found the inspiration for the huge and boldly simple landscapes for which he became so well known.

Maligne Lake, Jasper Park is one of Harris's finest works. Here he creates a complete feeling of unity among the mountains, sky, and water. The huge snow-capped peaks tower over the lake but are joined to it by their reflection. The clouds, their shape reflected in the mountains, are also mirrored in the lake.

The composition is kept in perfect balance but gives no feeling of boredom. This is largely because of the important tensions at work in the painting: curves against angular shapes, light against shadow, solid forms against reflections. Even the quiet colours form a kind of opposition to the lively shapes of the mountains. Each part of the painting exerts tension to check and control an opposite part, and thus the whole work is held in balance. Although achieved in different ways, this is the same kind of effect that Dessaillant aimed for in *L'Ange gardien* (p. 26) and Jackson was creating in *Grey Day, Laurentians* (p. 137). In all these paintings balance depends upon tension, for without tension, balance could not exist.

Harris's painting seems to open out into a mystical universe, but at the same time it shows the artist's belief in a law and order in nature. Yet it is far from being a copy of nature. All the forms have been made so simple that they suggest mountains,

Composition #1, 1940, oil on canvas
62″ x 63-1/4″ (157 cm x 161 cm)
The Vancouver Art Gallery

clouds, snow-caps, and shadows; they do not
describe them. And because of this *Maligne Lake,
Jasper Park* is only a step or two away from being an
abstract painting.

In 1912 Wassily Kandinsky, a Russian painter,
published a book entitled *Concerning the Spiritual
in Art*. This book has had a tremendous influence on
the development of modern painting. In it Kandinsky stated his belief that man's deepest feelings
about the spiritual values in life, such as truth,
goodness, harmony, and beauty, can only be expressed in painting by purely artistic means. That is
to say, that by combining forms and colours, an
artist can express these values without using familiar or realistic subject matter.

In some of the works we have already seen, such
as Pierre Le Ber's *Marguerite Bourgeoys*, Thomas
Davies's landscapes, and Ozias Leduc's *L'Enfant au
Pain*, the same idea was present. Even though there

was a recognizable subject, the meaning of the
painting did not exist in that alone, but in the forms
themselves.

Kandinsky took the theory one step further; he
was among the first artists to paint pure abstract
works. In his early attempts, and in those of other
painters, the forms and colours were taken from the
visible world. But the later abstracts came to depend
completely on relationships of pure forms and
colour for their meaning.

Kandinsky, like Lawren Harris, believed in
theosophy and the idea that the Creator exists in
nature, His creation. For Harris, *Maligne Lake,
Jasper Park* was an expression of his reverence for
creation. From there, like Kandinsky, he began to
experiment with pure abstracts. In these he wanted
to express his belief in the spiritual values that he felt
when looking at the grandeur of the Rocky Mountains or the vast, lonely spaces of Lake Superior.

Composition #1 was painted in 1940. It was
Harris's first painting done in Canada after living in
the United States for six years. While he was in the
United States, he had devoted himself entirely to
abstract painting. To him it was 'an art as pure as
music', in which he could express deep feelings
'with power and subtlety of meaning'.

Composition #1 still has connections with landscapes. In it there are suggestions of mountains,
clouds, and a horizon line. But basically it is a
geometrical composition based on triangles and
circles, which were also ancient symbols in
theosophy and Eastern religions. Relationships of
forms in space, light and shadow, and colour also
play their part.

For the admirers of the Group of Seven's Canadian landscapes, Harris's abstract painting was a
rejection of all their aims. For Harris it was a further
step towards an understanding of the great mystery
of nature.

Emily Carr

1871–1945

Forest B.C., 1932, oil on canvas
51" x 35-3/4" (130 cm x 91 cm)
The Vancouver Art Gallery

Other than the members of the Group of Seven, Emily Carr is probably the most famous Canadian artist. Known from coast to coast for her painting and writing, she is almost a national heroine. It is sad that her talent was unrecognized at first and that her art was scorned by the public during most of her lifetime. As she wrote in her autobiography, 'My pictures were either hung on the ceiling or on the floor and were jeered at, insulted; members of the "Fine Arts" joked at my work, laughing with reporters. Press notices were humiliating.'

Yet she might not be particularly pleased by her present fame either. Emily Carr was a modest, sensitive person who was deeply hurt by her rejection. Because of her great sincerity as an artist, nothing would have delighted her more than a genuine understanding of her work. But to earn fame by becoming fashionable would certainly have troubled her.

Emily was born in Victoria, British Columbia. She was the youngest of three sisters and had one younger brother. 'Our childhood was ruled by Father's unbendable iron will,' she wrote. But apparently her mother was gentle and understanding. By the time she was fourteen, both her parents were dead.

When Father died I was still at school getting into a great deal of trouble for drawing faces on my fingernails and pinafores and textbooks. When I moved up a grade, the new teacher said, 'Ah, another good Carr!' but was disappointed.

After Father and Mother died my big sister ruled. She was twenty years older than the youngest of us.... The biggest sister owned everything and us too when Father died.

Her childhood obviously affected Emily greatly. She was completely different from her sisters – sensitive, imaginative, and rebellious. All her life she longed for them to approve of her work, but they thought it ugly, and the only praise they gave her was for her picture frames.

The sisters supported charities, Sunday schools, and missionaries. They 'filled our house with long-faced samples. Missionaries roosted on us during migration, others hopped into meals while waiting for boats.' Among other things, Emily was 'rebellious about religion'.

When she was eighteen, she left Victoria to study art formally in San Francisco. She remained there for about six years, receiving a solid academic training. On her return home she taught art classes for children. Since her eldest sister claimed every inch of the house, Emily made her studio in the barn with the cow. Always devoted to animals, she said, 'I did not really mind sharing with cow – I was really not keen on her smell but she cosied things.'

During this time Emily first visited an Indian mission on the west coast of Vancouver Island. Though she only did a little sketching, she was aware that 'unknowingly I was storing, storing, all unconscious, my working ideas against the time when I should be ready to use this material.'

In about 1899 Emily left Victoria for England to study at the Westminster School of Art in London. She hated living in a large city but found the countryside too gentle and tame compared with the open spaces of Canada. She considered the English stuffy and dull. 'The make-believe gentility of Miss Green's Paying-Guest-House became intolerable to me.' While she was in England, Emily became very ill and suffered from poor health for the rest of her life. On her return to Canada after a five and a half year absence, she was thankful to be back in the open spaces once again.

But she found Victoria and Vancouver almost as stifling as London. She was invited to become the art teacher for the Vancouver Ladies' Art Club, but this was not a success and she was dismissed. They

Untitled, charcoal drawing
22-5/8″ x 17-5/8″ (57 cm x 45 cm)
The Vancouver Art Gallery

thought her too young, and she thought them too stupid. Instead, she opened her own studio, gave art classes to children, and started to paint seriously.

During this time she painted hundreds of water-colours and made sketches of the totem poles and Indian villages of the West Coast. 'Indian Art broadened my seeing, loosened the formal tightness I had learned in England's schools. Its bigness and stark reality baffled my white man's understanding.'

Emily was also very sensitive to Indian design and was outraged by those who changed it in order to make money. 'I loved the beautiful Indian designs, but I was not happy about using Indian design on material for which it was not intended and I hated seeing them distorted, cheapened by those who did not understand or care....'

Although Emily produced a lot of work during this period, she was not satisfied with the quality of it. In 1910 she left for further study in Paris, hoping to develop a style that would allow her to express her strong feelings more forcefully. Unfortunately, she again became ill and had to return the following year. She was then forty years old.

Her experience in France, though, had helped her considerably. She had seen the work of the Expressionists and the Fauves, and in her new Indian canvases she used a bolder, broader technique based on what she had learned. This untitled and undated charcoal drawing of totem heads and abstract forms of trees is probably from this period. It shows a forcefulness and strength of design that her earlier art lacks.

But despite the artistic quality of her work, it was not popular in conservative Vancouver and did not sell. Discouraged, she moved to Victoria, bought an apartment house, and tried to make her living as a landlady. Loathing this existence, she became extremely depressed and stopped painting altogether. The only things she still enjoyed were her menagerie of animals and the pottery that she made and decorated with Indian designs.

In 1927, when she was fifty-six, her life suddenly changed. Eric Brown, director of the National Gallery, persuaded her to enter fifty canvases in an exhibition of West Coast Indian art that he was preparing. He also arranged for her to meet the members of the Group of Seven, and on her return from the exhibition she started painting again.

Lawren Harris was her greatest inspiration. He believed in her work, understood her changing moods, and encouraged her to be herself. He also suggested that she move away from Indian subject matter towards more general scenes of nature.

Forest B.C. (p. 143) is a result of her new enthusiasm and energy. The powerful forms of the forest trees surge, twist, and unite in a work that almost resembles sculpture. The colours too swirl across the canvas like waves of the sea or mighty winds. The painting is far more than a mere description of tree trunks; it suggests the force of life itself.

Without any direct reference to the Indians who inhabited the forest, Emily Carr has captured the same sense of awe and mystery of nature and its gods that the Indians had expressed in their powerful totem poles. Even in her earlier charcoal drawing, she had shown her understanding of the spirit of Indian art, which recognizes these gods within nature.

In *Forest B.C.* and in the work she did during the last ten years of her painting career, she shows her struggle to express her own feelings about nature. 'I sat before the woods, lost, frustrated. I had let myself be bound. It was not handling of paint but handling of thoughts which overwhelmed me.'

Despite her successes, Emily Carr remained a modest person who needed encouragement. Lawren Harris understood her well and he wrote to her saying, 'It is no good to tell you that your work does not warrant despair. Every creative individual despairs, always has since the beginning of time. No matter how fine things are, there are always finer things to be done and still finer ad infinitum. . . . We have to be intense about what we are doing but think what intensity does, what it draws into itself. . . . Keep on working, change your approach, perhaps, but don't change your attitude.'

Lemoine FitzGerald

1890–1956

Doc Snider's House, 1931, oil on canvas
29-1/2" x 33-1/2" (75 cm x 85 cm)
The National Gallery of Canada, Ottawa

Landscape, 1950, pencil
8" x 5-3/4" (20 cm x 15 cm)
Winnipeg Art Gallery

Lemoine FitzGerald was born in Winnipeg and spent most of his life there. During the winter of 1921 he studied in New York at the Art Students' League, but returned to Canada the following year. He began teaching at the Winnipeg School of Art in 1924, and five years later he became principal, a position he held for twenty years. From 1932 to 1933 he was a member of the Group of Seven in name, if not in style or spirit.

Although FitzGerald painted some magnificent canvases in oil, the majority of his work was done on the small, intimate scale of drawings in pencil, crayon, pastel, ink, and watercolour. He was a quiet person, who was sincerely dedicated to his work. In

148

a letter his friend Bertram Brooker wrote,

You are not a large producer, of course, but when you do show something there is evidence of long contemplation and patient workmanship in it, whereas so many people seem to dash off things in time for the show.

FitzGerald neither painted many oils nor exhibited them frequently, but his numerous drawings reveal the same careful thought and patient technique.

It is interesting, though, that despite the precision of everything he did, FitzGerald felt his technique was far less important than the feelings he wanted to convey.

Consider technique as a means by which you say what you have to say and not as an end in itself. What you have to say is of the first importance, how you say it is always secondary.

Doc Snider's House (p. 147) was painted in 1931. The subject matter is simple, but the painting is elegant and delicately composed. Forms, line, and space are balanced with great control. The colours are quiet, and details are kept to a minimum. The buildings give the composition a three-dimensional structure, while the positioning of the trees emphasizes the feeling of space. The trunks bend and curve towards and away from each other, creating delicate tensions and rhythms.

The meaning of the painting resides in its form, in cubic shapes, line, colour, and the relationships of one element to another. Although it is a realistic painting of a house and garden in winter, it is not far from being an abstract composition. Through nature, FitzGerald has worked towards finding the inner substance of forms. He once wrote,

It is necessary to get inside the object and push it out rather than merely building it up from the outer aspect. . . . This required endless search and contemplation; continuous effort and experiment and appreciation for the

Abstract, 1950, pencil
8″ x 5-3/4″ (20 cm x 15 cm)
Winnipeg Art Gallery

endlessness of the living force which seems to pervade and flow through all natural forms even though these seem on the surface to be so ephemeral.

In the two pencil drawings, done about twenty years after *Doc Snider's House*, the landscape has been reduced to even simpler elements. Line plays a vital role in the surface patterns and rhythms. But space and the relationship of parts are also important.

It is evident that no one object can be segregated in space without the feeling of something around it, and usually it is associated with other objects. The appreciation of the relation of one object to another and their effect on one another will help to suggest the solidity of each.

Darker areas emphasize the shapes of lighter areas, showing them not only as they look on the surface but also as they are in reality. Thus even a drawing of a tree trunk, divided lengthwise by light and shadow, may reveal an underlying form in nature, and not just a surface pattern.

In his *Abstract*, FitzGerald has taken his analysis of the essential parts of a woodland scene one step further. With the most delicate lines and subtle shading, he conveys a sense of depth and transparency in a continuing attempt 'to get inside the object and push it out, rather than merely building it up from the outer aspect'.

Yet at the same time, the light areas and dark areas are combined into interesting patterns of varying tones. Besides his remarkable skill with line, FitzGerald had a strong sense of texture. In his drawings, watercolours, and oils he used fine strokes of the pencil or brush to convey varieties of surfaces that appeal to the sense of touch.

Always searching and probing for the true nature of objects, FitzGerald also produced many fine still lifes. Bottles, jars, and bowls of fruit became subjects of precise drawings made after 'long contemplation'.

In the last five years of his life, FitzGerald experimented with pure abstraction. It was during this time that he produced his beautiful *Green and Gold*, now in the Winnipeg Art Gallery. Delicate in colour, the fragile shapes are subtly shaded like the forms in his drawings. Balancing each other, they seem to float in a space that is as important to FitzGerald's work as is the relationship of objects.

Bertram Brooker

1888 – 1955

Sounds Assembling, 1928, oil on canvas
44-1/2″ x 36″ (113 cm x 91 cm)
Winnipeg Art Gallery

Bertram Brooker was seventeen when he emigrated with his family from England. The Brookers settled in Portage la Prairie, where Bertram and his father worked as labourers on the railway. From that time until he was middle-aged, Brooker changed jobs many times. He was a bookkeeper, a movie-house operator, a film script writer, a journalist, and an advertising man.

Later in his life he turned to more serious writing and had nine books published. His novel *Think of the Earth* won the first Governor General's Award for fiction in 1936. The same year he published a mystery novel and his second *Yearbook of the Arts in Canada*. Brooker was a man of great energy and had many interests, including music, but throughout his life art remained his major form of creative expression.

In 1921, when he was thirty-three, Brooker moved from Manitoba to Toronto. During the next ten years the Group of Seven dominated the Canadian art world, at first receiving loud attention in their struggle for acceptance, and later setting a standard for Canadian painting. The one member of the Group who was changing his style was Lawren Harris. The Arts and Letters Club in Toronto had been a centre for the arts since 1908, when it was founded. It was here that Bertram Brooker met Lawren Harris and Arthur Lismer, who encouraged him in his painting.

Through Harris and F.B. Housser, an important writer on Canadian art, Brooker became interested in theosophy. Kandinsky's book *Concerning the Spiritual in Art* also influenced him greatly. Being a music lover himself, Brooker was particularly interested in Kandinsky's idea that abstract art is the form of expression closest to music.

Brooker's first exhibition was held in 1927 at the Arts and Letters Club. Though there is no copy of the exhibition list, it is thought that many of the paintings displayed were those related to music. In these works Brooker translated musical forms into visual ones, and he himself described them as 'expressions of musical feeling'.

Sounds Assembling was painted and exhibited in a Group of Seven show the following year. It attracted a great deal of criticism and such comments as 'abstraction is not a natural form of expression in Canada'. This was a rather strange reaction, since Toronto critics had been interested in the international exhibition of abstract art shown in the city the year before. It seems that abstraction was acceptable for foreigners but not for Canadians.

Sounds Assembling is a vivid personal description in form and colour of a musical composition. The smoothness, sharpness, changes in direction, grouping of forms, spaces, and colours all have the power of suggesting the visual shape of a musical composition.

This painting was among the many pure abstracts that Brooker painted during the 1920s. But after 1929 he completely changed his style, in part because of a close friendship with Lemoine FitzGerald which was developing at that time. FitzGerald's great talent for drawing in a precise and delicate style had obviously impressed Brooker deeply, and in a letter to FitzGerald, Brooker wrote,

Your attitude toward your work and your companionship on the few days I had with you have had a very considerable effect on me. It has changed not only my approach to things, but also my appreciation of other people's work. If I tried to put my finger on it I should say that it has made me more honest and studious and less impatient for quick results. So far its effect has been that I have been perhaps too realistic – in a small way I mean – but I hope to grow out of that to a bigger appreciation of form – particularly. To boil it down to one word – form is

151

Shoes, c. 1946, watercolour
11-1/2″ x 15″ (29 cm x 38 cm)
Winnipeg Art Gallery

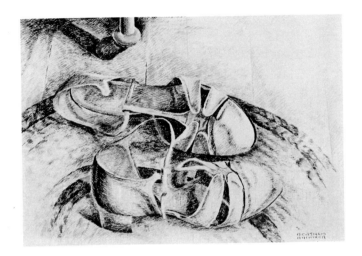

the thing that obsesses me. Colour is no longer a thing that interests me for its own sake, as it did.

The forms that Brooker has used in *Sounds Assembling* took shape in his own imagination as he listened to music, but their variety is limited. In his later work, though, forms in the visible world began to interest him more and more. In them he saw great possibilities for variation and combination, even in so plain a subject as a pair of shoes lying on a braided mat beside a small water pipe. Here the design is completely realistic, but the artist has recognized the underlying forms in his subject. For this reason it too is almost an abstract arrangement of shapes.

It seems that Brooker saw these realistic drawings and watercolours as a kind of stepping stone towards a return to abstraction. In a letter to FitzGerald he wrote,

I am more committed than ever to go more deeply into drawing. Somehow I feel that after this apprenticeship to naturalistic painting has served a little more fully, I shall perhaps go back to more abstract things with a greater command of mediums and do something quite different.

Brooker did not remain a complete realist, but it was many years before he returned to the pure abstractions of his earlier days.

David Milne

1882–1953

Glass Jar 1, 1946, watercolour on paper
14" x 21-1/2" (36 cm x 55 cm)
The Robert McLaughlin Gallery, Oshawa

'Most of my painting has been done direct, finished and left alone,' David Milne once wrote. 'I never had much luck in working up sketches, if the sketch had intense feeling in it, it had everything needed, why touch it? If it hadn't it had nothing of value. Why bother further with it?'

The only thing that really mattered to Milne was to catch his own vivid sensations the instant he looked at something. It was not the subject that was particularly important; it was the force of the impression that concerned him. And that, he felt, had to be captured immediately.

The kick, when I see these things, is instantaneous. Then I usually make a very slight line sketch in pencil, a few lines only, and go over the values, hues and arrangement in my mind – really paint it in my head, as a matter of fact. I have done all this the instant I saw and felt it. This short memorizing, ten minutes or so of conscious thought, is merely recapitulated fixing. That is usually the end, but some I paint next day, in a month, a year later, it doesn't seem to make any difference.

David Milne was born in Burgoyne, near Paisley, Ontario, in 1882. His first job was as a teacher in a country school nearby, but at the age of twenty-one he left to study art in New York. He worked at the Art Students' League for several years, supporting himself by doing commercial design but continuing to paint on his own.

In 1913 he exhibited in the famous Armory Show in New York, an exhibition that included the work of several well-known European artists, whose 'modern' ideas enraged many of the American critics. Milne had little financial success during these years in New York but was well received critically. In 1916 he and his wife moved into the country and settled in Boston Corners in New York State, and there he continued to develop a personal style of his own. Even at this stage of his career, his strong sense of pattern is evident in designs that seem almost abstract in their balance of light and dark areas.

In 1918 Milne joined the Canadian army and was sent to Europe. After the war he worked as an artist for the army but returned to Boston Corners the following year. It was not until 1929, after he had spent twenty-six years in the United States, that Milne returned to live permanently in Canada. For the next twenty-five years he spent most of his time in small towns in Ontario but lived for six years in the bush. Like Tom Thomson, he has become an almost legendary hermit of the wilds, but this is an exaggeration. Though he spent a considerable amount of time painting on his own, he kept in constant contact with his friends and made frequent visits to Toronto.

As an artist, Milne's main aim was to shock his viewer into an immediate response to the visual image. To do this he condensed what he saw in nature into a kind of shorthand that could be 'read' quickly. 'The thing that "makes" a picture is the thing that "makes" dynamite — compression. It isn't a fire in the grass, it is an explosion.'

Hill Reflected, Bishop's Pond (p. 155) and *Glass Jar I* (p. 153) were painted over twenty years apart, and though in many ways the style has changed, the impact is still the same. They both have the force of an explosion.

Hill Reflected, Bishop's Pond was painted after Milne returned from Europe to the United States. Although the pattern is still fairly dense, it is more open than some of his earlier work. It also shows his individual use of line and dry patterned brushwork.

In a black and white reproduction, his balance of tone can be seen quite clearly. The darker area of trees and reflections on the right is balanced by the larger area of paler tones. Meanwhile the excitement of the patterned water is contrasted, and

Hill Reflected, Bishop's Pond, 1920
watercolour on paper
17-3/4″ x 21-3/4″ (45 cm x 55 cm)
The Art Gallery of Windsor

balanced, by the sweeping curves across the hills. The visual impact of the forms is startling, but the quiet colours act as a balance. This controls the emotional effect, though the eye is kept alert and interested.

Glass Jar I was painted some years after Milne returned to live in Canada. Though it is a small painting, it has great strength. Milne preferred to work on a small scale because he felt he could 'register the feeling more rapidly without exhaustion'.

In *Glass Jar I* he has shown his amazing ability to handle space as well as objects; the open areas of Milne's paintings are as important as the actual images. These 'open and shut' spaces, as he called them, give a sense of great importance to the image.

It is obvious from this watercolour that Milne had complete control of his medium. Only the minimum of lines were required to suggest his subject. The force of the work lies in its colour and composition. The brilliant oranges and rich purple and red of the flowers seem almost to burn against the pale background and the dark areas in the corners. Arranged on a diagonal, the composition is kept stable by the upright cylinder of the glass jar and the weight of the dark corners. The curves of the jar, empty and clear above but heavy with liquid below, echo the lightly suggested curves of the flowers. These also balance each other in weight and outline.

Glass Jar I creates an impact that is almost breathtaking, yet it is a work that remains in the memory long after leaving it. Somehow it seems wrong to analyze a painting like this. It is rather like pulling the petals off a daisy to admire the way it is formed. However much we may admire the skill and control of the artist, he would not have wished this to interfere with a spontaneous sharing of his vision.

Carl Schaefer

b. 1903

Ontario Farmhouse, 1934, oil on canvas
41-7/8″ x 49-1/4″ (106 cm x 125 cm)
The National Gallery of Canada, Ottawa

There is something very personal about Carl Schaefer's work. It is straightforward and realistic, but it also shows his honest search for ways to express values that are extremely important to him.

Schaefer was born in southern Ontario. His mother died when he was still a boy, and so he went to live with his grandfather on a farm near Hanover. Having grown up close to the land, he knows it well, and it has always been the basis of his painting.

Schaefer studied at the Ontario College of Art in Toronto when George Reid was the principal. At that time Arthur Lismer was vice-principal and J.E.H. MacDonald was teaching there. He studied under them both, and they, along with A.Y. Jackson and Lawren Harris, had a considerable influence on him when he was young. Schaefer's later work, though, has taken a more intimate and personal direction.

In 1926 he went north on a sketching trip. Though the landscape obviously impressed him and he experimented with various styles to convey its character, he showed no signs of being inspired by the North, as the Group of Seven had been.

During the 1920s Schaefer also experimented with formal geometric painting, but did not work in the same abstract, decorative style of Lyman and the Contemporary Art Society of Montreal.

It was not until about 1932 that he seems to have felt completely at ease with his choice of subject, the countryside in which he had grown up. He was then teaching part-time to support a young family. Times were difficult during the Depression, and so in the summer months the family would return to the farm near Hanover.

Although Schaefer's style became realistic, there are traces of the angular shapes of abstraction in *Ontario Farmhouse*, which was painted in the middle of the 1930s. But despite its realism, the meaning of the painting is symbolic, suggesting the idea of permanence within change.

The house, raised on a hill, is important as a symbol of strength and endurance, but it is also important because it is a home. Although the wind is tearing at the trees outside, there is a warm glow coming from the neatly curtained windows. The chair on the verandah seems to suggest quiet relaxation on summer evenings.

But now the summer is drawing to an end. The potato patch is still green, though the grain has ripened and will soon be cut. Yet everywhere there is promise that the cycle of life will continue. Even the dead tree becomes a symbol of continuity, of endings that steadily change into fresh beginnings. The sky too reflects the theme. Storm clouds gather overhead, but through them shine beams of light, suggesting the calm that soon will follow.

The farmhouse, typical of the Ontario farm architecture of the day, is both realistic and symbolic, but at the same time it represents another blend of opposites. The building is strong and sturdy, a fortress against harsh weather and the troubles of life. But the fretwork and wrought-iron railing, broken in one place as things so often are in real homes, exist for the sheer pleasure of decoration.

The style of the painting emphasizes a theme that binds all time together. On the one hand, its straightforward realism clearly describes the reality of the present moment; on the other hand, its analyzed geometric shapes give the painting its quality of timelessness.

Later in his career, Schaefer chose to paint in watercolour rather than oil. This medium seemed to allow him the opportunity of being more personal and more immediately in touch with his subject. And it is this personal relationship to the land and the objects of daily life that seems to be of ultimate importance to him.

Charles Comfort

b. 1900

Young Canadian, 1932, watercolour
36″ x 42″ (91 cm x 107 cm)
Hart House, University of Toronto

Born in Edinburgh, Charles Comfort came to Canada with his family to settle in Winnipeg when he was twelve years old. There he received his early training in art and later studied at the Art Students' League in New York. During his career he became well known for his portraiture, his mural painting in many public buildings, his work as a war artist, and his teaching at the University of Toronto. He was also director of the National Gallery of Canada from 1960 until his retirement in 1965.

Although he painted in oils, Comfort has always been particularly interested in watercolours. In fact, *Young Canadian*, a portrait of Carl Schaefer, is one in a series of large watercolour portraits. It was exhibited with two of Comfort's other works at the Tate Gallery in London.

Young Canadian was painted during the hard years of the Depression. Although it is a portrait of one individual, it also represents many strong and able young men who moved from place to place, suitcase in hand, looking for work. In a triangular composition, the artist has deliberately emphasized the large hands, hanging loose and idle, and the questioning, almost fearful, expression on the man's face.

Comfort's portrait of Carl Schaefer and Théophile Hamel's *Self Portrait* (p. 54) make an interesting comparison, since both paintings are of young artists. Hamel, like Schaefer, seems to be questioning what the future will bring, but while he looks relaxed and confident, Schaefer's appearance gives no sense of self-assurance. Rather, the uncertainty of his future is obviously causing him great worry and concern.

Both portraits are based on triangular compositions, but the style of painting and the treatment of light produce totally different effects. Hamel controls his light so that he can move quietly from light to shade and back again, while Comfort treats light dramatically to produce a deliberately stark and abrupt effect.

The background of each painting is also in keeping with its mood. Hamel is seated in front of a gentle, dreamy scene full of curving lines and forms. Comfort, though, has given Schaefer a background of harsh angular shapes that reflect the many sharp angles, and few curves, in the figure itself.

The tall farm buildings suggest storage places for wheat, reminding the viewer of the grain that became valueless during the Depression years. Meanwhile the young Canadian sits idle and discouraged – a symbol of wasting youth.

Jack Humphrey

1910–1967

Draped Head, 1931, oil on panel
16-3/4" x 13-1/2" (43 cm x 34 cm)
Hart House, University of Toronto

Born in Saint John, New Brunswick, Jack Humphrey spent most of his life there, with the exception of his early training in Boston and New York and a visit in 1929 to Germany, where he studied art. While he was in Europe, he was impressed by a variety of styles that had not affected much Canadian art at the time. But the influence Humphrey's European experience had upon his work remained with him throughout his career.

An interesting and unusual feature about Humphrey's art is its variety. In his landscapes, he seems to have allowed his energy and personal feelings to take control in a way that had been encouraged by Hans Hofmann (1880-1966), the famous German abstract artist under whom he studied. But in his portraits, his style remained quiet and controlled and always extremely sensitive. His variation in approach can probably best be explained in his own words, 'Painting is worthwhile when it is not a creature of habit.'

Draped Head, painted shortly after he returned from Germany, is actually a portrait of himself, but it is also a study of forms, planes, and their relationships. The painting is strong and effective enough to enjoy without any explanation. But in order to understand its technique, we must briefly consider the work of one of the giants of European painting, the Post-Impressionist artist Paul Cézanne (1839-1906).

Although Cézanne was interested in the work of the Impressionists, he was disturbed by the way in which solid objects were being completely dissolved in their later paintings. Cézanne wanted his art to convey a solid and lasting sense of nature. Though he did not talk of God, he, like the earlier classical artists, believed that there was order and purpose in life. But his method of expressing these ideas differed from theirs.

Classical artists since the Renaissance had aimed at creating illusions of the visible world through the use of careful drawing, shading, perspective, and every means possible to suggest real life. Cézanne's aim, though, was to find the underlying geometric structure and forms within nature and to build these up on his canvas in planes of colour. In this way he was able to model his surface as if it were composed of solid geometric forms.

But while Cézanne wanted to restore a feeling of solidity to his art, he also wanted to capture the vitality of the living world, the as-it-is-at-this-moment quality that the Impressionists had caught. His aim was to combine a sense of the permanence of nature and the lasting values of life with a feeling of the importance of this particular moment.

Pablo Picasso carried Cézanne's theory one step further. He agreed that all objects have an underlying geometric form. But, he said, all we see when we look at an object is what is visible from where we stand. We see the front and perhaps the sides and the top. But this is not the whole form of the object. What we cannot see is as much a part of it as what we can see.

Picasso set about analyzing the shape of the object. He looked first at the front, then at the sides, top, bottom, and inside. In fact, he examined every surface, or plane, separately. He then placed these views together, one at a time, on top of each other.

The finished painting looked rather like a flat pack of differently shaped cards turned in different directions. By using this process, Picasso arrived at a complete knowledge of his object, though the result would not resemble the object at all if it were only seen from one viewpoint at a time. This flat style became known as Cubism, and it is so extremely important in the history of modern art that it has been called 'the parent of all abstract art forms'.

At its most extreme, Cubism was so carefully and intellectually thought out that it became a kind of mental game. Since little room was left for expression of feelings, it was a style that did not last long in its pure state. But this analysis of three-dimensional forms into two-dimensional flat shapes has been an important basis for many kinds of abstract art.

Humphrey did not go as far as Picasso had in his work, but *Draped Head* does show the strong influence of Cézanne. It is a powerful painting. The head has a serious, simple, and solid quality that is as timeless as a mathematically ordered Greek statue. The strong planes of colour with which it is built up suggest a knowledge of the whole form and not just of the surface. With firm brush strokes, and areas of colour carefully placed in relationship to each other, the artist has managed to model his form as if it were carved rather than painted. But despite the feeling of solidity and solemn stillness that he has achieved by this modelling technique, Humphrey's choice of colour, which contrasts the warm tones of the face with the cool tones of the cloth surrounding it, gives the head a vital sense of life.

John Lyman

1886–1967

Lady with a White Collar
(Femme au Collet Blanc), 1936
oil on board
24-1/8″ x 17-3/8″ (61 cm x 44 cm)
The National Gallery of Canada, Ottawa

John Lyman was an artist of considerable importance in the development of modern art in Canada. In fact, he was the key figure in a movement that led away from the patriotic painting of the Group of Seven. Lyman was concerned that, under the Group's influence, art in Canada was in danger of becoming 'souvenir painting', as he called it.

We have seen that although each artist in the Group of Seven had his own individual style, the Group as a whole was deeply concerned with painting Canada as Canada for Canadians. In John Lyman's opinion this was a dangerous aim for other artists to follow. It could lead to paintings that were only pleasing pictures and had no serious meaning in the language of art. 'The real adventure,' he said, 'takes place in the sensibility and imagination of the individual.'

As is the case with so many artists, John Lyman's work was deeply affected by his training and personal experiences. He was born in the United States of American-born parents who became Canadian citizens. Lyman was brought up in Montreal and studied at McGill for two years, but he received most of his schooling in Connecticut. At the age of twenty-one he went to Europe and started a course in architectural design in London, but a few months later he moved to Paris and enrolled at the Académie Julian. In an exhibition at the Salon he first saw a work by James Morrice. Lyman was greatly impressed by it and made friends with the artist. In 1909 he enrolled in a new art school that had just been opened by Henri Matisse, the famous Fauve artist. Matisse and the Canadian Morrice were to become the two great influences on Lyman's work.

Like Morrice, Lyman remained abroad for many years and did not return to live in Canada until 1931, when he was forty-five. He had exhibited in Montreal during the time he lived in Europe, but his work was laughed at and scorned. He was treated in much the same way as the Group of Seven had been in their early days, and as every new art movement is still treated.

When we considered James Morrice's *The Ferry, Quebec*, we noted that it differed from earlier works because of the artist's greater concern for it as a formal expression than as a pleasant view. Although Morrice used the scene in front of him as material for his painting, he was not describing it so much as extracting sensations from it that he could then translate into colour and form.

This was the main theme of Matisse's own painting and teaching. As we saw in Tom Thomson's *The Pool*, the original Fauve approach to art was very emotional, and strong feelings were expressed in thick brush strokes of pure but varied colours. But of all the Fauves, Matisse was the artist concerned with form as well as colour. In his later work his shapes generally became simpler and flatter, and his compositions displayed large areas of plain colour.

Matisse's aims can be seen in John Lyman's *Lady with a White Collar* (p. 163). His subject is dignified and elegant. She is both a human being and a formal artistic pattern. But to maintain such a balance is not an easy task. Either a figure can become so flat and pattern-like that the work is no longer a portrait, or it can become too realistic, approaching the 'souvenir' landscape style of the followers of the Group of Seven – merely a shallow description of what we see.

There is nothing new in the basic problem. All portrait painters have to decide whether they are going to emphasize the realistic look of a person, or try to convey all they can about their subject's character, or aim for effects of pure painting, as Morrice had done in his landscape *The Ferry, Quebec*. Most good portrait painters attempt to reconcile the three approaches, though each emphasizes his own particular concern.

It is interesting to compare Humphrey's *Draped Head* (p. 160) with Lyman's *Lady with a White Collar*. In the Humphrey portrait there is an emphasis on a solid three-dimensional form. The face is built up with levels of colour, and there is a subtle blending of greens in the drapery. The strong outlines of the head do not take away from the general feeling of solidity; rather, the head resembles a piece of sculpture.

Lyman's *Lady* is flatter and more linear. Though there is still some suggestion of three-dimensional form to convey the sense of a living person in space, the main emphasis is on the long, elegant lines and plain surface pattern. Here the face is simpler in construction than Humphrey's portrait. Light and shade play bolder parts. While the colour in Humphrey's painting is built up as if it were modelled, Lyman's depends on strong contrast of flat areas. It is a striking pattern – bold, simple, and effective.

Lyman was impressed by the artists painting in eastern Canada and exhibiting in Montreal during the 1930s, among whom were Jack Humphrey and Goodridge Roberts. He considered their work genuine art, whereas he felt many of the painters in Toronto were merely copying the style of the Group of Seven.

In 1931, Lyman and three other artists opened a school in Montreal. For economic reasons it did not last long, but the artists clearly stated their aims when they said, 'The essential qualities of a work of art lie in the relationships of form to form, and colour to colour. From these the eye, and especially the trained eye, derives its pleasure and all its artistic emotion.' From these ideas developed the Contemporary Art Society, the founding group for modern painting in Montreal, established in 1939.

Goodridge Roberts

1904-1974

Still Life with Detail from Velazquez Print, 1963
oil on canvas
48″ x 36″ (122 cm x 91 cm)
The Art Gallery of Windsor

This painting by Goodridge Roberts is so alive that it hardly seems accurate to call it a still life. Although the artist has shown a collection of attractive and decorative objects, they alone are not responsible for the success of his painting. The vitality of the canvas comes from the brilliance of the colour and light, the bold and rich texture of the paint, and the fascinating effects of space.

We have already seen several still lifes – by Légaré, Plamondon, Leduc, and Milne; later we shall see others. Though each artist has painted his objects in a completely different way, each has faced the same basic challenge. Still lifes are pure painting, in which the artist relies solely on the language of painting for his effects. Form, space, texture, colour, and light are the only means he has to convey his message. He has no story to tell, no moral statement to make, and no criticism to direct against society. The message of his painting depends entirely on our aesthetic sense, or the pleasure and understanding we receive from seeing.

In addition to being a fine painting in its own right, Goodridge Roberts's *Still Life* clearly shows how art grows out of art. Roberts has deliberately included a detail from a famous seventeenth-century Spanish painting and has drawn attention to it by mentioning it in the title of his work.

But he has also proven that a good artist never copies; instead, he re-creates. He looks at the art of the past and strives to understand its essential qualities. He then paints his own work, including in it the values that he feels have meaning for all men in all times. Yet every artist's work remains his own, something that grows out of his own personality and the period in which he lives.

In his *Still Life*, Roberts has combined a wide variety of objects of different colours and shapes. Hanging on the wall behind them is a detail from Velazquez's *Surrender of Breda*. The actual paint-ing depicts a battle scene, though the detail is merely a glimpse from behind the lances of the soldiers into the landscape beyond. Why, we may ask, would Roberts have chosen to include a detail of a Velazquez painting, and why this particular one? It is probable that each part of this question has a different answer.

It is only because of the title of Roberts's work that we know the scene at the back is a detail of a painting at all and not a view through a window, as we might have expected. But since Roberts specifically mentions that it is a detail of a Velazquez painting, we realize that it is important for our appreciation of the *Still Life*.

Velazquez (1599-1660) was a painter who was fascinated by light. Since he believed that our sense of what we see is entirely dependent on light, his canvases radiate light from direct and reflected sources. Because of his theories, Velazquez had a great influence on the Impressionists, who two hundred years later proved scientifically what he had discovered by observation.

The vitality and life of Roberts's painting is also largely dependent on light, and by referring to Velazquez, Roberts acknowledges his debt to him. It is true that here the clarity, the contrasts of light and shadow, and the rich variation of colour belong to Roberts's own work. A knowledge of Velazquez, though, helps us to put Roberts's painting in a historical series, beginning with Velazquez and continuing with the Impressionists and the Fauves. An understanding of the historical development helps us to see how this particular painting relates to a fundamental question that has already been examined by many other artists from many different eras.

But why did Roberts choose a small detail from the *Surrender of Breda*? The answer here is not concerned with history but with the effects of space.

Roberts's painting suggests a series of planes in which the objects recede from the front to the back of the scene. But the artist has deliberately left us in a state of uncertainty. We are not sure whether we are looking at real space that goes plane by plane back into a far distance or into a fairly shallow space that ends with the wall. This uncertainty creates a kind of movement within the painting.

At first glance, we can believe we are in the real world, looking at a table on which solid objects are arranged in a series of planes. Behind this is a window with a sill crowded with more objects. Beyond the bars of the window are fields stretching towards the horizon. But then, of course, we remember that it is not a window; it is a flat painting on the wall, and this knowledge changes our whole perception. Though we accept that Velazquez's painting suggests space beyond the lances of the soldiers, we know that in reality it is only a flat canvas.

The square area now tends to move towards us and reduce the feeling of space. We tend to perceive the flat surface patterns of line and colour, rather than solid objects arranged in planes. In fact, Roberts's approach to space now seems quite similar to Tom Thomson's in *The Pool* (p. 125).

Goodridge Roberts is probably best known for his landscape painting, though he also painted many still lifes and nudes. For him the actual subject matter was less important than the relationship between things. He wrote, 'A pale blue bowl is an enveloping tropic sea, the dome of a summer sky, a protecting embrace. A stone jar crammed with green-leaved twigs is a rocky bluff from whose summit the dense green forest radiates and strains into the air.' Roberts thought and painted like a poet, but this is not really surprising, since his father and uncle were both well-known writers and his cousin was Bliss Carman, the famous Canadian poet.

He first trained in art at the Ecole des Beaux-Arts in Montreal and later at the Art Students' League in New York. Here he received his introduction to the work of Picasso, Cézanne, and Matisse, the latter two being particularly important influences on his own style. Roberts's description of the emphasis of the training he received in New York may also increase our understanding of his work and particularly this *Still Life*.

As a student under Max Weber I had learned the importance of seeking for the true relationships of all shapes and colours to one another and to the whole structure of the design. His method in painting involved a constant comparison of each object in all its aspects to every other object. In applying the paint to the canvas there was a constant affirmation and re-affirmation of the relationship of colour to colour and shape to shape. As the painting progressed each object grew to assume its proper role. There must be no doubt about the meaning of each part. This one must assert its boldness and that one its gentleness. Here colour must be bright and clamorous, there it must be faint and sweet.

PART VI

THE PAST AND THE PRESENT

Some works of art belong to no particular period or style. Often these are the works of untrained artists, ordinary men and women who create for their own pleasure or for their friends. Having had no formal training, these artists know nothing of current styles or fashions and are not involved in the continuing process of finding new ways of expressing ideas in visual form.

High art, as it is sometimes called, is the work of trained artists who seek to reflect the society in which they live, but it is also part of a long artistic tradition. Artists learn from the work of others before them and then develop new techniques and visual ways of expressing the ideas and beliefs of the ever-changing world. New styles evolve from this continuous stream of change. They serve their purpose in their time, and from them emerge other styles.

Untrained artists, though, are not involved in this artistic evolution, and so their work has a timeless quality that belongs as much to the past as to the present. The ex-voto paintings of early French Canada, for example, differ very little in style from the work of untrained artists today. Even the subject matter, though it may vary in importance from one period to another, generally remains similar. The ex-votos were religious works, as are many by Simone Mary Bouchard and Norval Morrisseau. Abbé Louis Nicolas drew the animals he saw and heard of in New France, just as Kiakshuk did some two hundred years later on Baffin Island. Hermann Moll and Arch Williams, also working two hundred years apart, drew similar scenes of the fishing industry in Newfoundland.

Portraits; accounts of daily life at home, on the farm, in the villages and towns; simple personal experiences, all provided, and continue to provide, popular subject matter for the untrained artist and his everyday audience.

It is interesting that although the work of these artists follows no particular style, strong similarities exist among the best of their paintings. Usually, very little effort is made to convey the sense of solid objects within space – sometimes because it is too difficult to do, but often because the artist has no need to create an illusion. What he has to say can be said on a flat two-dimensional surface. Surface patterns and rhythms, created by the repetition of shapes and lines, are both of considerable importance. In fact, love of design for its own sake often seems to be as vital as subject matter.

There is considerable confusion among critics and their readers over the terms used to describe such work. Primitive, naïve, and folk art are the three main terms, but there is no clear and accepted definition of any of them. They are frequently used interchangeably. But since there are three distinct sources of art produced by untrained artists, the terms may be used to distinguish them.

Primitive art is a term that may be used to describe the work of artists in isolated societies who have not been exposed to the major civilizations or have not been heavily influenced by them. The work of African tribes, for example, or of Eskimos or North American Indian tribes, whose styles and images are uniquely their own, could be identified as primitive art.

Folk art is a useful term for the work of people who live in groups within the major civilizations but retain their own distinct customs and traditions. Ukrainian art in Canada, for example, preserves the intricate geometric patterns that have been handed down from generation to generation. Other groups who have established their own customs and way of life in certain districts have also depicted them visually. The Folk Painters of Charlevoix County, for example, were a group of French-Canadian artists living in the Charlevoix area of Quebec in the

1930s. Their farms and villages were central to their lives, as was their strong belief in the Catholic faith, and their art was a reflection of their background.

Naïve art is a broader term that can be used to describe the work of any untrained artist. Naïve painting obviously varies greatly in quality, because the artist has had no instruction in technique. But fine naïve art has a simplicity and charm that makes up for any awkwardness in drawing or lack of artistic knowledge.

Finally, there are some artists who have had formal training but who choose to work in a naïve manner because they admire the honesty of untrained painters.

Naïve painting, like children's art, is direct and uncomplicated. It expresses what the artist sees or imagines in the simplest way possible, and because of this it is easy to understand and enjoy. At last, it is beginning to be seriously accepted as an art form – a sincere visual expression of pleasure in the everyday world by ordinary men and women.

Simone Mary Bouchard

1912–1945

The Three Kings, c. 1930, oil on canvas
22-3/4″ x 31″ (58 cm x 79 cm)
Private Collection

From the time of the birth of Jesus until the fourth century A.D., Christmas was celebrated on January 6. After that time Christmas Day was moved to December 25, and January 6 became the Feast of the Epiphany. This day is still kept to celebrate the arrival of the Three Kings from the East, who brought gifts to the stable in Bethlehem.

Many of us may think of this event as having taken place hundreds of years ago and of the yearly celebration as an occasion held in memory of it. But in Simone Mary Bouchard's imagination, the Three Kings were actually present every year at their feast on January 6.

Because her painting (p. 171) is so delightful, child-like, and bright with colour and detail, it is easy to think of the subject as a kind of fairy tale. But to the artist it probably had a very special meaning. Just as Sister Marie Barbier painted the Child Jesus and hung His portrait over the bread oven so that He would prevent her loaves from burning, so Mary Bouchard felt the living presence of the Three Kings on their particular day.

For Mary Bouchard a feast was exactly that – a feast and a happy occasion. Accordingly, she has shown all her brothers and sisters gathered around the multi-layered and splendidly decorated cake. Everyone is dressed in his best clothing, and the party is made even more lively with the music of an accordion and violin.

It is probable that the room in the painting looks just like the Bouchard family parlour did then, since details from daily life and scenes from Mary's own imagination meet comfortably in her art. She makes the pictures on the wall, the model of Notre-Dame on the mantelpiece, the ferns, the pattern on the carpet, and the Three Kings themselves all belong to the same world.

Mary Bouchard and her two sisters, who were also painters, were born at Moulin St-Césaire, a mill near Baie St-Paul in Quebec. From this area came a number of untrained artists who have since been called the Folk Painters of Charlevoix County. The term folk better describes these artists than do the terms naïve or primitive, because their work is based on their own particular district, and it shows the customs and way of life of the country people who lived around them.

The work of all three Bouchard sisters has become quite widely recognized. Mary was a member of the Contemporary Art Society in Montreal and exhibited there frequently. Marie-Cécile, who was eight years younger, started painting when she was eighteen, and her work was also exhibited in Montreal with that of her two sisters. Her painting career ended when she entered a convent in 1947. Edith, the youngest of the three, was born in 1924 and did not start painting until after Mary died and Marie-Cécile entered the convent. She too exhibited her work in Montreal until she became a nun.

The home of the Bouchard sisters and the neighbourhood in which they lived occupy a central place in all their paintings. In one of them Mary is seen fashionably dressed in high heels and a large hat. She is sitting on the arm of a chair in this same parlour with the draped curtains and flowing fern behind her. The sisters also painted scenes of the inside and outside of the mill, some of which show the nearby woods and fields with horses grazing.

All these paintings have a direct and human quality, resembling that in the early ex-votos of Quebec. *The Three Kings* is a statement of Mary's religious belief that she has presented in the simplest, most straightforward way possible. The Magi have been invited into the very midst of the Bouchard home. As if they were neighbours from next door, the Kings share with the family the Feast of the Epiphany.

Jean Paul Lemieux

b. 1904

Lazare, 1941, oil on masonite
39-3/4″ x 32-7/8″ (101 cm x 83 cm)
Art Gallery of Ontario, Toronto

Jean Paul Lemieux is an artist who frequently represents the passing of time in his paintings. In fact, the subject of time and how to depict it has always been a problem and a source of interest for artists. Life takes place within time. Each of us and everything around us changes in time, and because of this every subject that an artist paints is in some way affected by it. The season of the year and the hour of the day affect the light in which he paints. Movement that changes the position of objects also happens within time. Even space is altered with passing time, because objects that are moving change the space around them.

Since it is such a complex subject, the problem of representing time has no single answer. In the past, artists have worked with it in a variety of ways, according to their different ideas about time and their different feelings about its effects. In the present day the passage of time seems to concern artists even more. Later we shall consider some of their problems and solutions.

In *Lazare* (p. 173) Lemieux has returned to a method of depicting a time sequence that was used hundreds of years ago. Basically, this method required the artist to arrange his story in its proper order so that it could be read from left to right. In the religious works of the early Christian church, figures and little scenes crossed the painting in regular bands, or registers, like rows of printed words.

Later this arrangement became looser, and though the story could still be read from left to right, the scenes were arranged in a more flowing composition. This type of time sequence, similar in some ways to a modern day filmstrip, was used in early Italian Renaissance painting of the fourteenth century. Lemieux has always been interested in this period of history, and there he seems to have found his inspiration for *Lazare*.

The events that Lemieux describes take place during war, and his whole story can be followed from beginning to end. In the top left-hand corner enemy planes fly overhead, dropping parachutists who fire upon the villagers. A man is shot and falls to the ground. The central scene is of the funeral service in the church, while the next is of the funeral procession winding its way up to the graveyard. The final scene shows the dead man rising from the grave.

This little section obviously recalls Lazarus, or 'Lazare' in French, the brother of Mary and Martha, who was raised from the dead by Jesus. It was at that time that Jesus said, 'I am the Resurrection and the Life: he that believeth in Me, though he were dead, yet shall he live. . . .' These are the words that are still repeated at every Christian burial service, and thus the painting links the past and the present not only in its stylistic treatment of time, but also in its statement of religious faith.

Lazare has that simple, direct force of naïve painting, partly because it was based on early fourteenth-century Italian painting and partly because the artist has always been interested in the natural, unspoiled quality of folk art. Lemieux has done much in his lifetime to encourage, but not interfere with, the work of talented untrained artists.

Jean Paul Lemieux was born in Quebec City and received his early training at the Ecole des Beaux-Arts in Montreal. In 1929 he went to Paris for further instruction, including courses at the Académie Colarossi. After leaving Paris the following year, he returned to Canada, where he devoted himself to painting and teaching in Montreal and Quebec.

More and more from the 1950s onward, Lemieux's work has become simpler in form and more monumental. His figures, typified by those in

es Promeneurs, 1963, oil
_2″ x 58″ (107 cm x 147 cm)
Collection of Dr. A.C. Ritchie

es Promeneurs, are large and lonely, trapped in the process of aging and of time that passes by while they remain apart. Even in families or groups each individual occupies his own world, sometimes in confined spaces, but often in great, wide landscapes that offer no protection. Grandparents, mothers, fathers, children, all live alone, in constant contact but far apart. Even within their own lives time makes them change, and the child loses touch with the adult.

Lemieux, of course, is not the only artist who considered time as an element of his painting. We have seen the work of many others who have done so. Lemieux has simply treated it more obviously.

Time is one of the themes of Ozias Leduc's _L'Enfant au Pain_ (p. 106), for instance, though Leduc has not treated time in its process of passing. On the contrary, time is frozen in his painting. It is as though we stopped a film sequence of life at one particular moment so that we could enjoy it forever. Ozias Leduc has given us this rare moment – the chance of saying stop, this is what life is all about, this is its meaning.

Another painting in which time plays a part is Michel Dessaillant's _L'Ange gardien_ (p. 26), but

here time is again treated differently. Dessaillant has represented time in motion by depicting an action that is in the process of happening. It is not a question of time passing, in the sense of looking backwards and then forwards, as Lemieux has shown us. Dessaillant has allowed us to be present at the very moment that his great angel arrives on earth to protect the little girl. We can almost hear the rush of air caused by his huge wings in flight.

Mary Bouchard described yet another aspect of time. When she invited the Three Kings into the living room of her Quebec home, she was closing the gap of the nearly two thousand years that have passed since the Magi entered the stable at Bethlehem. To her, that day and every yearly celebration of the Feast of the Epiphany are one and the same.

Time is so much a part of our existence that it always has been, and always will be, a question that human beings must face. And to complicate matters still further, time is intimately bound to space, for it is within space that time moves. This might recall William Blake's seemingly very simple but actually rather profound poem on page 107. It seems that we are left with yet another question, but it is one that we shall be considering again in later paintings.

Norval Morrisseau

b. 1930

Windigo, undated
tempera on heavy light-brown building paper
61-7/8" x 31-7/8"(157 cm x 81 cm)
Glenbow-Alberta Institute, Calgary

This is a painting of the Windigo, an evil spirit who feeds on human flesh and grows so tall he touches the clouds. He lives in the North and threatens his victims with cannibalism or death from winter starvation. The Ojibway and Cree have many legends about the Windigo, and some fear him so much that when they hear him shout they fall down in a faint.

Norval Morrisseau, whose Indian name is Copper Thunderbird, is an Ojibway. For nearly twenty years he has retold the legends of his people in words and pictures. In the past, these stories were handed down by word of mouth from generation to generation, since the Ojibway had no written language until the nineteenth century. Morrisseau, for example, learned them from his grandfather Moses Nanakanagos, and he is determined to preserve them as they were told to him.

Some of these legends may go back hundreds of years; some may have been altered by contact with other tribes; others undoubtedly resulted from the Indians' association with Western culture. The belief in a Windigo is an ancient one. These legends, however, are not superstitious fairy tales or quaint little pastimes. For the Ojibway they are the truth and the explanation of life's mysteries. Just as the Three Kings were as real to Simone Mary Bouchard as her own brothers and sisters, so the Windigo is completely real to Norval Morrisseau.

At one time, the legends of the Ojibway had a reality for all their people, as the stories of the Bible had for all Christians. But as time passes and new contacts are made with other ways of life, beliefs change. The Christian religion has the Bible to keep its tradition alive, but the Ojibway legends could die forever if they are not recorded now.

Because he fears the loss of his people's legends, Morrisseau has tried to remember the stories he was told in order to preserve them for the future. But he wanted to do more than describe them in words, and so he painted them in strong, simple images like this one. He knows he is an artist and accepts it, not proudly, but as a fact. He has said,

My idea is, why I draw them – see, there's lots of stories that are told in Ojibway. But that wasn't enough for me. I wanted to draw them – that's from my own self – what they would look like. And I never knowed anybody who would be interested. And I thought if they could be some place for a hundred – two hundred years – not for myself, for my people. Even if I don't get no money I would be glad to paint them just for people to see.

When his paintings were first exhibited in Toronto, they sold immediately. But even this did not convince Morrisseau that the legends would survive. The danger is that paintings can be bought as mere decoration, rather than as vital statements of belief. Therefore, he wrote down these beliefs and traditions and gave them to someone he trusted to have them printed in words everyone could understand. Morrisseau did not attempt to do this himself, since he has had little formal education.

Even if we did not have the written legend, Morrisseau's painting would still convey the fear and horror the Ojibway had for the Windigo. The huge, angular figure towers over the Indian village – his face like a skull, his hair of jagged icicles, and his nails like twisting, curling claws. The monster eats whole beavers in a gulp, while the beavers appear to have swallowed people. The painted image of the Windigo is terrifying enough; the details of the legend only strengthen the effect.

Some believe that if an Ojibway dreams of the Windigo during a period of fasting in which he is searching for a vision, he will become the Windigo from time to time during his life. On those occasions the demon will inhabit the Indian's body, which will grow and grow until it touches the clouds. The

Indian, in his Windigo form, will then set out to devour any meat that he can find, including his fellow men, since he is hungry for human flesh. At that everyone for miles around falls down in a faint. When the Windigo has at last satisfied his great hunger, he shrinks back to human size. Then the Indian awakes, no longer hungry, remembering nothing of what happened but feeling icy cold. He will remain in a normal state until the next time that the Windigo chooses to occupy him.

Among most Cree and Ojibway, the Windigo is an explanation of why, during winter starvation, some persons are seized with a craving for human flesh. Such individuals are believed to have been possessed by the Windigo and must be killed. Needless to say, all the Indian tribes who know of the Windigo fear him and fear that at the end of a long, hard winter, they or a member of their family may fall under his spell.

William Kurelek

b. 1927

Manitoba Party, 1964, oil on board
48" x 60" (122 cm x 152 cm)
The National Gallery of Canada, Ottawa

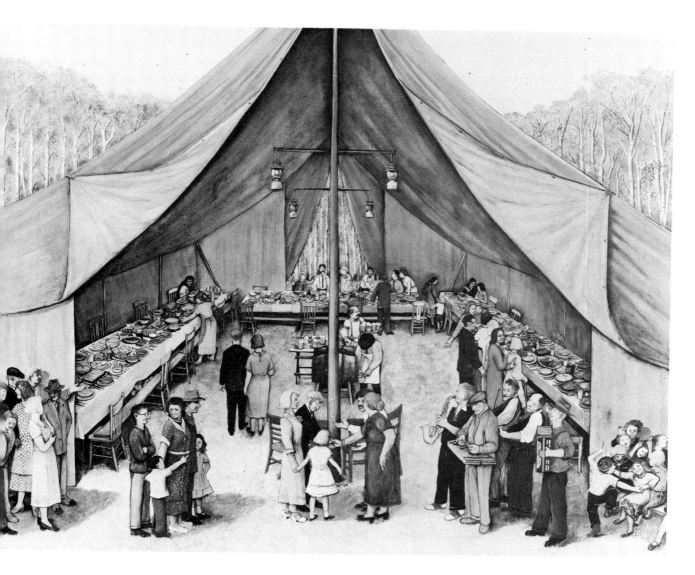

William Kurelek was born in Alberta of Ukrainian parents. The Kurelek family owned their own farm near Edmonton until 1932, when they were forced to leave as a result of the Depression. They moved to Stonewall, near Winnipeg, where they managed to buy another farm, and there William spent the rest of his childhood.

Farm life on the prairies is the subject of many of Kurelek's paintings. Some of them were done when he was a young boy, but many of them were based on recollections of his youth. Painted in 1964, *Manitoba Party* was, he said, 'a combination of two memories of parties under a circus tent at our neighbours, the Tomycks, near Stonewall where our family farmed; both a wedding and an anniversary.... The scene, he says, shows 'typical half-Ukrainian, half-Canadian aspects of such a community celebration.'

As in many of his other paintings, here Kurelek has chosen a symmetrical composition with the tent pole dividing the canvas down the middle. From a central position, we look straight into the tent. The tables on either side draw the eye into the picture space. By using a straightforward, balanced composition the artist is free to concentrate on the detail and variety of the scene. Little groups of people waiting to begin the lavish feast converse excitedly with one another, and Kurelek has treated the actions and dress of each figure individually.

Manitoba Party is a genre painting that recalls the work of Krieghoff and the German painters who were continuing the tradition of 'Peasant' Bruegel. Pieter Bruegel, the famous sixteenth-century Dutch artist, obviously influenced William Kurelek directly. *Manitoba Party*, for example, is closely related to *Peasant Wedding*, one of Bruegel's best-known paintings.

By associating his work with Bruegel's, Kurelek is emphasizing the connection between events of the past and present. He seems to suggest that the simple everyday life of a farming community has changed little over the years. *Manitoba Party* shows only one of the many similar celebrations that took place in the Netherlands four hundred years ago, in the Ukraine during his grandfather's time, and in Canada during the 1930s.

Kurelek left for England in 1952 after taking a degree at the University of Manitoba, working at several jobs, and studying for six months at the Ontario College of Art. He stayed there for seven years, employed as an apprentice to a picture framer and painting on his own. Some of his works were accepted for the Royal Academy summer exhibitions.

During this period of his life Kurelek suffered an emotional crisis that resulted in his conversion to the Roman Catholic faith. Although he had been brought up in the Greek Orthodox church, he had later become an atheist. But with his conversion to Roman Catholicism he acquired a deep and lasting religious belief.

His faith has greatly influenced his work. In 1959 he spent five weeks in the Holy Land, doing research for a series of paintings based on the Gospel of Matthew. He has kept these works, which tell the story of Christ from the Last Supper until the Resurrection, so that slides made from them may be used in missionary work.

Another Dutch artist who has had a strong influence on much of the work of William Kurelek is Hieronymus Bosch (c. 1450–1516). Bosch, who lived a generation before Bruegel, is probably one of the most extraordinary figures in the history of Western art. His paintings are like strange dreams, filled with weird creatures in fantastic settings. Though some of his works are obviously meant to convey stern religious and moral lessons, others are so imaginative that they are almost impossible to interpret.

Like the works of Bosch, many of Kurelek's paintings have clear moral messages that he feels compelled to make. Others are simple statements of his religious faith, and some are poetic and mystical. Despite his limited formal training, Kurelek has become a very successful artist whose work is widely known and collected. For the most part he paints scenes from daily life in the towns and countryside as well as religious subjects. But in nearly everything he paints, he includes symbolism for his viewer to interpret.

Kiakshuk

– 1965

Hunter and Birds, 1961, stone-cut
" x 12"(23 cm x 30 cm)

On west Baffin Island there is a small settlement called Cape Dorset, where some of the most skilled Eskimo carvers and printmakers live. Although carving is an ancient art of the Eskimo people, printmaking did not begin until 1957. James Houston, an artist who had been working with the Eskimos since 1948, introduced them to the technique. Houston stayed in the North for twelve years, and during that time he worked hard to encourage the Eskimo artists and arrange for the sale of their work in the South.

Kiakshuk was among the first Eskimo sculptors to begin printmaking. He was an old man when he made these two prints and died shortly afterwards in 1965.

Kiakshuk was a believer in Shamanism, an ancient Eskimo religion practised for generations before Christianity was introduced into the North. According to this belief, the world is controlled by spirits that can invade the human being and be driven out only by the power of the Shaman, or witch doctor. Because these spirits are usually unseen but can take any form, they are greatly feared.

Kiakshuk lived by hunting, which in the past was the only means of surviving in the North. The men in each family hunted and fished, while the women made food and clothing from the creatures they killed. Similarly, the arctic animals and birds lived by preying on each other. Attack and defence are the two laws of survival, and for a hunter like Kiakshuk killing is a reality of life.

Because the subject is so vital to him, Kiakshuk's prints are usually connected with his occupation. The women printmakers, who are not hunters themselves, tend to treat animals and birds more decoratively. But the choice of subject matter by both men and women is generally wide and varied: scenes of daily life in this world and the spirit world, real creatures and imagined monsters, happy themes and grim ones. The imaginative power of the artists is remarkable.

Kiakshuk's *Hunter and Birds* (p. 181) has a strong expressionistic design full of energy and movement, but his work is also well contained and balanced. In it he conveys a sense of the violence and fear that had been a constant part of his life. The scene depicts the struggle for survival. The hunter, even with his gun, seems almost dwarfed by the huge, ferocious birds that surround him. Above him on the right, a great hawk attacks a pair of ravens, who fight back to protect their young. Kiakshuk emphasizes the fierceness of the scene by using jagged lines to suggest the tearing claws, sharp beaks, and bristling feathers of the birds. Even the awkward shapes of their bodies increase the sense of threat.

This print was made by the stone-cut method, a technique that can be used to give very bold effects, as Kiakshuk does here. The most popular type of stone for printmaking is serpentine, a green stone with a fine grain.

Stone-cuts are made by the relief method, in which the design to be printed is left untouched, while the background and details are cut away. This process is the reverse of engraving and etching, both intaglio methods, in which the design is cut into the surface and the background is left solid.

Kiakshuk was the first of the Eskimo carvers to produce a copper-plate engraving; he had learned the method from James Houston in 1961. In *Loon's Head and Other Creatures,* which he did the following year, Kiakshuk has used this technique. The effect is quite different from that of the stone-cut. It is not as bold or dramatic, and many more details have been introduced. But the design has form and rhythm – the great loon's head balances the various smaller creatures, which themselves are linked by curves and counter-curves.

Loon's Head and Other Creatures, 1962
Copper-plate engraving
8" x 11-3/4" (20 cm x 30 cm)

It is also highly imaginative. Only the loon's head appears above the surface of the water, so that the bird can observe the activity going on above. There, many strange little animals and birds watch the terrifying sight of an Eskimo being attacked by a bumblebee. Kiakshuk claimed that all Eskimos know that the sting of the bee brings instant death.

To us, the engraving might appear to be a delightful fantasy. The huge loon, the goat with the crumpled horns, the dancing goose, and the furry bumblebee are all enchanting creatures. But for Kiakshuk fear and danger are never far below the surface of his art.

Arch Williams

b. 1909

Fish Drying, Goodridge Premises, 1907
1974, oil on canvas
16" x 24" (41 cm x 61 cm)
Private Collection

Arch Williams's ancestors emigrated from Wales to Newfoundland sometime before 1620. Now four generations of his family have lived in the house where he and his wife have brought up their seven children. Every day for seventeen years, Arch Williams fished with his father and uncle off the headlands near the village where he lives – every day except for one spring in 1930 when he fished out of Boston. For thirty-one years he worked as a bookkeeper for the fish buyers in the community. Now that he has retired, he has other interests. He has served as vice-president of the local Historical Society and clerk of the Community Council. He also gardens and paints.

Arch Williams is an untrained artist who has a remarkable sense of design. Because he has had no formal training, the quality of his work is uneven. Some of his canvases are outstanding; others less so. Never having studied the methods of formal design, he does not understand why some of his paintings are more successful than others. But he has produced so many canvases of high quality that his accomplishment cannot be considered accidental. Arch Williams has a natural talent.

He is not an artist who paints from nature, setting up an easel and copying what he sees. Arch, as he is always called, works at home, painting from memory and imagination. If he feels like adding some houses or painting extra details, he does so. But he is basically faithful to his memories. Recalling how his village looked around the time of the First World War, he said, 'The fishing flakes and a lot of buildings are gone now, but except that our house was painted red then, it still looks just the same.'

Many of his paintings, like *Fish Drying, Goodridge Premises,* 1907, describe the past. This one recalls a time two years before he was born, and others go back still further. The past and the present seem very close together in Newfoundland. Though separated by two hundred years, Hermann Moll's scene of drying fish (p. 14) is remarkably similar to Arch Williams's.

In *Fish Drying, Goodridge Premises,* 1907, Arch has divided his canvas into satisfying proportions, locking his design together so that it pleases the eye. It is a realistic scene that tells exactly what Arch wants to tell, but it is also a work of art.

The strong block of houses, set together like building blocks, divide the painting at eye level, three-quarters of the way up the canvas. This gives a stable base from which the details can spread out. The large front drying-yard, with its stylized fish and shell-shaped nets, is painted in pale shades. Blue-greys and muted yellows effectively contrast with the dark, but smaller, area to the left. The black and white buildings catch the eye, though they are plain enough to set off the lively pattern of the drying fish. The blue sky, green fields, and hilly ridge provide an interesting background, while the neat white fences add an appealing and human touch.

Arch Williams's other successful paintings show the same strength of design. In all his best works he creates a balance between strong structure and interesting details. This balance gives his paintings a quality that makes them more than merely delightful pictures – which, of course, they also are.

PART VII

NEW DIRECTIONS

circa 1940 to 1976

During the first half of the twentieth century, Canadian artists had cautiously begun to experiment with a new approach to art, but it was not until 1940 to 1945 that contemporary methods and ideas were able to develop fully. Canada had always been conservative in its attitude towards the arts; anything new or experimental was looked upon with suspicion. Even in the early years of this century, society tended to tolerate artists rather than accept them. Many artists left the country for years, discouraged by the lack of interest in their work. Even the Group of Seven had had to struggle for recognition and, once accepted, were often admired more for their nationalism than for their creativity. Emily Carr was violently rejected during most of her lifetime, and David Milne was largely ignored.

The abstracts of Bertram Brooker and Lawren Harris, painted in the 1920s and 1930s, were regarded with distaste, although abstraction had already been firmly established in Europe years before. The first exhibition of Cubism was held in Paris in 1907, and Wassily Kandinsky published *Concerning the Spiritual in Art* in 1912. But in Canada the full impact of contemporary ideas and styles was not felt until 1940.

While a conservative attitude towards art existed among the general public, it was also encouraged by the older methods of teaching. The academic system of copying reproductions of the Old Masters and drawing from models was still firmly supported. Arthur Lismer, who felt strongly about the need for encouraging free creative expression, resigned from the Ontario College of Art because his ideas were not accepted. Fred Varley and Jock Macdonald met the same rigid attitudes at the Vancouver School of Design and Applied Arts, and they too resigned. L'Ecole des Beaux-Arts in Montreal was another major art institution that remained strongly academic.

It was in 1940 that Canadian art entered a new era. That year Alfred Pellan returned to Canada after spending about twelve years in Paris, where he had come into contact with the great upsurge of artistic change that had been sweeping through Europe since the end of the last century. On his return at the beginning of the Second World War, Pellan brought with him new ideas and styles, and great enthusiasm. He became an important teacher.

Montreal was the birthplace of contemporary Canadian painting, and Paul-Emile Borduas, another Quebec artist, was one of its principal founders. He gathered around him a group of eager students, anxious to experiment and break away from the tired repetitions and rigid attitudes of the past. They called themselves *Les Automatistes*.

Borduas, in the new twentieth-century definition of the word, was a romantic. A follower of Kandinsky, he felt that the imagination and the subconscious mind were the paths to understanding the meaning and mystery of life. His influence and teaching have been of tremendous importance in the development of Canadian painting during the last thirty years.

But, as has happened throughout the history of Western art, another movement evolved whose concern was more with the mind than with the imagination. Under Guido Molinari and others who based their theories on the Dutch artist Piet Mondrian, a group of artists in Montreal began painting hard-edge abstracts. In contrast to Borduas's work, their style of painting was based on mathematical precision and, again in twentieth-century terms, on a kind of classical clarity, order, and balance. This group, known as *Les Plasticiens,* supported theories that linked them to new developments in New York, whereas *Les Automatistes* were more closely related to Paris.

Contemporary painting in Toronto did not really begin until the 1950s with the formation of a group called Painters Eleven. Their first exhibition was held in 1954, and, by the time they disbanded in 1959, abstract art had become generally accepted by the public. During the 1960s, in fact, about eighty-five percent of works of art sold in Toronto were painted in an abstract style.

In the fifties and sixties Vancouver, Regina, Winnipeg, and London also developed as important art centres, experimenting with new styles and techniques.

Artists throughout the country began receiving more encouragement from the government and from the general public. The Canada Council, formed in 1957, started its program of grants for study and travel. Sums of money were given to galleries for the purchase of contemporary art. The National Gallery as well as provincial and commercial galleries were also involved independently in the promotion of Canadian painting. By the time of Expo 67, art in Canada was no longer merely a hobby of wealthy collectors; it was becoming accepted and enjoyed by an increasingly large portion of the general public.

Now, in the 1970s, Canadian art and artists are, for the most part, receiving wider recognition than they ever did before. Exhibitions are held regularly in the numerous public and commercial galleries and are well attended. The government has become a major patron of the arts and buys and commissions large-scale projects. High-quality printmaking by leading artists has encouraged the public to buy contemporary works of art.

Certainly it is difficult for all but a few artists to make a living from their work alone, but the situation has improved greatly. New materials are leading to new techniques. The visual arts are constantly expanding into broader areas. Painting, in the traditional sense, has not been abandoned but is being combined more and more with other media.

Canadian art can now take its place in the world. Whether or not it can be identified as typically Canadian is open to question, but there is no doubt that Canada has artists today who are respected in every nation.

Paul-Emile Borduas

1905 – 1960

L'Etoile Noire, 1957, oil on canvas
63-3/4" x 51-1/4" (162 cm x 130 cm)
The Montreal Museum of Fine Arts

Ozias Leduc was Borduas's first art teacher. Both men were born in the little village of St-Hilaire, near Montreal, and like Leduc, Borduas came from a poor family. When he was seven years old, Paul-Emile became seriously ill, and it was probably during his long recovery that he first became interested in painting.

Borduas had had only five years of schooling when he began work under Ozias Leduc as a church decorator. But during this time he also studied for a degree at the Ecole des Beaux-Arts in Montreal. When he was twenty-three, he went to Paris and saw the work of major French artists for the first time, but he soon returned to Montreal, where he continued to work with Leduc and began teaching art.

Paul-Emile Borduas could be called one of the founding fathers of modern painting in Canada. In his work he carried the process of abstraction one step further than earlier artists had done. Morrice, Lyman, and FitzGerald had relied on the forms of nature, and even Lawren Harris and Bertram Brooker had based their work on them. Harris's *Composition #1*, for example, is strongly suggestive of a mountain landscape, and Brooker's *Sounds Assembling* is a visual description of what he heard in a musical composition. Borduas, though, painted canvases that described his inner feelings about an experience but had nothing directly to do with the visual world. Therefore this type of style is called non-representational, or sometimes non-figurative or non-objective, painting.

Borduas was deeply impressed by children's art, which showed a total acceptance of the world of imagination and dreams. And it was partly through his teaching of children that he came to realize his own aim as an artist – to capture a reality that exists beyond the visible world.

At this time he became interested in Surrealism,

or Automatism, a style that was developing in Europe during the 1920s. Its aim was to capture the process of thinking as it actually happens by allowing a painting to emerge automatically from the subconscious mind directly onto the canvas.

Inspired by these theories, Borduas started painting his first non-representational works in 1941. These early paintings have no apparent organization. Free forms and colours float in endless space – the space of a dream world. They are a direct result of the theory that the subconscious should be given complete freedom and the painting be allowed to flow from it without interference by the conscious mind.

A number of artists, including many of Borduas's pupils from L'Ecole de Meuble in Montreal, were impressed by his ideas and work. Banding together, the group called themselves *Les Automatistes*. Their work inspired one of the most important movements of modern Canadian painting. In 1948 the group became involved in Quebec politics when they issued an important document called *Refus Global*. Just as in art they wanted to work in a style that was free of controls, in politics they demanded freedom from rigid systems and authorities.

In 1953 Borduas moved to New York, where he met various artists who called themselves Abstract Expressionists. Followers of Kandinsky's theories, their ideas were similar to Borduas's. Their common aim was to express inner feelings through form and colour without copying anything from nature.

But Kandinsky also believed that even if an artist allowed his inner mind freedom of expression, his training and experience could make him automatically produce work with form and order. This is because form and order are not only basic principles of art; they are also basic laws of nature. Indeed, Piet Mondrian (1872-1944), another extremely important European artist to influence Borduas, shared Kandinsky's mystical beliefs. But Mondrian considered that spiritual values could only be expressed in their pure form in balanced, ordered, and geometric abstracts.

L'Etoile Noire (p. 189), and other later abstracts, show a balance that Borduas seems to have been searching for—a balance between the free expression of the subconscious mind and the basic order of nature. In *L'Etoile Noire* each form exists individually and separately, but it is also related to the others in an informal structure. The horizontal forms are balanced against the vertical forms, but not rigidly or in a mechanical way as if they were artificial objects. Instead, they are almost like living things, capable of change but depending upon each other in an informal relationship. The weight of each shape is balanced against the space around it. The small 'star', for example, is as important as the larger blocks because of its distance from them and the tension that is created by this distance.

The title *L'Etoile Noire* (The Black Star) suggests a certain link with the world we know. But it is a world we know through the imagination more than through the eyes. Certainly the painting suggests the vast space we see on starry nights. But space also relates the 'star' to the larger blocks, just as in Borduas's mind it contains and holds all living things of the world in balance.

Unfortunately, no reproduction of a painting can replace an original. In a reproduction we lose contact with the subtleties of the paint, the texture, the highlights and shadows, and the fine shades of colour. But most of all we lose the direct contact with the artist himself.

L'Etoile Noire is a personal creation. The artist was allowing his feelings to leave him automatically and take a concrete form in the painting. His hand, holding a palette knife, was his instrument, and, as if he were finger painting, he has had an almost physical involvement in the process. When we look at the original, we are close to feeling the actual act of creating it. We can almost feel the paint being smoothed out softly and evenly or being pulled and sculpted into ridges, which catch the light on one side and leave delicate shadows on the other. *L'Etoile Noire* is a painting that provides endless opportunities for thought and feeling but can only be experienced by many careful viewings.

Alfred Pellan

b. 1906

Végétaux Marins, 1964, oil on plywood
48-1/8″ x 32-1/8″ (122 cm x 82 cm)
Art Collection Society of Kingston

Alfred Pellan's *Végétaux Marins* (Plants of the Sea) is part of a long tradition in the history of art—a tradition inspired by the living, growing things of nature and all their extraordinary forms. Plants and animals have been painted not only for their beauty but also because mankind depends upon them for survival. Because *Végétaux Marins* is part of this tradition, it is linked to man's artistic beginnings.

The earliest prehistoric cave paintings were of bison, cattle, and deer. Thousands of years later the Egyptians painted plant and animal life on the walls of their tombs, so that after death they would have food, shelter, and clothing. The Minoans, who were more concerned with life on earth, decorated household objects with plants and animals. The wall paintings of Pompeii and Herculaneum show that the Romans too painted nature with skill and delight. In medieval and early Renaissance art, animals and plants took on new roles as symbols for teaching the Christian faith. Later, some of the world's most famous artists, such as Leonardo da Vinci and Albrecht Dürer, looked at every part of nature, filling their sketch-books with their studies.

Thus nature has served as one of the major sources of art through the centuries. At different times it has been used as direct subject matter, as background setting, or as a source of themes for self-expression. Today it is often used as the basis for abstract painting.

But in addition to being part of a long tradition dating back to man's earliest art, *Végétaux Marins* is also a link between the beginning of life on earth and twentieth-century science: in artistic symbols it suggests the process of evolution. Scientists tell us that life began in the water from single cells. Through millenniums of time, more complex structures developed and multiplied with infinite variety. Sheltered in their protective nests or webs, creatures of jewel-like beauty evolved—each one an indi-vidual being made up of many, many parts. Out of this complexity emerged the creatures that fill the world we know today.

In the future, the scientists tell us, we may have to return to the sea so that the plant and animal life there can support what is living on the land. Using slides and microscopes, scientists magnify drops of water and the tiniest structures in order to learn more about them. But while doing this, they dis-cover the most beautiful patterns of form and colour. In many ways Pellan's painting is like a microscopic slide: a jewel to look at, rich in colour and intricate in design.

Alfred Pellan has seen more of the developing modern art forms in Europe than almost any Canadian. Living in Paris from the 1920s to 1940, he was strongly influenced by the styles of many of the modern European masters.

Born in Quebec in 1906, Pellan received his early training at the Ecole des Beaux-Arts in Montreal between 1920 and 1925. He excelled as a student and won many awards, including a scholarship to study in Paris. Shortly after his return to Canada in 1940, Pellan accepted a teaching post at the Ecole des Beaux-Arts. Since that time he has become known as one of the great artist-teachers in Canada.

Because Pellan was always an eclectic artist, it is often possible to see a variety of influences in a single painting. *Végétaux Marins,* for example, suggests the rich patterns of Matisse but also shows definite links with the themes of Max Ernst, a German surrealist who painted imaginative visions based on the mysteries of nature. But in *Végétaux Marins* Pellan's love of glowing colours and intri-cate designs seems more important to him than the mysteries that haunted Ernst. This painting, how-ever, is more than mere decoration; it is a poem about life and creation.

Jean-Paul Riopelle

b. 1923

Pavane (Triptych), 1954, oil on canvas
9' 10" x 6' 7"; 9' 10" x 4' 11"; 9' 10" x 6' 7"
(300 cm x 201 cm; 300 cm x 150 cm; 300 cm x 201 cm)
The National Gallery of Canada, Ottawa

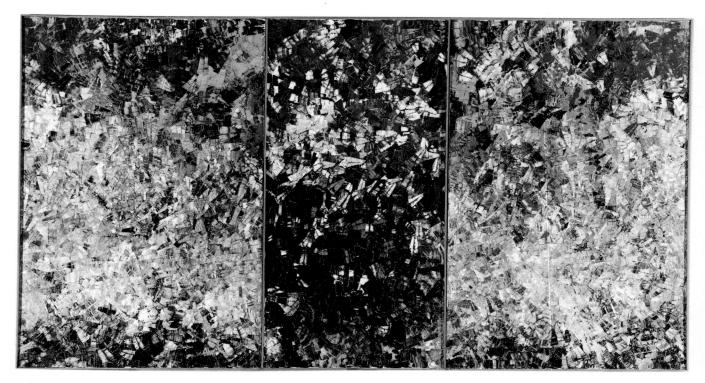

Today Jean-Paul Riopelle is one of the most internationally known Canadian painters, though he has not lived in Canada since 1948. He was born in Montreal, where he received his early instruction in art. But his academic training was formal and conservative, and he was expected to copy the works of the Old Masters, not even from originals but from prints. For a long time he had no contact at all with the development of modern art outside Canada.

Though Riopelle studied for a while at the Ecole des Beaux-Arts, his early work was mainly influenced by Borduas. Through Borduas he became interested in the writing and painting of the Surrealists, and in 1946 he exhibited with *Les Automatistes*. He was also one of the artists who signed *Refus Global*, a document that demanded

freedom from authority in Quebec but was also a symbol of a desire for artistic freedom.

Riopelle views this period of his life as the major influence on his developing style, but there were other important influences as well. By this time he was travelling to France, Germany, and the United States, meeting important European and American artists and studying their work.

In Europe, for example, he would have seen the paintings of van Gogh, which had impressed him in his youth. It is likely that Riopelle's emotional use of colour and thick impasto treatment of paint are partly a result of his admiration for van Gogh's canvases. Also in Europe, Riopelle would have seen the brilliant stained-glass windows of the medieval churches. These splendid mosaics of colour could easily have been one source of inspiration for

Pavane.

Another important influence was probably the work of Jackson Pollock, the American artist. Pollock's method, sometimes called action painting, was perhaps the most extreme step an artist could take towards being totally automatic. He no longer used a brush or palette knife but dripped his paint onto a canvas from a height of several feet. In doing so, he attempted to rid his work completely of any interference by the conscious mind. According to his theory, the order that appeared in a finished work of art was a direct expression of the order that existed within the artist's subconscious. Pollock's canvases are very large and the design covers the whole area. Because of the size, the viewer feels he is inside the work instead of looking at it. He is left to respond in a personal way to the patterns, shapes, similarities, and contrasts.

Riopelle never actually dripped paint onto his surfaces, but he did paint very large canvases that he totally covered with thick strokes of paint, applied with a palette knife. His idea, like Pollock's, was to express his subconscious feelings and present them directly to his viewer. In his paintings there are no objects set against a background. Space is created by the relationships of colours, some sinking back, others looming forward.

Pavane is a triptych, or one painting divided into three parts. This form allows the artist to break his design into three separate sections, each having its own unity. A triptych can be made more interesting though if an artist builds up similarities and tensions among the sections.

The triptych form relates Riopelle's work to ancient times. As far back as the days of the early Christian church, artists had used the triptych as a way of associating three different religious scenes in the minds of their viewers. Though Riopelle has not given his painting a religious meaning, the form he has chosen does connect it with the past history of art.

The title of Riopelle's painting also recalls the idea of past times. A pavan is a Spanish dance dating back to the sixteenth and seventeenth centuries. It was originally thought to be named after the Spanish word *pavo* meaning 'peacock', which might have referred to the rich costumes worn by the dancers. The dance itself was performed to slow music with a stately rhythm.

Riopelle gives us these small clues that associate his painting with the outside world, then leaves us to enjoy it for itself and respond to the effects of light and colour. Like little pieces of richly coloured glass, the strokes of paint seem to catch the light in some places and recede into the shadows elsewhere.

The paler side panels emphasize the darker central one but create a feeling of tension as well. It seems as though they have been interrupted while reaching out to meet each other. Yet despite the strong relationship between the central and side panels, each panel has an interesting and subtle balance of its own. Bright areas of colour are weighed against dark areas and seem to lift the glimmering paler fragments upwards. The whole canvas is alive with movement as the patterns constantly change like a kaleidoscope.

Riopelle's *Pavane* is an example of Abstract Expressionism. It is abstract because it does not copy anything in the world, and expressionist because it expresses feelings rather than rational ideas. Yet its impact is also impressionistic, relying on the effects of colour and light and the artist's skill in combining them. But while the Impressionists attempted to paint the world exactly as the eye sees it, Riopelle does not start with what he sees in the world, but with what he feels about the experiences he has had.

J.W.G. 'Jock' Macdonald

1897–1960

Legend of the Orient, 1958
lucite on masonite
54″ x 48″ (137 cm x 122 cm)
Private Collection

Canada has been fortunate over the years to have had some fine and dedicated teachers of art whose influence has been of great value in the development of Canadian painting. It is true that teaching has been a necessity for some artists, since in a new country it is often difficult to make a living from the sale of paintings alone. Nevertheless, some outstanding figures have emerged for whom teaching has become more of an art than a necessity.

In the nineteenth century Robert Harris, George Reid, and William Brymner devoted much of their lives to teaching. In the early years of this century, Arthur Lismer stands out as the great artist-teacher of the Group of Seven. Paul-Emile Borduas, Alfred Pellan, and Jock Macdonald were three others to make outstanding contributions in this field.

In 1926 Macdonald arrived in Canada, where he had been offered the post of head of the Department of Design and Applied Arts in Vancouver. He was born in Scotland and had been trained as a designer at the Edinburgh College of Art. Later he worked for a Scottish textile company but started teaching a year before he came to Canada.

On his arrival in Vancouver, Macdonald met Frederick Varley, who was also teaching at the School of Design. Both of them found the atmosphere dull and unimaginative, and so together they founded the British Columbia College of Art. Unfortunately, neither was a skilled administrator and the college only survived for two years. But the influence of their teaching made a considerable impression on the Vancouver art community.

In 1947 Macdonald took a position at the Ontario College of Art, where he taught until he died thirteen years later. Younger artists, particularly William Ronald and his brother John Meredith, remember Macdonald as one of the most important influences upon them, both because of his teaching and his generous artistic and financial encouragement.

Macdonald's training as a designer, rather than as an academic painter, may have been partly the cause of his interest in abstract art. Training in design, as we have seen with the work of Tom Thomson, stresses simplification of subject matter into its most basic parts and concentration on shapes, colours, and their relationships.

While Macdonald was in Vancouver, he became involved with a group of people, in various artistic fields, who were also interested in philosophical and mystical ideas. Among his friends were Frederick Varley, Emily Carr, and perhaps most importantly, Lawren Harris. Because of Harris, Macdonald too became interested in theosophy and Kandinsky's *Concerning the Spiritual in Art*.

Like Borduas, Macdonald also developed an interest in the direct and spontaneous paintings of children. Colour fascinated him, and in his early abstracts it almost seemed to take control. During the 1940s he produced a series of small watercolour automatics but later moved on to larger canvases painted in oils and other media.

In 1954 he went to Europe for a year to visit and study. Later, through his former pupil William Ronald, he made important connections in New York. Macdonald invited Clement Greenberg, an extremely influential American art critic, to Toronto to meet a group of artists who were particularly interested in colour. Jock Macdonald and Jack Bush, among others, were greatly influenced by Greenberg's advice. Macdonald later wrote that 'Greenberg gave me such a boost in confidence that I cannot remember ever knowing such a sudden development before.'

Legend of the Orient is a painting that is based on the relationships of forms and colours. In fact, the pleasure that comes from viewing the painting is largely a result of the variations of colour that the artist has used: the gradations of blue that flow through the largest area, the sudden shock of clear yellow that cuts in from the left in an angular shape, the mysterious black form on the right with its startling patch of red, the softly mottled gold below, and the turquoise above, divided from the blue by a shimmering white band.

The painting is given a sense of depth by the overlapping colours and becomes more than a totally flat design on a two-dimensional surface. Yet the surface composition is strong. The darkness of the black area is contrasted with the more lively yellow so that the two tend to draw together. The blue and the turquoise are more closely related, but spill over at the top of the painting. The strong patch of red, however, acts as an eye-catching focus and holds the colours within the frame.

Macdonald shows us the heaviness of black and the lightness of yellow, the brightness of red and the richness of blue. But he also introduces shapes and textures for us to feel: angular, smooth, harsh, and soft. The variations within each area of colour also give different effects of texture: smooth black, almost gritty gold, and flowing blue.

Both the colours and title of this work are suggestive of the haunting and mysterious character of the Orient. It is possible that the painting is based on a specific legend, but because the forms are generalized and the painting is composed of the three primary colours, red, blue, and yellow, it is also possible to read it as a more general expression. Whatever way we choose to interpret it, our associations must be made personally through a series of connections that are stored in our own minds and imaginations. Macdonald, like a poet, speaks of one thing but means many things all at the same time.

Colour, form, and texture are important in *Legend of the Orient,* but despite Macdonald's interest in abstraction, he never entirely rejected the visible world. He would have been in complete agreement with Georges Braque (1882-1963), one of Europe's greatest abstract artists, who said, 'To arrive at abstraction, one must start from nature, and to start from nature means to find a motif. To lose contact with nature is inevitably to end up with decoration.'

198

Ernest Lindner

b. 1897

Decay and Growth, 1964, watercolour on paper
29-1/2″ x 21-1/2″ (75 cm x 55 cm)
Norman Mackenzie Art Gallery, University of Regina

Ernest Lindner, in a quiet and unobtrusive way, has had a great influence on the artists of western Canada. Now in his late seventies, he is looked upon with respect and affection by a generation of younger painters. Some of them he has taught; others have learned by looking at his work. But all of them have been impressed by his realism and penetrating honesty. In a century in which ideas and artistic styles have become more and more complex, it is evident that Ernest Lindner has revealed some very basic truths.

Clement Greenberg, the New York critic and promoter of colour-field painting, said of Lindner's work, 'I find more imagination and modernity in Ernest Lindner's sharply focused rendering of a tree trunk than in the largest part of current abstract painting.'

Lindner was born in Vienna in 1897, the youngest of thirteen children. Since his youth he has known fine craftsmanship and appreciated good design. His father and his grandfather were skilled wood-workers who manufactured carved walking sticks, parasols, and luxury goods. They established a small factory, where they employed jewellers and other specialized craftsmen. In this early period of his life, Lindner began to show great interest in drawing and painting.

During the First World War he enlisted in the Austrian army and was wounded in an air crash in 1916. Between the end of the war and 1926, when he immigrated to Canada, Lindner worked in several businesses, none of which succeeded.

On his arrival in Saskatchewan he had to work as a farm labourer because of the strict Canadian immigration laws. The Depression and the prairie droughts followed soon afterwards. During this time he found whatever work he could, including some occasional commercial design, but he spent his spare hours drawing and painting.

In 1928 Lindner studied under Augustus Kender-dine, taking night classes in art until 1935 and teaching part-time from 1931 onward. In 1936 he became the only full-time art instructor at the Saskatoon Technical Collegiate Institute. Later he became head of the Art Department, where he remained until he retired in 1962.

After his retirement he was able to devote himself to his painting. During the 1960s he began a watercolour series of detailed forest scenes. These are deceptively simple works of art, realistic in style and straightforward in symbolism. But the longer and more closely they are looked at, the more beautiful and profound they seem to become.

In an introduction to an exhibition of his work in 1967, Ernest Lindner wrote,

I paint what I can't say in words. I try to express my thoughts and feelings as I observe life in the forest, on the prairie, in people, everywhere. Life as revealed in the smallest growth is, to me, most meaningful. Forms change, life goes on.

In *Decay and Growth* (p. 199), as the title suggests, Lindner is expressing his feelings about the continuity of life. This old tree trunk has been a part of the forest growth for generations and has been exposed to many cycles of summer and winter weather. The bark is gone, and the wood is scarred and crumbling. But on the surface grow a variety of lichens, mosses, and fungi, each different and rich in texture and colour. At the foot of the tree, in the fertile soil created by the decaying wood, new growth appears, small seedlings that will replace the old, weather-worn stump.

Like Carl Schaefer, Ernest Lindner emphasizes the order and cycles of nature. Both artists have lived close to the land and have drawn strength from it, but their artistic methods are quite different. Schaefer tends to stylize, or to find the basic shape of a form and emphasize it. In his watercolours particularly, he uses stylization as a way of giving impressions and creating designs.

Lindner, though, looks intently at small sections of a forest scene, as if examining them under a microscope. He then paints every little detail: tiny leaves, the shell-like shapes of lichens, and the hairy fronds of moss. Everything becomes extremely important. In Lindner's paintings, as in Thomas Davies's, the particulars of life play their own individual and necessary role in the general cycle of nature and time.

The great German artist Albrecht Dürer (1471—1528) used the same technique in his famous studies of animals and in his beautiful watercolour *A Patch of Grass*. By emphasizing every tiny whisker on a hare and every blade of grass in a clump of sod, he expressed his wonder of nature.

Since 1969 Lindner has produced a series of large pencil drawings he calls 'human landscapes'. As well as being interesting works of art, they are skilful and sensitive studies that reveal his concern for fine craftsmanship. His human landscapes include nudes and detailed drawings of hands and feet in which every vein and wrinkle stands out clearly. In form, composition, and meaning they are a continuation of his search for a way to express the union of individual parts in a whole.

Jack Shadbolt

b. 1909

Winter Theme No. 7, 1961, oil and lucite on canvas
42-3/8″ x 50-3/4″ (108 cm x 129 cm)
The National Gallery of Canada, Ottawa

Jetty from a Bridge, 1960, conté crayon
17″ x 14-1/2″ (43 cm x 37 cm)

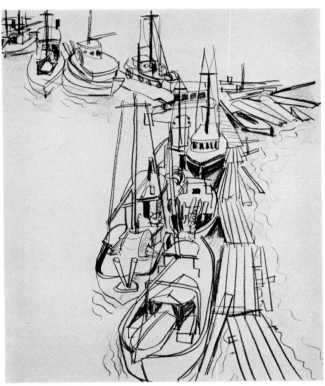

It is unusual to have the chance of following the growth of a painting step by step from the original sketch to the final work in oils. It is even more rare to find an artist who will talk about the process in words. Jack Shadbolt, though, has written a great deal about his personal experiences as an artist and about the mysterious unfolding of ideas into visual forms and colours.

As well as being a painter, Shadbolt is a teacher and poet, and all three of these interests have affected his approach to art. Although he was born in England, British Columbia has been his home since he was a small child. He began his career as a high-school teacher, but at the age of twenty-four he decided to study art and trained in Paris before the Second World War and New York afterwards.

In his book *In Search of Form*, Shadbolt tells how *Winter Theme No. 7* grew out of the memory of scenes he had viewed and known since his childhood. With the help of preparatory sketches, he also explains his difficulties in deciding on the particular form that this or any painting would take. For Shadbolt the form of a painting is not a copy of what he sees; instead, it is a way of describing the meaning of what he sees.

Winter Theme No. 7 began early in his life. Because he had grown up in Vancouver, ships and dinghies, harbours and piers had been a part of many of his experiences. Later, travelling in Europe, he saw other scenes of 'the pier or small breakwater or jetty with its cluster of almond-shaped dinghies like seed pods around a stem or like beetles eating a leaf.' The similarities he recognized among many harbour scenes encouraged him to find a form to express the meaning that all these scenes had for him.

Views of harbours are a popular subject for photographs and tourist souvenirs. But Shadbolt wanted to do more than make pleasing pictures. By using his canvases to reorganize the objects he saw around him, he hoped to emphasize their relationship to each other and to suggest their relationship to other things in nature.

Once he became aware that a particular form, based on his experiences of many harbours, was starting to take shape in his mind, Shadbolt began to work on paper. He made his first working sketch from an earlier straightforward drawing he had made while looking down from a high viewpoint on sailing boats tied to a pier. He reorganized the group of boats and surrounded it with a dark ink wash, creating dramatic contrast of light and dark. The design was spread across the surface with the basic left to right diagonal that appears in the final painting.

Night Marina, 1960, india ink
13" x 16" (33 cm x 41 cm)

He then worked on many variations of this scheme, changing the relationship of background sea and clustered boats. As his sketches grew more abstract, the individual objects became less and less recognizable but more closely related to each other and locked into one overall design.

By the time he had finished his series of preparatory sketches, he felt at ease with his theme. He had reduced his experience of many harbour scenes into one form that had the meaning he wanted to convey. The move from drawing to painting brought further problems, but, once he knew his basic form, he could concentrate entirely on the effects of light, colour, and texture. In many ways the finished work is close to the original sketch of boats tied to a wharf. But now it is no longer a description of one particular scene; it suggests wider meanings and relationships.

What are these objects that we see? Are they boats, or cocoons, or seed pods? And where are they now? Is the structure a harbour, or a fence, or are these roots of sprouting plants? Meanings are neither restricted nor defined, because the artist, like a poet, is not telling but suggesting. It is up to us to meet him halfway. His meaning lies in form and colours, and we must respond to what is offered.

The whole painting seems alive with an inner energy. The brilliance of the colours is made even more intense by the black background. The exploding white mass on the left, echoing in different places across the canvas, increases the feeling of excitement. There is a sense of nature's growth, held in check for the moment, but waiting to burst forth. The promise of spring grows out of the darkness of winter.

An underlying, grid-like form and a balanced tension of verticals and horizontals suggest the order and control of nature. But on top, the 'cocoons', though enclosed in their winter shells, seem ready to burst their bonds.

Boats, cocoons, seeds, roots, sprouting growth – whatever way we choose to read it, as a vertical composition or as a view from above – the painting conveys a sense of suppressed energy. And it suggests, though it does not define, a waiting time in the cycle and mystery of nature.

Alex Colville

b. 1920

Visitors Are Invited to Register, 1954, gouache
28-1/4" x 23-1/4" (72 cm x 59 cm)
Saskatoon Gallery and Conservatory Corporation

Visitors Are Invited to Register (p. 205) is a subtle painting. As quiet and ordered as it may seem on the surface, there is an undercurrent that is mysterious and almost menacing.

The figure, who stands alone in this bare little church, has his back to us. We are not encouraged to meet him as an individual but instead to share his experience. Yet at the same time, because he is set in a scene we are watching, we are made aware of his isolation.

The interior of the church is quite realistic. The ceiling even shows stains from the water that has leaked through it. But there is a strange sense of unreality here as well. The scene we look upon seems like a frozen moment in a dream, and a rather disturbing dream at that.

There is nothing personal or inviting about this little deserted church; in fact, it has a prison-like quality. The tight little boxes that contain the family pews do not seem to offer much spiritual comfort, but instead they suggest the need for stern discipline and self-control. It seems unlikely that many visitors would want to enter, despite the notice on the pillar that invites them in.

Because the interior of the church is divided into geometrical shapes (boxes, windows, pillars, balcony), the atmosphere seems logical and disciplined. But there are strange contrasts and oppositions that disturb the surface calm. Two staircases lead to a level above, presumably to the balcony that we can see. But while the lower floor is defined precisely, we are left rather unsure about where these staircases end or what exists above.

The most disturbing element in the painting, though, is the long black stovepipe that cuts across on the left and drops down to the floor at a sharp, awkward angle. Its solid blackness and its odd shape make it stand out like a menacing intruder in the quiet order of the grey and green interior.

Visitors Are Invited to Register suggests a delicate balance between the ordered world we know and the disordered world of dreams. In fact, one of the major themes of Colville's work is the balance of opposing forces: the conscious mind and the subconscious, man and nature, gentleness and violence, security and fear. Colville's paintings show scenes of everyday life, but they also become a meeting ground for life's conflicting forces and the balancing of tensions.

Life is neither black nor white, good nor evil; rather, it is a blend of all of these. But a balance is a very delicate state that is difficult to maintain. In Colville's work, there is often an underlying sense of the danger of tipping the scales too far one way or the other.

Colville is a serious artist. He believes art has an important role in life and should be more than mere decoration. He also believes that art can teach us how to be more complete human beings. Because of these ideas, which are reflected in his painting style, he is a classical artist. He searches for a balance between his subject matter and his form, while satisfying the eye, mind, and emotions.

One of the great influences upon his art was the work of the early Italian Renaissance painter Piero della Francesca. In fact, while he was in Europe, Colville studied Piero and admired his work so much that he copied the position of several of Piero's figures directly into his own work.

Piero was an artist who painted forms in a three-dimensional style that resembles sculpture. His figures have an almost mathematical perfection and balance – smooth and simple, like Greek columns. They are often set in surroundings, similar to Colville's little church, that emphasize the order and geometry of the space. The paintings themselves have a feeling of quiet serenity and of time standing still.

Alex Colville is one of Canada's outstanding modern artists, whose work is as well known in Europe as it is in this country. He has also contributed greatly as a teacher of art at Mount Allison University in Sackville, New Brunswick.

He was born in Toronto in 1920 but moved to the Maritimes with his parents when he was a child. There he went to school and later earned a degree in Fine Arts at Mount Allison University. Because the Second World War was then in progress, he joined the Canadian army and became an official war artist. On his return to Canada he became a professor of painting at Mount Allison and taught there for seventeen years. His influence upon a generation of younger Maritime artists has been another of his great accomplishments.

Jack Bush

b. 1909

Dazzle Red, 1965, oil on canvas
81″ x 104″ (206 cm x 264 cm)
Art Gallery of Ontario, Toronto

Jack Bush's *Dazzle Red* is a sophisticated painting. In order to enjoy it fully, it is helpful to learn something about colour and its theory by studying a colour wheel. The colour wheel arranges the colours of the spectrum (p. 119) in a circle, showing clearly how each one is related to the next or to its opposite. But even without a formal knowledge of colour, *Dazzle Red* can give great pleasure if we allow our eyes to travel back and forth across the canvas, letting the colours work on our senses.

Like other recent paintings by Bush, *Dazzle Red* is composed of subtle relationships of colour that give the work its meaning. It is a non-representational painting in which the artist has deliberately removed any meaning that can be drawn from outside. In the other non-representational paintings we have seen, such as Borduas's *L'Etoile Noire* (p. 189) or Riopelle's *Pavane* (p. 194), there was some suggestion in the title of a meaning outside the painting. But the title *Dazzle Red* gives only one clue, and it is a vital one – this painting is *about* colour.

How do we approach a pure abstract like this one? First, by allowing the colours to work on us. Some of the relationships are soothing; some vibrate. We may feel jarred by the combination of pink, red, and green, but relaxed by the blue and green. We can feel the effects of the colours, and we can think about them. The next stage of understanding comes after looking closely at the composition. Why are some of the bands of colour divided horizontally and others diagonally; why are some of them narrow and others wide? This, then, is our first approach to the painting — examining the effects of colour and questioning the composition. Afterwards the painting deserves thought and feeling. It is not a work that gives up its secrets easily.

What colours has the artist used and how has he used them? *Dazzle Red* is based on the three primary colours – red, yellow, and blue – from which other colours can be mixed. But here the only colour that the artist has chosen to keep flat and even is the red; all of his other colours have texture.

The blue has been applied unevenly, its visible brush strokes giving a greater sense of life and even of gentle movement. The yellow, which also has an uneven texture, has been made deeper by the addition of red. It is warmer than a pure yellow but less vibrant. But the pure red and yellow-red are now closely related to each other and form a direct opposite to the cool green and blue. The green, which also has a great deal of life because of the uneven distribution of paint, is not a primary colour. Being made up of blue and yellow, it is related to each. But it is a direct opposite to red and so vibrates against it. The brilliance of the pink stripe across the red also adds to the vibrancy of the top of the painting.

With his colours the artist has created a series of harmonies and discords, or tense combinations and relaxed combinations. Then, to make his painting even more interesting, he has used a composition that continues the theme of tension and relaxation. Finally, though, he has drawn everything together in complete harmony.

At the bottom of the painting he has placed his heaviest and darkest colour, the deep blue. This lies quietly in a horizontal line like a firm but living base. Above it is the green, which meets the blue gently and with no tension. This is a wider band, cool but lively in texture and movement.

The meeting of the red and the green sets up the first strong tension. This is partly because the two colours are direct opposites and partly because they meet at an angle. A diagonal line, as we have seen in other paintings, is less stable than a horizontal one.

The dazzling red, smooth and pure, with the pink stripe slashing across it, again on a diagonal, seems to lift up the top of the painting. It is only because of the weight of the blue band and the liveliness of the green that the two halves of the painting are kept in balance.

Meanwhile the deep yellow vertical bands hold the design in at the sides. On the right, the band is straight and steady, and the colours cross the canvas almost at right angles to it. On the left, the added weight at the top of the band controls the lifting effect of the red and pink. But because it is a diagonal itself, it strengthens the force of the other diagonals going across.

This is a painting that is alive with contrasts and tensions, but, by balancing them against each other, Bush has reached a feeling of final stability. It is also a very skilful painting, carefully thought out to appeal to the mind and the emotions. But it is not easy to appreciate quickly and deserves to be looked at carefully, with wandering eyes and an open mind.

Jack Bush is one of the most important abstract artists working in Canada since the 1950s. He was born in Toronto, and his early training there and in Montreal led him to paint traditional landscapes and portraits. He also worked as a commercial artist. But a visit to New York in the early 1950s changed his direction towards more abstract forms of painting.

Returning to Canada, he and several other Ontario artists who were experimenting with abstracts formed a group known as Painters Eleven. They exhibited together for eight years. During this time Clement Greenberg was invited to Toronto, where he saw Bush's work and encouraged him to continue with his colour-field paintings. *Dazzle Red* is one of these works and a fine example of Bush's particular talent as an artist. Bush, now dedicated to colour-field painting, believes that his serious contribution to art began only within about the last fifteen years.

Ronald Bloore

b. 1925

Untitled Mural, undated, oil on masonite
146-1/2″ x 142-3/4″ (372 cm x 363 cm)
Confederation Centre Art Gallery and Museum
Charlottetown

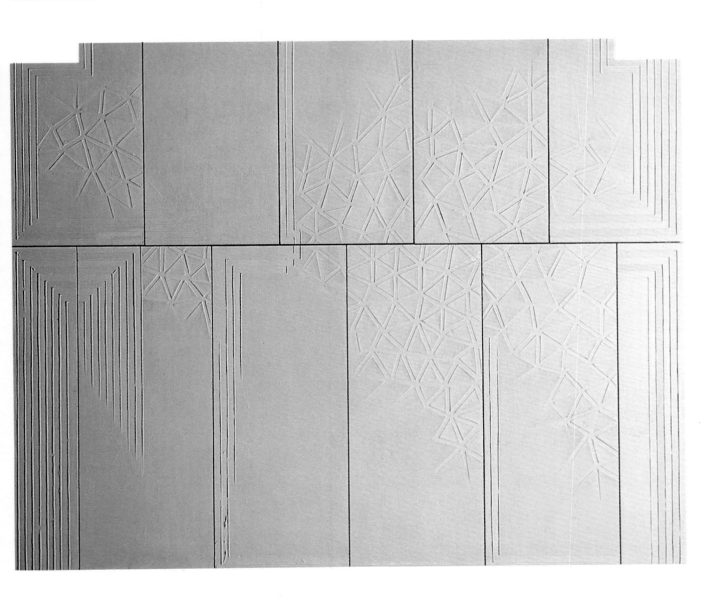

Ronald Bloore, like Jack Bush, is an artist who has developed a mature style that differs considerably from that of his earlier work. Like Bush, he is reluctant to show many early paintings and has even destroyed much of the work he did before 1959. Although the beginning of his present style can be traced to this date, Bloore's greatest artistic changes occurred after 1963, a year he spent in Greece, Turkey, Egypt, and Spain. He was greatly influenced by his study of ancient architecture and sculpture, and his experience of the brilliant contrasts of sun and shadow have significantly affected his work as well.

But Bloore's influence on Canadian painting began several years before this visit. Born in Brampton, Ontario, he studied art history at the University of Toronto and in New York and London. He was also a lecturer at Washington University in St. Louis and the University of Toronto before 1958, when he became director of the Norman Mackenzie Art Gallery at the University of Regina. In 1966 he became director of art for York University in Toronto. Bloore's solid academic background in art history and archaeology has contributed greatly to his style and tastes.

But it was in Regina, as a teacher and organizer, that he made his first contribution to the development of modern Canadian painting.

During the 1930s Augustus Kenderdine (1870–1947), an artist born and trained in England, was appointed head of the new art department of the University of Regina. Kenderdine owned some property at Emma Lake in the wild country north of Prince Albert, and he encouraged the university to open a summer school for the arts there. Eventually this became one of the most influential art centres in western Canada.

In 1959 a group from the school, including Ronald Bloore, invited Barnett Newman, an impor-

tant New York artist, to lead a session at the workshop. Newman's own concern was with colour – large areas of pure colour, broken only by a few lines that set up gentle rhythms in infinite spaces. He had considerable influence on the Canadian artists at Emma Lake, and on the basis of his ideas, a group called the Regina Five was formed.

Bloore was actively involved as a member of this group and as an organizer of the workshop. In 1962 he invited the New York critic Clement Greenberg to Emma Lake. Greenberg had already made a strong impression on the group of Toronto artists known as the Painters Eleven because of his concern with colour-field painting and formal structure. But Bloore, though interested in Greenberg's ideas, was developing an independent style, which was later strengthened by his studies and experiences in Europe and the Middle East the following year.

As early as 1959 Bloore had been experimenting with all-white paintings. His canvases, some of which resemble Borduas's later works such as L'Etoile Noire, emphasize line, the texture of paint drawn up into ridges or finely cut into the base, and subtleties of light and shadow. The whiteness, which substitutes for colour, also provides an extremely sensitive background for suggesting space and depth.

When Bloore was in Egypt, he was impressed by the simplicity and geometry of the architecture and sculpture he saw there. Middle-Eastern wall designs, Trajan's Column in Rome, relief sculpture in Greece, all these influences can be seen in his work since 1963.

Preserving the flatness and solidity of the surface of his work is important to Bloore. He is careful not to distort his surface by penetrating it with deep holes or building it up with high ridges that create extreme contrasts and emotional disturbances. Having emphasized the flat purity of the surface, he then inscribes it with subtle patterns and moulds fine designs on it, which catch the light and cast shadows. While these give wonderful effects of shimmering space, they also keep the surface and depth in balance.

One of Bloore's most important works is the mural commissioned for the Confederation Centre Art Gallery and Museum in Charlottetown in 1967, Centennial Year (p. 211). Since the mural was designed for a particular position in the building, it was carefully related to the space provided for it, as well as to the architecture of the building.

Although it is one unit, it consists of eleven parts, or panels, each with its own character and design but related to the adjoining parts and the whole. In keeping with Bloore's own particular style, the surface remains flat and intact, though divided logically and geometrically. The divisions of space are carefully thought out and proportioned.

In fact, everything Bloore does in his work is precisely calculated and designed. Even the casual network of triangles, which prevents any sense of mechanical geometry, is carefully sketched beforehand. But the seemingly unorganized arrangement of triangular shapes gives an impression of frost patterns on a window, or snowflakes, or the imprint of birds' feet on sand and appears quite natural.

The creamy white-tinted surface of the mural fades in and out of space, an effect that is emphasized by the subtle patterns and their relationships. The arrangement of lines on the left could suggest a passage that moves away from us, while those on the right meet like two walls at right angles.

Meanwhile the 'net' sometimes billows outwards and sometimes rolls inwards. Within an organized, geometric framework there is the suggestion of organic growth. Living matter is kept in balance with formal structure; solids balance spaces.

Underlying the whole work is Bloore's intellectual and emotional understanding of the fundamental nature of ancient sculpture and architecture. While each art form has its own particular qualities, each contributes to man's environment in terms of decoration, function, and the expression of the balance of life.

Guido Molinari

b. 1933

Mutation Sérielle Verte-Rouge, 1966
acrylic on canvas
81″ x 98″ (206 cm x 249 cm)
Art Gallery of Ontario, Toronto

Throughout history there have been two major kinds of artistic expression: intellectual and emotional. Some artists paint mainly on the basis of what they think; others, on the basis of what they feel.

Antoine Plamondon and Joseph Légaré, for example, were both fine early Canadian artists, though their styles differed greatly. Plamondon's paintings were ordered and disciplined; his work was carefully thought out to express his ideas about life. But Légaré's approach was far more emotional. He allowed his imagination to guide his painting, and he encouraged his viewers to follow him.

In our own time Paul-Emile Borduas and Guido Molinari have been leading representatives of these two different kinds of artistic expression. Borduas and *Les Automatistes* believed that art should be allowed to flow directly and freely from the subconscious mind onto the canvas without the conscious mind interfering. By allowing their paintings to develop in this way, *Les Automatistes* felt that they were in touch with the inner spiritual forces of man – forces that relate us all to something beyond the visible world.

But Guido Molinari supported the views of another group of artists who called themselves *Les Plasticiens* and worked in Montreal during the 1950s. In their opinion, art was not a product of the subconscious mind at all, but a carefully thought out, organized arrangement of form and colour.

Molinari was born in 1933 of Italian parents. His father was a musician, and one of his grandfathers was involved in the plaster casting of sculpture. As a result of his background, Molinari was exposed to the arts at an early age, and he knew members of *Les Automatistes* and other Montreal artists. In 1948 when *Refus Global* was published, Molinari was still at school. He was also taking night classes at the Ecole des Beaux-Arts, but he found the methods there too dry and academic. Later he continued his studies at the School of Art and Design at the Montreal Museum of Fine Arts for a short time.

The work of *Les Automatistes* interested Molinari, and he experimented with their technique. In order to test their ideas about direct expression from the subconscious mind, he painted several canvases blindfolded. Molinari also tried Jackson Pollock's method of dripping paint onto a canvas and considered Borduas's theory that an almost personal relationship can develop between painter and paint applied with a palette knife.

None of these methods satisfied Molinari's organized and intellectual mind, and by the middle of the 1950s he allied himself with *Les Plasticiens* in their opposition to *Les Automatistes*. *Les Plasticiens,* a group that Molinari never actually joined, drew up the following formal statement of their aims:

Les Plasticiens are principally concerned in their work with the 'plastic' facts: tone, texture, form, line, the ultimate unity of these in the painting, and relationships between these elements. . . . *Les Plasticiens* are not concerned at all, at least consciously, with possible meanings in their paintings.

In fact, they were advancing the theories of James Morrice even further than he himself had done. While Morrice believed that a painting is a work of art to be enjoyed for itself alone, he did paint recognizable landscapes. But *Les Plasticiens* claimed that their works had no deliberate relationship with anything outside the painting.

Mutation Sérielle Verte-Rouge is an example of what is now called hard-edge painting. It has been said that Molinari started using the technique after watching masking tape being used in car painting to prevent the colours overlapping. But the same type of style was also used at the time by New York artists, and so it was not actually Molinari's invention.

Like Jack Bush's *Dazzle Red* (p. 208), *Mutation Sérielle* is a painting that depends on the effects of colour. But there are some important and interesting differences between the approaches of the two artists. Molinari used an acrylic paint, applied in brilliant bands of flat colours that look deliberately artificial. Bush, though, has used more subtle oils and in some places has applied his colour with an uneven texture to suggest a sense of life.

In Molinari's painting every band is the same width and every edge is straight; the entire work has a strict mathematical, even mechanical, order. In Bush's canvas the bands of colour vary in width and their dividing line is often an unstable diagonal. Molinari's painting honestly acknowledges the modern, man-made world of technology in which we live. Bush, though, suggests a more natural world, neither even nor constant, in which he can find a state of balance by opposing one force against another.

By making these visual statements, it may seem as though these artists are concerned with meanings outside their subject matter, even though they claim not to be. All real art has meaning. Otherwise it would be pointless and no more than mere decoration. But the meaning of *Dazzle Red* and *Mutation Sérielle* is conveyed by forms, colours, and their relationships alone, rather than by any definite connections with outside objects.

The pleasure that comes from *Mutation Sérielle* can only be felt after looking at the painting over and over again. In doing this, the eye will find ever-changing patterns and rhythms that resound like musical notes, then fade away. The eye groups and regroups combinations of colours that give different effects of their arrangement in space. Some sections, or even individual bands, loom forward;

others fade back. Some combinations of colour seem to soothe the eye, while others vibrate and, like waves of sound, spread outwards from their source.

Mutation Sérielle Verte-Rouge is not a symbol for anything; it has no stories to tell or connections to make. Because of this it is a very personal work that must be experienced by each viewer individually.

Yves Gaucher

b. 1934

Circular Motion
(En Deuxième Phase: Rythmique Circulaire), 1965
acrylic on canvas
84" x 84" (213 cm x 213 cm)
York University Art Gallery, Toronto

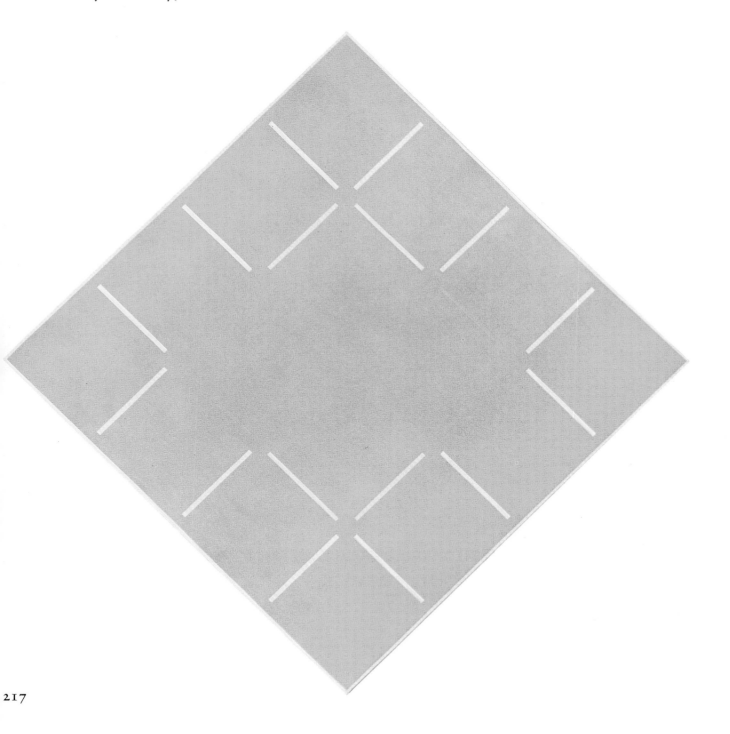

Yves Gaucher was brought up in Montreal in a family where music was an important part of daily life. His mother was a serious musician, and every member of the family played a musical instrument. In fact, although Yves was interested in art from a fairly early age, jazz was his major interest until he was twenty. After leaving school when he was seventeen, he played in several bands, but he had had no formal training in music and was not satisfied with his achievements.

In 1945 he enrolled in the Ecole des Beaux-Arts, but he did not remain there long. Gaucher, who has always been a rebel against conventions and accepted standards, became interested in printmaking, and he bought his own press. Continuing to work on his own, he soon became widely recognized for his prints. His early experimental work was rather loose and free in comparison with the style he developed by the 1960s.

By then he had found his own artistic direction, and today he still works with the same subtle relationships of colour and line that create incredible effects of space and rhythm. His knowledge and serious interest in music, which he continues to develop on his own, has been one of the main influences on his art.

The relationship between the visual arts and music is not a new one. Throughout the history of Western culture there have been many links, though they have been expressed in different ways. Medieval architects, for example, used the same mathematical order and rhythms that were the basis of music to design the great cathedrals of the Middle Ages. Occasionally sculpture was also related to music. In one medieval monastery courtyard, the monks could read the chant they had to sing by looking at the carvings on top of the surrounding columns.

Later, once painting became based completely on recognizable forms from the visible world, connections were still being made between the two arts. Either they were expressed directly, such as in Ozia Leduc's *L'Enfant au Pain* and Robert Harris's *Harmony,* or they were left to the viewer's imagination. In some of J.E.H. MacDonald's canvases, for example, the huge, heavy forms set in wide space might easily remind the individual viewer of grand musical compositions.

With the development of abstract art, painting and music became even more closely related. Kandinsky stated in *Concerning the Spiritual in Art* that abstract art is the form of expression closest to music. Based on this idea, Bertram Brooker, who also had a keen interest in music, painted some of the first Canadian abstracts, including *Sounds Assembling.*

Piet Mondrian, another very important European abstract artist, believed that these spiritual values could best be expressed through balanced, geometric abstracts. Mondrian, who influenced Borduas as well as Guido Molinari and *Les Plasticiens,* has obviously affected Yves Gaucher as well.

The other single figure to influence Gaucher's art was Anton von Webern (1883-1945), a musician whose work has interested him for some years. Webern's music has a classical quality of order and balance but also has complex patterns of rhythm. His style is simple, in the sense of not being cluttered with details, and it is concentrated, requiring the listener's attention.

Circular Motion (p. 217), like Webern's music, has order and balance, but it also has patterns that flash in and out, grouping and regrouping. By choosing a square canvas but hanging it on the diagonal, Gaucher has achieved a sense of liveliness within order. The feeling of a whole structure resting on a single point is exciting, but the balance of the design prevents any suggestion of fear that it will collapse.

It is a proven fact that colours affect the emotions in some people perhaps more than others. Psychologists have not been able to decide precisely why this happens, only that it does. The reason may lie partly in the undeniable effects that light and darkness also have upon us.

The light, bright yellow of Gaucher's *Circular Motion* is lively and exciting. For most of the lines in the design he has chosen a pale blue, another primary colour, but one which is lighter in weight that the yellow, because it is paler. The opposition of primary colours and the effect of the blue lines flashing in and out further increase the sense of liveliness. The white lines in two of the corners complicate the patterns while adding variety. Meanwhile the yellow lines in the other corners sink into the background and suggest a sense of depth and space.

Gaucher is a master of colour and balance. In his later work the effects of these have become more and more subtle. His colours, or lack of them in his all-white works, create amazing effects of space, in which intricate rhythms are formed by delicate lines of varying lengths. These are related to each other so carefully that the spaces between them are as important as the lines themselves.

Another Canadian artist who possessed this instinctive sense of interval, or the quiet resting place between objects, was David Milne. He, like Gaucher, also used colour and line in a subtle and sophisticated way. But in other respects the work of these two artists differs greatly. For Milne the work of art was always more important than the actual choice of subject, yet he always painted from nature. In Gaucher's work, there are no direct connections with nature at all. His is a purely abstract style – the only style, perhaps, in which music and painting can be this closely related.

19

Michael Snow

b. 1929

Venus Simultaneous, 1962, oil on canvas and wood
79" x 118" (201 cm x 300 cm)
Art Gallery of Ontario, Toronto

Michael Snow is one of the most unusual and interesting Canadian artists of the last twenty years. He is unusual because he does not limit himself to one medium. Art in all its aspects is important to him, and he has been involved in music, writing, film-making, and in many kinds of sculpture and painting. He is interesting because he never allows his art to remain the same; instead, he is always progressing and exploring. Not only does Snow experiment technically in his work; he also explores the very meaning of art and its relationship to life.

For Snow, art and living are inseparable. Without living there is no art, and without art we lose an important understanding of the form and meaning of life. But art, for Snow does not only mean pictures hanging on a wall, or classical music in a concert hall, or an untouchable piece of sculpture in an art gallery. Art is a part of life; it involves us all, since each of us creates art in one way or another.

An artist is a person who looks at life more closely than most people do and tries, with all the different media he can find, to make its meaning clearer. By putting living into a form we can grasp, such as a painting, a film, or a poem, an artist becomes a translator of life. Naturally, he does not have all the answers, but he can at least ask questions that may help us to find some answers of our own. Because Snow's ideas about the relationship of art and life are complex, his work is not easy to understand. But his intelligence and skill make the effort of following his experimental mind worthwhile.

Michael Snow was born in Toronto. His father was a Canadian of English origin and his mother a French Canadian. He was educated at Upper Canada College and received his art training at the Ontario College of Art.

He is married to Joyce Wieland, an artist who shares his great interest in the various media. Both of them have worked independently of the many Canadian art movements of the last twenty years. But Snow's work has been influenced by some of the most experimental and intellectual European art forms of this century. In 1962 he and his wife moved to New York but returned to Canada in 1971. While they were there, Snow gave several one-man exhibitions and became internationally known for his film-making.

In 1959, when he was making a collage – a work of art made of cut-out forms pasted on a background – Snow created his *Walking Woman*. He used this figure, which he devised almost by chance, again and again for ten years, exploring every possible variation. She appeared in painting, sculpture, wallpaper, T-shirts, and a Coca-Cola advertisement. She also appeared in the huge, flat, silver figures that stood near the Canadian pavilion at Expo 67 and reflected the people as they walked past. There she became a work of art within life, a mirror of life, constantly changing.

The *Walking Woman* was never meant as mere decoration. In all the different media and materials, she took on different roles and characteristics. Through her, Snow was exploring all the ways in which we are affected by what we see. By changing her position, size, material, colour, and the medium in which she was used, he was conducting a serious experiment about the way a single form can act upon us. But only by retaining the same form could he 'control' the effects of it.

Venus Simultaneous, painted in 1962, is one of the most important of the *Walking Woman* series. Here there are eight of the figures in a variety of forms. They are combined in one painting that seems quite simple, but that is actually a very complex exploration of time, space, and relationships.

The title gives a clue to its meaning. Venus, the Greek goddess of love, has always been a symbol of womanhood and of art in its most perfect human form. The word Venus, then, links the idea of a living woman and an artistic creation. Venus also associates the *Walking Woman* of today with a figure that has been used throughout the history of art.

The word simultaneous suggests that time has been condensed in this painting. Each figure, though seeming to move forward, is caught and held there simultaneously. But this is only one frozen moment, like a single frame that has been stopped in a filmstrip.

What happens, though, once time continues or the filmstrip starts up again? The figures in each space move forward into the next. But what kind of space is it? What is real life and what is picture space? Which is the living Venus and which is the painted one?

Moving from left to right, the first woman is partly in and partly out of the painting. Half of her is in real space; half in the flat picture space.

The second woman is only an outline with a frame around her. She has no solidity and the paint shows right through her.

The third woman is solid, though she is only partly in real space and partly within the painting. She also seems to be behind the second woman, but how can she be if woman number two is only an outline on a painted surface?

The fourth woman looks like a figure cut out of the heavily painted surrounding area. Her shape is more like a hole in the surface of the canvas than a solid object on top of it.

But the woman in front of her is like the solid figure that has been cut out of the dark shape. She seems to be in front of the entire canvas, but is she real or is she part of the picture?

The next figure, number six, is barely suggested by the purple line. In fact, it is only because our eyes have grown accustomed to the shape that we recognize her as a woman at all.

Number seven is obviously a painted figure, unlike solid number three or number five in front of the canvas. But her existence is much clearer than that of outlined number two, and she is standing outside a frame and not within it.

The last figure looks like the outline of a piece of Greek sculpture carved in stone, a pillar used in the temples to support the roof structure. But even this stone figure has a ghostly green shadow behind her, like other shadows that float across the canvas.

In *Venus Simultaneous* Michael Snow poses many questions about what we see and how we see it. He examines what actually exists and what we assume exists because we are used to accepting what we have learned or been taught. He considers the nature of time and space, and he questions the relationship of art to the real world. As complex as his work may be, he is still producing some of the most interesting visual ideas in Canada today.

Maxwell Bates

b. 1906

Interior with Figures, 1961, oil on masonite
36″ x 48″ (91 cm x 122 cm)
Confederation Centre Art Gallery and Museum
Charlottetown

Maxwell Bates exaggerates what he sees in order to emphasize what he feels. Sometimes his paintings may seem cruel, but this is only because he is concerned with kindness. The people he attacks or ridicules are those who are thoughtless and stupid. For the suffering and unfortunate he has great understanding.

Bates constantly seeks to capture the truth that lies behind the surface of things. For him every person is a human being whose inner strengths and weaknesses are concealed by outward appearances. People put on masks, make-up, and fancy clothes, like actors in a play, in order to hide from the world their private selves and secret fears.

The man and woman in *Interior with Figures* are ordinary people whom Bates has not made to look like great heroes or symbols of noble virtues. But they do suggest a kind of courage and endurance, not obviously or dramatically, but in a quiet human way that is deeply moving.

Neither of them is a beautiful person. The man has dark shadows under his eyes from the disappointment and worry of daily living. But like armour against the world, he wears a perky little bow tie, making him appear self-confident and smart. His wife, bright with lipstick and earrings, wears a cheap but fashionable sweater in shades of violet matching her husband's tie. This his-and-hers effect links the two in a rather touching way. They are similarly related to their living room, which has curtains of the same colour and a floor and background to match.

There is nothing grand in their surroundings. The bulb of the hanging lamp is barely covered by the green shade. A loaf of bread and an open can stand on the table. But in the background there are the modest luxuries that brighten up their lives, a bottle on the shelf to the right and a bouquet of yellow flowers on the left.

The closeness of the two people, linked to one another by the overall design and related by colour to their surroundings and shared experiences, gives the painting a sense of tenderness. Unlike Lemieux's family (p. 175), where each person is isolated and alone, this husband and wife seem to draw their strength from each other. The gentleness of the couple's relationship is emphasized by the subdued colours of the painting: shades of violet and blue-green with the happy splash of yellow in the flower vase.

In this way the painting stresses the quiet, inner values of everyday life rather than its outward drama. It is not a realistic work but an expressionistic one, where the artist has deliberately exaggerated what he sees in order to express his own feelings and to capture those of his subjects. This approach to painting has interested Bates since he was quite young. Even some of the work he did in his teens shows his concern for conveying people's feelings rather than their outward appearance.

When he was twenty-five, Bates left Calgary, his home, and went to England to study painting and architecture. He was there for several years before the Second World War broke out. In 1940 he joined the army but was taken prisoner. At the end of the war he returned to Calgary, leaving again in 1949 to study art in New York under Max Beckmann, the famous German Expressionist painter. What particularly interested Bates in Beckmann's painting was his expressionistic use of figures and his subtle handling of colour. Colour remains one of Bates's major interests. In *Interior with Figures* and many other paintings, he uses it both to strengthen the meaning of his art and to delight in the effects of colour itself.

Jack Chambers

b. 1931

Sunday Morning #2, 1969-1970, oil on wood
48" x 48" (122 cm x 122 cm)
Collection of Joan S. Currie

Sunday Morning #2 (p. 225) appears to be a straightforward work, painted in a simple realistic style. But the true meaning of the painting cannot be found on the level of what we actually see. In fact, it is a serious work of art and an almost religious statement of faith by the artist. Here Jack Chambers is using his own subtle approach to the old problem of representing time and space, which was handled in their different ways by Lemieux, Bouchard, Leduc, and Dessaillant.

We see two little boys watching television in their night clothes, warm and secure despite the cold winter day outside. An unusual painting hangs on the wall, and in the window hang three stars that introduce the idea of Christmas time. There is nothing else to suggest a Christmas theme, no decorations or wrappings to force this point upon us. But the stars and a spruce tree outdoors, directly below them, work quietly on the mind like tiny clues.

On the surface, the painting is clearly describing the here-and-now of this particular Sunday morning in a suburban house. But once the viewer has time to consider the many suggestions Chambers places before him, the painting begins to take on new dimensions.

Christmas was the birthday of Christ, the child who brought a message of peace and hope to a troubled world. Each Christmas repeats the message, just as each child, like the Infant Jesus, renews the hope of life and peace. The title of the painting, *Sunday Morning,* strengthens this idea of hope and renewal. It was on a Sunday that Christ rose from the dead and promised mankind eternal life. Thus the suggestions of Christmas, Sunday, and childhood all work together in putting forward the idea of fresh beginnings and the promise of continuing life.

It is true that Chambers has not given obvious clues to lead our thinking in this direction. Often, though, an artist is reluctant to force his images too far. Instead he introduces them quietly and naturally into a simple setting, leaving them to expand and take hold in the viewer's mind.

But for all his suggestiveness, Chambers insists upon **the** importance of the here-and-now; this particular moment on a Sunday morning is the subject of his painting. We are left, however, with some questions about his specific choice of subject matter. Why are the boys watching television? Why is the scene placed before a window? Why is there a painting on the wall?

Of course, the answer could be that this is how the room looked and the artist was interested in presenting a realistic scene. But again, we could ask why the artist chose this particular view. After all, it could have been any other.

These questions seem to bring us back to the problem of time and space and the roles they play in our lives. The boys are watching a television program that is probably coming from hundreds of miles away. The picture on the screen appears to show a man in German or Austrian dress waving a flag. But whatever the program or the subject, time and space have been condensed into the television picture. It is now as much a part of the boys' experience as the inside of the warm room, the cold, snowy street outside their window, or the painting on the wall. Each of these is a part of a separate world: the world of present reality, the world of television, or the world of art. Yet, at this moment, all worlds are one for the children.

As viewers of this painting, we are actually looking in on a very complex combination of time periods and spaces. Yet, on the surface, the scene appears to be a simple one; certainly for the two children it is an accepted part of their daily lives.

It is easy to say, especially of so straightforward a

subject as this one, that a great deal more can be
read into a painting than appears to be present.
Some people may read it one way; others in quite a
different way. But this is one of the greatest
pleasures of art; it is there for each person to enjoy
on his own. Although it is the artist who originally
creates the work, once it exists, it belongs to the
world of the imagination. And if the viewer can
meet it imaginatively, then he too becomes a
creator, giving it his own understanding and appreciation. The only really successful way to kill a
work of art is to ignore it and not to spare the time to
think about it seriously.

Because Jack Chambers's paintings are realistic
and apparently straightforward, there is a danger of
their importance being overlooked. Yet Chambers
is a serious artist who is deeply concerned with
looking beyond the surface of what we see.

Born in London, Ontario, he began his art studies
there, but in 1954 he enrolled in the Royal Academy
of Fine Arts in Madrid. Winning a number of
scholarships, he lived and studied in Spain until
1961, and there he would have seen the work of
some of the greatest European painters. Even in
Sunday Morning #2 there are suggestions of some
of the Old Masters, particularly of the still, quiet
atmosphere of Vermeer and of Velazquez, whose
fascination with light and its reflections off different
surfaces influenced generations of later artists.

Claude Breeze

b. 1938

Sunday Afternoon: From and Old American
Photograph, 1965, acrylic on canvas,
104" x 66" (264 cm x 168 cm)
Department of External Affairs, Ottawa

Cruelty, torture, ignorance, and prejudice are not new vices; they have existed in every country throughout history. In Canada, however, commentary on society and its weaknesses has not been a popular subject in art. Even today it still does not receive much attention from professional artists.

In *Sunday Afternoon: From an Old American Photograph*, however, Claude Breeze is making a raw and violent statement against inhumanity. It is not a 'pretty' picture, and in 1965 when it was painted, it probably shocked many people who felt that 'Art' should be appealing and decorative.

Unfortunately, it is probably less shocking today than it was then — less shocking because violence has since become the most common subject of popular visual material. Being part of a daily diet, images of violent death, torture, and suffering have become more acceptable as facts of life. As a result, the horror that we should feel in viewing *Sunday Afternoon* may be muted and dulled. But Breeze is attempting to shock and disgust us by revealing the true nature of violence. He is attacking violence with violent artistic language.

In *Sunday Morning* (p. 225) Jack Chambers used the theme of childhood and the meaning of Sunday to suggest hope and the renewal of life. In *Sunday Afternoon* Claude Breeze questions whether even hope of renewal is possible. By the afternoon the message of the morning seems to have been forgotten. This couple, their hands tied behind their backs, hang helplessly from a tree. They are being burnt on a funeral pyre made up of hundreds of bodies with arms and hands outstretched as if appealing for help.

In Chambers's *Sunday Morning* there is an idea of repetition and renewal of life through all children; in Breeze's *Sunday Afternoon* there is also an idea of repetition, but one of continuing cruelty and prejudice. Chambers brings a message of hope from the past into the future; Breeze is expressing his anger and frustration that out of this past and present there seems to be little hope for the future.

There are details in *Sunday Afternoon* that make the painting even more moving. In the bottom right-hand corner there is an inset, similar to the type that often accompanies newspaper photographs of disasters with such captions as 'the victim seen in happier days'. In the top left-hand corner is another suggestion of what might have been. A cheerful yellow road leads up to a green field where a tree stands laden with fruit. There is a blue sky overhead, and everything seems to suggest springtime and innocence, surely an image of the Garden of Eden.

Both details, the inset and the green field, seem to strengthen Breeze's statement that the violent scene need not happen. This is no disaster brought about by fate or chance; it is a deliberate act of cruelty towards helpless victims. This painting is Breeze's plea for compassion and humanity. It would be a mistake to limit the range of his statement by thinking that it represents only the 'racial problem in the United States which could, of course, never happen in Canada'. Cruelty, violence, and prejudice are human problems that can occur anywhere. Breeze has merely chosen this incident as an example, or an image, for all such events.

In fact, Breeze's work belongs to a type of Expressionism that was developed in Germany early in the twentieth century. It was a style that arose when artists began to see a sick and troubled world which had lost all decent human values. This sickness reached a climax with the horrors of the First World War. Violent colours, misshapen figures, exaggerated proportions, and deliberate ugliness were some of the methods the German Expressionists used to convey their strong feelings. Sometimes their paintings were deliberate attacks on people they felt were greedy, thoughtless, or cruel; at other times their works were expressions of pity, concern, and understanding for the victims.

In Canada, Maxwell Bates and Claude Breeze have both been influenced by the ideas and style of the German Expressionists. There seems, however, to have been no obvious reason or direct influence on Claude Breeze to explain why he followed this particular style.

He was born in Nelson, British Columbia, in 1938 and studied with Brian Fisher at the University of Regina. Among his teachers were Ernest Lindner and Ronald Bloore, whose styles are both very different from his own. In 1959 he attended the Vancouver School of Art and since that time has exhibited widely and taught occasionally.

It is now ten years since *Sunday Afternoon: From an Old American Photograph* was painted. It is worth noting, though, that it was bought by the Department of External Affairs of the Government of Canada. We can hope that it will serve as a reminder that violence and prejudice threaten all men everywhere.

Brian Fisher

b. 1939

Enigma, 1966, polymer acrylic on cotton canvas
68″ x 68″ (173 cm x 173 cm)
The Agnes Etherington Art Centre
Queen's University, Kingston

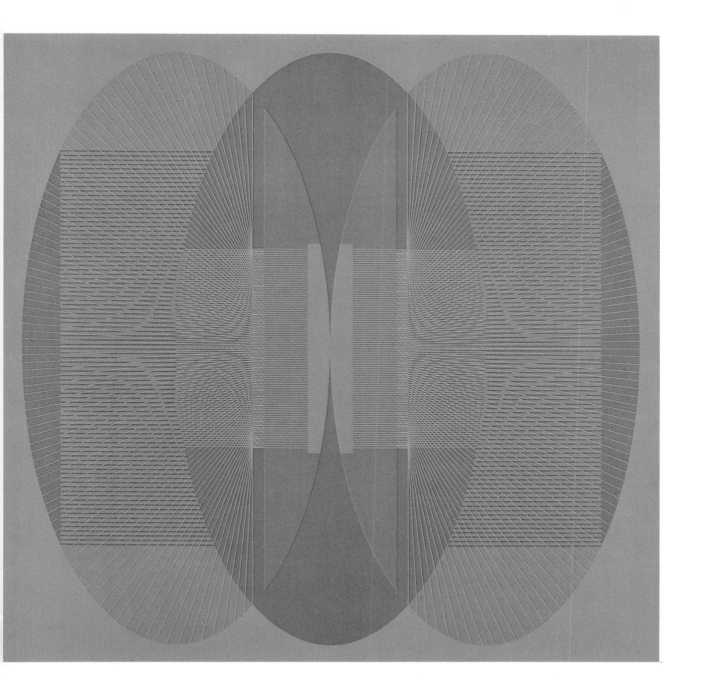

Brian Fisher's art is an interesting combination of opposites. His paintings are modern in structure but traditional in meaning. They represent the mathematical precision of machinery and fine instruments, but they also suggest aspects of nature. Because the images are painted 'constructions' on canvas, they have a solid and immediate quality, but at the same time they encourage us to drift into endless space.

Fisher is a successful young artist who has exhibited widely. His work is included in many important collections and displayed in several public buildings. Born in England of Canadian parents, he came to Canada as a child. He received his art training at the University of Regina and later at the Vancouver School of Art. Between 1962 and 1964 Fisher studied in Europe.

While in Regina he worked under several members of the Regina Five, who have had considerable influence on him. For example, he shares with Ron Bloore a cool, intellectual approach to art which he expresses in abstract painting.

His work is based on Constructivism, a style developed in Russia in the early part of this century. It took the form of light, airy pieces of sculpture made of many different materials, including glass, wire, and fine metal. Later the style spread to Europe, where it has influenced several forms of architecture and decoration.

Basically, the Constructivists felt that the effects of movement in space are more important in art than the effects of solid objects in space. This is because they believed we experience a greater feeling of space when a sense of movement is suggested than we do by looking at the relationship of solid, stationary objects. As we have seen in many other paintings, an artist can give specific meaning to his work by conveying the sensation of space. Space relates us to the world around us and can also create the impression of an unending universe.

Like the work of the Constructivists, Brian Fisher's *Enigma* (p. 231) seems to float like a huge web, gently supporting the blue egg-shaped form in the centre. Mathematically precise in structure, it suggests the diagrams and patterns produced by the most modern scientific instruments. *Enigma* is based on three egg-shaped forms, the outer two like delicate wings of the inner one. At first the eye is led towards the centre by the converging lines. From there the patterns form and reform, sometimes dividing, sometimes uniting, but constantly moving. The solid forms are positive, like the known material objects of the world, while the delicate threads of the web lead us into the unknown space beyond.

Yet despite the sense of constant movement and change, there is no hint of chaos. Everything is held together and controlled by logic and order. The image appears to have the same constancy as the cycles of nature. The more the viewer is drawn into the design, the more involved he becomes. Gradually the mind becomes one with the image and is totally absorbed into it.

This effect of uniting the mind and the object is part of the ancient Eastern philosophy of Zen Buddhism, a subject which interests Brian Fisher. In Zen, the individual is taught that beauty is not something apart from the human being, but something in which he becomes part. By dissolving his mind into an object of beauty, man approaches the truth of life.

This idea, in different forms and variations, is closely related to many of the works of art we have seen. Ozias Leduc's *L'Enfant au Pain* draws the viewer into a private little world so beautiful in form that it is totally absorbing.

Lawren Harris, Borduas, and many others who followed Kandinsky's theories also sought to involve the viewer totally in their art. But they felt that a realistic description of the visible world might only distract the viewer from an understanding of its most fundamental truths. They chose abstraction as a means of absorbing the viewer's feelings and thoughts in the basic truths of the spirit.

Brian Fisher too absorbs his viewer into his art, where he combines modern abstract design and ancient philosophy. A blend of the past and present, his art rests on mathematics, the most ancient of sciences and one of the main foundations of philosophy.

John Meredith

b. 1933

Ulysses, 1968, oil on canvas
72″ x 96″ (183 cm x 244 cm)
The Vancouver Art Gallery

John Meredith has said, 'Art should always be a mystery. It isn't possible to totally explain any work of art, anyways, since it is this mysterious quality which makes art so beautiful.' In fact, he treasures the mystery of painting so much that he once protested to an interviewer, 'Don't try to explain it all away.'

Meredith's paintings are among the most difficult of any to discuss, since their style is unique. He works in images, shapes that for him are the visible

forms of feelings, ideas, beliefs. All of these unite in his art; they spread out like drops of oil on water into patterns of intense personal meaning.

But, since art exists for the viewer as well as the artist, we must see if it is possible for us to understand such highly personal imagery. Does the artist give us the clues we need to share in his part-dream, part-thought, part-feeling world?

Because each of us has a different personality and set of experiences, the direction of our minds and

234

feelings will differ too. As we have already seen, Abstract Expressionist painting depends on the power of images that affect each viewer in particular ways. Shapes, colours, lines, spaces, and their relationships to each other are the only means an Abstract Expressionist has to make suggestions. But we the viewers must reach out to meet him, trying to overcome the distance between his mind and ours, and trusting that he is leading us into a new and valuable experience.

What are the clues Meredith gives us in his painting to help understand it? First there is its title, *Ulysses*, which is the Roman name for the Greek hero Odysseus. In the *Odyssey*, an ancient poem by Homer, Odysseus (Ulysses) travels through the world, facing many trials and adventures on his voyage home. Though the *Odyssey* is an exciting story, it is also an allegory for a man's personal trials in the world.

Meredith's title, then, gives us a clue that this painting can be seen as a man's journey outwards from his own little world into an outer world, and finally into the spaces of the universe. The titles of other works by Meredith show his concern with the idea of man's search for himself and the meaning of life. Two of his works are entitled *Journey* and *Seeker,* while another, entitled *Atlantis,* recalls the mythical land lost under the sea and sought for thousands of years.

But after the artist offers us his title, he leaves us to explore the painting and make our own connections. Sometimes his works have no title, and then we are left entirely alone with his forms, his colours, and his very personal use of line.

Many of Meredith's paintings are based on circles, a symbol of unity and eternity in many Eastern religions. We know that Meredith is very interested in Eastern thought, and particularly the idea of union between man and the universe.

Ribbon- or flame-like shapes are another favourite design of Meredith's, and he uses sharp V-shaped angles and waving, rippling forms to contrast with each other. But the most characteristic feature of his style is a distinctive 'nervous' line. Sometimes almost shaky, other times like lightning flashing across the canvas, it is energetic and imaginative, though seldom quiet and soothing. In his later works his lines have become textured, with little hairy fibres bristling off them, so that they occupy space and depth instead of remaining flat.

Meredith's colour is often rich and usually used to strengthen the meaning of his forms. Here, for example, the blue suggests the colour of the sea and sky on Ulysses' journey home. But whatever colours Meredith chooses for his themes, he intends them to assist the meaning, and not to be used as accepted artistic rules.

John Meredith's actual surname is Smith. But he and his brother, William Ronald, another well-known Canadian artist, chose to use only their given names professionally. The Smith family was not wealthy, but the father, being talented in drawing himself, encouraged his sons with their art.

Meredith was born in Fergus, Ontario, and at the age of eighteen he enrolled in the Ontario College of Art in Toronto. There he studied under Carl Schaefer and Jock Macdonald. Macdonald, an Abstract Expressionist, encouraged Meredith to develop his own individual style. Indirectly, Borduas and *Les Automatistes* had a similar influence upon him.

Of all artists painting in Canada today, John Meredith is one of the most unusual. He is a loner in his life and in his art. His world is a private one, and the greatest compliment we can pay him is to allow his paintings to speak for themselves.

Mary Pratt

b. 1935

Salmon on Saran, 1974, oil on panel
18″ x 30″ (46 cm x 76 cm)
Collection of Dr. Michael J. Langford
St. John's, Newfoundland

Mary Pratt is a very direct artist who is interested in the surface of things – in light and shadow, colour and texture. She enjoys looking at objects and painting them as they appear, instead of searching for hidden meanings. But this is not to say that her paintings have no meaning; rather, their meaning exists within the subjects themselves. 'The things that turn me onto paintings are the things I really like. Seeing the groceries come in, for instance. Or cooking. I'm getting supper and suddenly I look at the cod fillet spread out on the tinfoil and I think, "That's gorgeous. That's absolutely beautiful."'

As a wife and mother of young children, Mary Pratt did little serious painting until about 1965. She was born in Fredericton, New Brunswick, and had studied art in school and at Mount Allison University in Sackville. Now she, her husband Christopher, and their children live in a rural part of Newfoundland.

'One morning,' she says, 'as I started on the usual round of tidying I was startled – quite "caught" by the appearance of our bed. The sun filled the turned-down sheets with light. The great red bedcover curled under the heavy pink blanket and dripped onto the floor. I painted all that morning, working as quickly as possible, oblivious to the schedule of housework I had been so carefully following, trying to record this unexpected "presence" before the sun moved too much.

'I began to see other ordinary things in the same

way and painting quickly on small boards, I tried to catch them all.

'But I couldn't. I had to work too fast. I wasn't doing justice to many of the best things – fish, soufflés – most food and many surfaces that required light to stand still.'

In order to solve the problem of the changing light, Mary Pratt began to use the new technique of taking coloured slides of her subject. At first she felt a little uneasy about it, since it meant sacrificing some of the excitement that comes in the special moment of recognition. Also, as she says, 'A lot of people argue that this isn't really Art.' But, as she sensibly comments, 'I think it's silly not to use everything your civilization offers you. Until I began using a camera, my subject matter was very limited. I couldn't do fish, or meat, or cakes, or any of the things I really enjoy....'

Mary Pratt speaks so clearly about her own intentions that it would be impossible to improve on her own words.

I suspect the romantic and the nostalgic. I identify with the precise and the definite. The painters I like best are the seventeenth and eighteenth century genre painters, particulary Chardin. I'd like to do as well by textures like tinfoil and Saran wrap as they did by cotton and linens. I don't go in for old things; if I had my way, I'd have a kitchen full of the newest, most modern cooking utensils on the market, and I like elegant futuristic fibreglass furniture better than antiques. And yet, I like my pictures to look old. That is why I paint in oil, rather than using acrylics like most other photo-realists. I put on the paint with the same kind of tiny sable brushes that Queen Victoria used for her watercolours. When it comes to drawing my approach is quite different. A drawing isn't a celebration in the way a painting is. You have a piece of paper on your knee, and you're using a fine graphite pencil, and you're making a kind of personal investigation of the thing you're drawing....

Mary Pratt's paintings are, as she says, 'celebrations'. They are moments captured on canvas when she recognizes an object for its own special importance and beauty.

The salmon, lying on a sheet of Saran wrap, is neither seen nor portrayed in a romantic way; it is not a symbol or a poetic image. In fact, it is nothing but itself – a fish, ready to be cooked. As if to insist upon its reality, the artist makes no attempt to hide the blood on the wrapping, and the redness actually contributes to the design.

The result is beautiful. The colours of the salmon are reflected in the clear film of the saran that surrounds it in a hazy cloud. Deep blues and reds move to purple, violet, pink, and all the subtle blends in between. The scaly surface of the fish and its bony tail contrast with the fine texture of the Saran. Light, flickering off the wrapping, makes wonderful patterns in the folds, while the shadows deepen the colours. The crinkles in the Saran are rather like abstracts in themselves.

The honest, direct quality of Mary Pratt's work seems to be in keeping with the character of Newfoundland. There is nothing soft or romantic about either. As she says, 'This is an abrupt, dramatic, light and dark kind of society. You're richer, you're poorer, you're wildly happy, or you're depressed. These extremes appeal to me.'

Greg Curnoe

b. 1936

View of Victoria Hospital, Second Series, 1969-1971
oil on plywood, wallpaper, stereo cassette
96" x 191-3/4" (244 cm x 487 cm)
The National Gallery of Canada, Ottawa

Greg Curnoe is more concerned with life and living than with 'Art'. In some ways his work is rather like Michael Snow's, but in others it differs considerably. Like Snow, he is unwilling to accept a division between art and life. But while Snow is continually asking questions, Curnoe makes statements of his own. Snow examines the meaning of art and its relationship to life, asking what it is, how does it function, what does it do for us? Curnoe shows slices of life in single paintings – life with all its unevenness and its disjointed bits and pieces of thoughts and feelings.

Although he studied art formally in London, Ontario, where he was born, and at the Ontario College of Art in Toronto, Curnoe remained unsatisfied with formal methods and approaches. Fine Art, he felt, had become a precious object, separated from the ordinary person and having little to do with daily living. Curnoe strongly believes that it is

the reality of life, much of it 'ugly' by old artistic standards, that we must recognize, accept, and, as he would say, 'celebrate'.

The idea of rejecting Fine Art because it had become meaningless in the modern world dates back approximately to the years 1915 to 1922. It came about largely as a result of the shock of the First World War. The movement was called Dada (French for 'hobby horse'), and one of its main supporters was Marcel Duchamp (1887-1968).

What, asked the Dadaists, is the point of producing beautiful art that no longer reflects the world in which we live? If the world is senseless, then art too should be senseless. Duchamp produced objects called ready-mades – a bottle rack, a urinal, a garden rake – as if daring the scholars and art critics to find meaning and inspiration in them.

Around the 1950s and early 1960s a new movement called Pop Art started in Britain. Again, it was

238

partly a result of war. But this time it was probably based less on horror and disgust than on a need to escape the serious patriotism and romantic attitude of wartime Britain. Attitudes that were expressed in songs like

There'll be blue birds over
The white cliffs of Dover
Tomorrow, just you wait and see

produced strong anti-sentimental, anti-Art feelings.

Fascinated by the new popular culture, particularly in the United States, a group of British artists started to look at advertisements, packaging, posters, neon signs, cartoon strips, and all the visual material of daily life. Although the movement began in Britain, it soon became popular in the United States as well. Brilliant acrylic colours, repeated objects, words and phrases, flat and often unrelated forms, all are features of Pop Art. In the United States, Andy Warhol became a king of Pop. Marilyn Monroe and Coke bottles, repeated over and over again, are like his signature, though car accidents, riots, and mug shots are other subjects he used.

Greg Curnoe's art is related to Dada and Pop, but from these ideas and methods he has produced his own personal form. Most of his paintings are based directly upon his own life and experiences, but the meanings of these particular incidents spread outwards to become more general concerns.

This view of Victoria Hospital in London, Ontario, happens to be the one that Curnoe could see from his apartment window. There is nothing romantic, idealized, or beautiful about the painting. Rather, it is an example of the business-like diagrams used in a variety of ways in modern life. The forms are basically flat, but the colours are bright, and the general effect is lively and interesting.

Curnoe worked on this painting over a period of two years, and during that time a great many things happened. As they occurred, Curnoe put a number on the painting and noted the particular event it represented on an accompanying chart. He also had a tape-recorder running so that he could capture everything he heard as well as everything he saw.

Two years of life are now condensed into one work. Every second we experience it, we also experience 63,072,000 seconds of living by sight, sound, and understanding. Art and life have become one in this work, and because it is a view of a hospital, where most of us begin life and end it, the meaning stretches on even further.

Esther Warkov

b. 1941

Memories of an Autumn Day, 1968, oil on canvas
62″ x 82″ (157 cm x 208 cm)
Beaverbrook Art Gallery, Fredericton

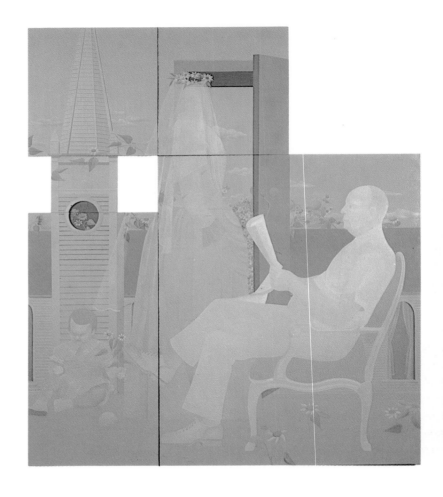

Esther Warkov is from Winnipeg and was born of Ukrainian-Jewish parents. She trained for three years at the Winnipeg School of Art and has exhibited often since her first exhibition in 1964. Her work was included in the Canadian pavilion art gallery at Expo 67, and she has paintings in collections throughout Canada and the United States.

Warkov's paintings describe a world of fantasy rather than fact. Because of this, she is not tied to the laws of nature or to the customs of society that govern the everyday world. She creates her own environment, where flowers can grow wherever she places them, where people have wings, or where apples and pears emerge from the barrels of guns. But she also paints a world of dreams. Many of her figures float like ghosts in a space that has its own kind of order, totally unlike the three-dimensional order of the world we know.

Time is also different for Esther Warkov. Hers is not the time of a clock or of fixed arrangements of morning, noon, and night. There are no clear beginnings or endings. Childhood, youth, middle age, and old age can all exist together as one.

When we look at Warkov's paintings, we must be prepared to enter them, not asking particular questions or expecting definite answers. Like dreams, they have their own clear logic at one moment that floats out of reach at the next. Explaining a dream in the morning is like trying to catch snowflakes, and Warkov's paintings belong to the same imaginative realm.

But even though she dislikes making definite statements, certain of her feelings come through very clearly in her art: her rejection of racial prejudice, her recognition of cruelty and violence, her delight in love and the process of creation, her sadness at the passing of time and the fact of death. All these feelings are present in her paintings.

Sometimes they exist together, sometimes individually, just as they do in the human mind and emotions. She makes no attempt to define them or give them labels, but with them she creates an atmosphere.

In contrast to this dream-like freedom of meaning, the forms she creates are clearly realistic. In fact, her style is related to the original form of Surrealism that developed in Europe in the 1920s. The Surrealists painted recognizable people and objects, but created an illogical relationship between them. For example, in one of his most famous paintings, Salvador Dali draped clocks and watches over weird forms of driftwood on a sandy shore. In a similar way Warkov has associated completely unrelated but identifiable objects in her drawing *Dalton Camp Having a Medieval Vision* (p. 242). By combining the logical and illogical, this approach to Surrealism differs from that of Borduas and *Les Automatistes,* who believed that the shapes of the forms themselves came automatically from the subconscious mind onto the canvas.

In some of her early works, Warkov experimented with Pop Art, using the bright and startling colours of commercial advertising. But later she turned to quieter colour schemes like the one in *Memories of an Autumn Day.* Often she uses one basic colour and varies the tones so as to imitate the sensation of dream and memory.

She treats her canvas shapes in a most original way. Instead of using the traditional rectangular, square, or even round canvas, Warkov chooses a variety of shapes, and often uses more than one in a single work. This allows her greater freedom to experiment with space and meaning. She can completely separate certain sections, as she does here, or create different spaces and tensions among the parts of a single whole, as Riopelle did in his triptych (p. 194).

Dalton Camp Having a Medieval Vision, pencil drawing
21″ x 16-3/4″ (53 cm x 43 cm)
The Art Gallery, Memorial University of Newfoundland

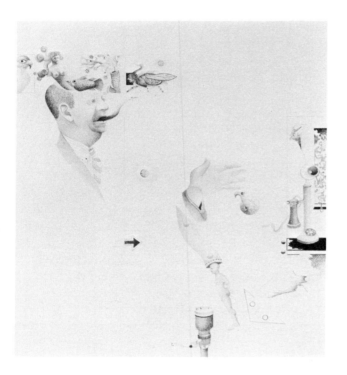

It is a little surprising that despite the inventive shapes of her canvases and the unrelated quality of her subject matter, Warkov's recent work has a quiet, classical feeling. In *Memories of an Autumn Day,* the vertical forms balance the horizontal ones; the figures are either facing straight outwards or are in profile, and there are very few diagonal lines. In itself, the little circular canvas is perfectly balanced and symmetrical; when it is hung, it balances the weight of the heavy lower right-hand part of the main canvas. The stillness of the figures and the quiet, cool colours also add to a classical feeling of calm.

The sense of order that is deliberately created by these artistic effects carries over to the meaning. An atmosphere of love, trust, and peace of mind seems to flow through the painting. Even the sad and ghostly sense of things past is controlled by the happy memories of spring flowers and a contented child.

Alexander Wyse

b. 1938

Detail of Exercising Flying Cows Over the Governor General's Grounds, 1975
wood, tin, nails, paint, glass (frame)
paper, ink, crayon, oil (painting)
overall dimensions 90″ x 21″ (229 cm x 53 cm)
Collection of the Artist

Those who have never seen a nude woman exercising her flying cow on the grounds of the Governor General's residence have not had the pleasure of sharing Alex Wyse's world. Perhaps these people might be even more surprised to see a train ploughing its way through a field of wheat, from which more nude women pop out, waving and shouting to enthusiastic passengers.

Of course Wyse's world is not entirely filled with nude women. Lions wearing Union Jack saddles; leather-capped airmen climbing out of biplanes; professional confetti-makers; brass bands and circuses; Baroque angels, who should be coyly seated on puffy clouds, but are unfortunately caught in a high wind; all these and more live in Wyse's world. Anything can happen there – and does. It is a meeting place for politicians waving flags, churchmen assembling marriage candidates, and tourist guides escorting wealthy customers to quaint Indian reserves.

In all his subjects, Alex Wyse enjoys himself thoroughly. Just when you might suppose he is setting himself up as a critic of society, you find him painting a work like *A Truly, Great, Rural Cabbage*. Just as you are about to express your amazement at the detailed craftsmanship of a handmade frame, you find that he has deliberately put a large patch on one side of it.

His world is overflowing and he talks '. . . of many things: Of shoes – and ships – and sealing wax – and cabbages – and kings'. Like Esther Warkov, he sets unrelated subjects side by side, simply because they come to mind that way. There is no point in trying to work out a logical explanation of the events he paints, because they are not put together with logic. Snatches of personal memories, feelings, and thoughts are woven together to produce magical scenes, filled with marvelous inventions and fascinating characters.

But there are certain threads that run through all his work, giving it a character that is his own personal style. Whatever the subject, his paintings are alive with humour, rich blends of colour, and the finest details. His humour, which is always present on the surface, may sometimes conceal his artistry. In the same way, the patch on his frame seems to be an almost deliberate disguise of his fine craftsmanship. The world is far from perfect, the artist seems to say, but let's not take it too seriously. It's better to enjoy it.

Alex Wyse was born in England and went to the Cheltenham College of Art for his early training. Later he continued his studies at the Royal College of Art in London, where he specialized in engraving. In 1961 he came to Canada and the following year was invited by the West Baffin Co-operative at Cape Dorset to teach copper engraving to the Eskimos. In 1961, Kiakshuk became the first Eskimo artist to produce a copper engraving, after he was shown the process by James Houston, who started the printmaking program in Cape Dorset. It was Alex Wyse, though, who really introduced copper engraving, and during his stay at Cape Dorset, he taught Kiakshuk, Pitseolak, Kenojuak, and many of the other Eskimo printmakers who are now famous.

Since that time Wyse has been working on his own, often combining his paintings with sculptural inventions that would please the most imaginative magician. Despite the light-hearted character of his work, it would be a mistake to think that it comes easily. The ideas may flow; the difficulty is in keeping up with them. Hours and hours of work go into his paintings, since everything is done in complete detail.

Following the techniques of an engraver, Wyse uses a similar method to set down his design, but he works with tiny strokes of his pen instead of an engraving tool. Once he actually begins painting, he

adds his colours layer by layer, strengthening the areas that need to be richer and darker and leaving those that are to be lighter.

The final effect is rather like looking through a series of veils. The foreground stands out sharply and clearly, but behind it level after level fades into the background. Yet to see this requires very close attention, because the whole process is so finely done and carefully detailed. The surface appearance is one of richly blended colours that act as a setting for the amazing activities of Wyse's characters.

Even the frames for the paintings, or the sculptures in which the paintings are included, are made with the most careful precision. Tiny pieces of smooth wood are nailed side by side onto a basic framework with tacks the size of pins. Then, as if the artist-sculptor-inventor was afraid he might appear to be showing off, the whole contraption is painted over, and a patch nailed on the side.

Exercising Flying Cows Over the Governor General's Grounds is one of Wyse's 'happenings' and not a regular event in the life of Her Majesty's representative. Part painting, part sculpture, part theatre, part invention, it is even, perhaps, part flying cow. It belongs in no category; it just happens. The script goes something like this:

MRS. PRESTON, *speaking to the cow.* You are doing beautiful, Mirabelle.

COW. I must say I feel a bit of a fool up here.

GENTLEMAN ON THE EXTREME RIGHT, *holding a placard that reads: Ban All Animal Shows.* It's nothing short of cruelty what you are doing with that animal, Mrs. Preston.

GENTLEMAN BESIDE MRS. PRESTON. Take no notice of the old fool, Mrs. Preston.

MRS. PRESTON. I simply ignore that kind of person.

GENTLEMAN FRIEND OF NUDE LADY SEATED ON A BOX ON THE LEFT. Your act is every bit as good as hers.

NUDE LADY ON BOX. I know but I am so nervous, darling.

GENTLEMAN WITH ONE LEG, ON EXTREME LEFT. Nothing but exhibitionism.

The message of the painting seems to be: Keep your eyes open next time you are wandering around the Governor General's grounds. You never know what you might see.

Ivan Eyre

b. 1935

Tanglewood, 1973, acrylic on canvas
62" x 143-1/2" (157 cm x 364 cm)
Winnipeg Art Gallery

Ivan Eyre was born and raised on the Prairies. He received his early training in Saskatoon, where Ernest Lindner was one of his instructors. He continued his studies in the School of Art at the University of Manitoba and later joined the staff. He has now been teaching there for sixteen years.

In his painting and sculpture Eyre seems to be searching for ways to express our need for personal freedom. Over the years his style has changed considerably, not once but several times. Yet his basic ideas and feelings remain the same, though they have now broadened and mellowed.

In his earlier works, he expressed his anger at the senseless society we have made. He depicted men and women, trapped and suffering, but unable to free themselves from their own systems. Humans and animals are lost in the chaos of wrecked machinery. The landscape is destroyed by the waste and litter of a society that has become a victim of its own inventions.

In these earlier canvases, Eyre conveyed his

meaning with sharp, jagged, angular forms, painted in clear and expressive colours. The symbols he used – enclosed spaces, torn metal, twisted shapes – all suggested his anger and frustration at needless human suffering.

But now Eyre's work is calmer. It seems as though he wants to stress the positive side of life – what we have and what we can make of it. In his new landscapes there are no figures; instead, there is a sense of vast, free space.

Tanglewood is a very large canvas, about twelve feet long and five feet high. Standing in front of it, the viewer becomes completely involved in the scene. Space, light, texture, and a feeling of unending green spread out across the valley to a high horizon line. Forms appear to billow out into the vastness of the green space.

In some ways *Tanglewood* is very realistic. It is a scene that could be experienced almost anywhere in Canada. But in other ways it is like an abstract painting, in which Eyre so skilfully captures the essence of one particular scene that what he depicts could apply to many other scenes as well. Yet the balance he strikes between the real and the abstract is very delicate and appears remarkably natural and unstudied.

In *Tanglewood* and his other recent landscapes, Eyre has chosen a style that is surprisingly close to that of two artists who might appear to work at opposite extremes: Ernest Lindner, under whom he studied, and Claude Monet, the great French Impressionist. Strangely, both artists were striving for the most realistic effects they could produce, although their work appears to be completely different.

Lindner studies the details of nature as if they were under a microscope. In his forest series he depicts clumps of moss, growths of lichen and fungi, and the bark of trees, though the effects seem very close to abstraction. These small segments of nature have a texture and structure rather like a sponge – cell upon cell build up into larger areas of living matter. In *Tanglewood* the texture of the trees has the same organic quality; this is living material that appears to grow before our eyes. Tiny flecks of paint are built up, like cells, into different forms related by colour and light.

Claude Monet, in his Impressionist paintings, was also concerned with capturing the effects of light on different surfaces. He was a realist in the sense that he wanted to record the fleeting reflections that the eye actually sees. But in his attempt to accomplish this, Monet, too, came close to producing abstract paintings. There are no solid objects, for example, in his huge canvases of water lilies, only the shimmering effects of light, colour, and reflection. The real world becomes patterns of colour on a canvas – but patterns that suggest endless depth and space. In *Tanglewood* Eyre's style resembles Monet's. The solidity of the trees and landscape is broken down into patterns of green and yellow that appear to rise and fall. The very size of the canvas seems to draw the viewer into a green world that stretches on and on endlessly.

Eyre, like Lindner and Monet, is looking closely at the real world. Yet taken only one step further, the shapes, colour, and texture of *Tanglewood* could cover the surface of the canvas with the billowing patterns of abstracts. Eyre's concern, though, is nature and our relationship to nature. In *Tanglewood* he is no longer fighting the forces of a senseless society. Instead, he seems to state that personal freedom can be found in an imaginative understanding of the living, natural world.

Gordon Smith

b. 1919

Sea Wall, Dunderave, 1972, oil on canvas
56″ x 65″ (142 cm x 165 cm)
The Canada Council Art Bank, Ottawa

Gordon Smith's paintings reveal a very delicate balance. They rest on a fine dividing line between landscapes which describe the world we know and abstracts which give it order and form. But they are also works of art, beautiful in their own right and independent of meanings or descriptions of things we have seen.

Sea Wall, Dunderave is composed of a subtle relationship of colour, form, and space that has both grace and elegance. These artistic qualities have a long history but are more important to some painters than to others. There are artists, like Michael Snow, who prefer to explore complex intellectual problems; others, like Claude Breeze, are more emotional in their approach; and still others, like John Meredith, allow their work to arise from their subconscious minds.

It is difficult to produce work that is elegant without being purely decorative. In some periods of history, painting and sculpture became so elegant that they almost lost their meaning, and without meaning, there is no real art. Sometimes, though, the meaning can damage the visual quality. Either the work can become so intellectual that its visible shape seems almost unimportant, or it can become so emotional that what we see is completely overwhelmed by the artist's feelings. Great skill and delicate control are needed to produce a truly beautiful work of art that balances meaning, feeling, and visual form. Gordon Smith is a perfectionist who constantly works towards achieving this balance.

Born in England, Smith went to the Winnipeg School of Art in 1934 and continued his training in Vancouver and California. He has been teaching since 1946 and has been a professor of Fine Arts at the University of British Columbia since 1956. His work, both painting and sculpture, is included in many public and private collections, and he has also exhibited widely in Canada, the United States, South America, and many European countries.

When he was at the Winnipeg School of Art, Smith studied under Lemoine FitzGerald. Although the two artists are different in many ways, their work shares a quality of refinement and elegance. Both artists also seek to preserve the delicate relationship between the visible world, the abstract structure, and a form that is pleasing to the eye.

Sea Wall, Dunderave is a fine painting that perfectly maintains this balance. It can be seen as an abstract composition on a flat surface, divided into areas of subtle colours and balanced shapes. But it can also be seen as nature in depth, with sand and water in the foreground and the sea wall, fields, and more water receding towards the distant horizon and sky.

Each area of colour is softly blended, giving the impression of life rather than of artificial bands of paint. The variety of shapes and the alternating sensations of flatness and depth also give the painting a sense of liveliness.

Sea Wall, Dunderave and James Morrice's *The Ferry, Quebec* (p. 115) make an interesting comparison. Both paintings have a cool, aesthetic quality that pleases the eye, and both maintain a fine balance between the visible world and the painted canvas. Morrice and Smith clearly show that a work of art can exist as a thing of beauty in its own right, giving us pleasure and adding something extra to our lives. But neither of them withdraws entirely from the visible world into pure patterns of decoration. Instead, they encourage us to look around and see nature with new eyes. By focussing closely on particular scenes, they have emphasized the underlying artistic designs that are present throughout the living world.

Marion Wagschal

b. 1943

Backyard, undated, acrylic on board
7' x 8' (213 cm x 244 cm)
Confederation Centre Art Gallery and Museum
Charlottetown

In *Backyard* Marion Wagschal has created a frightening modern version of the Garden of Eden. The members of this family, shown together in their garden, all have what they think they should want, but not one of them seems to be happy. The smile on the woman is not very convincing; the gentleman does not appear to be enjoying his rest; the child is plainly bored; and the poor dog might well be dreaming of far-away hills where he could run free.

Thick, leafy creepers surround the garden and the lush, green grass flourishes on its diet of chemical fertilizer. In the middle of the lawn grows a tree, heavy with fruit like the Tree of Life in the Garden of Eden, but this one produces pears, not apples.

In front of the middle-aged man in his plastic chair is a fancy table. The top is made of plate glass so that the driftwood legs can be seen more clearly. In case the gentleman feels hungry, there is a small cake on the table. But if it were not contained in a frilly paper cup, it might be mistaken for a live frog. After all, it is made in the shape of a frog and it is bright green, like everything else in the garden.

But although everything in this small backyard looks like an ideal advertisement for 'Outdoor Living on those Carefree Summer Days', no one looks content; no one is speaking, laughing, or even moving. Only a few feet apart, each person seems completely unaware of the other's presence. Even though the members of this family are living a luxurious suburban life, they are rather like Jean Paul Lemieux's *Les Promeneurs* (p. 175). Isolated from each other, not touching, not really living, they carry on from day to day. In *Backyard* we see three unhappy people living in a world of false values; they have lost touch with reality, with nature, and with themselves.

Nothing in this garden has been allowed to remain natural. Everything has been forced into the image of what an ideal home and garden should be.

In the process, nature itself has become distorted and threatening. The acid-green grass and the vines on the fence are so lush that the effect is almost choking. Even the pear tree, heavily laden with fruit, seems crude and grotesque.

The extremely realistic style of painting, Magic Realism, as it is sometimes called, seems to emphasize the artificial atmosphere of the scene. But the effect is almost surrealistic. Although there are no completely illogical relationships between objects, the crudeness of the green frog cake, the ridiculous combination of driftwood and plate glass in the table, and the absurdity of all the shiny pears on the tree make this reality seem like a dream.

By keeping the realistic and surrealistic aspects of her painting in balance, Wagschal is able to make her meaning quite clear. On the one hand, the painting is easy to read and leaves no doubt that it describes a scene from daily life. On the other hand, its intensely detailed style, which tends to associate it with the world of dreams, suggests how false and artificial this kind of life can be. In fact, she suggests it is a type of illusion.

Marion Wagschal is a young artist who was born in Trinidad. She received her training at Sir George Williams University and now lives in Montreal. Many of her paintings have a strange and haunting effect that tends to remain in the mind of the viewer for a long time.

Backyard is especially powerful. It is a very large canvas in which every detail is described with absolute clarity. The total effect, though humorous in some ways, is actually terrifying. Life and nature have become so distorted that all traditional human values seem threatened. Yet the artist's intention is not a negative one: in *Backyard* Marion Wagschal is rejecting the false values of an artificial society, but at the same time she is stating her belief in the true and honest values of the natural world.

Christopher Pratt

b. 1935

The Bed, 1971, oil on masonite
34″ x 27-1/4″ (86 cm x 69 cm)
Beaverbrook Art Gallery, Fredericton

Although Christopher Pratt may seem to be a realist, actually he is very close to being an abstract painter. He is one of several Maritime artists, working in a basically realistic style, who trained at Mount Allison University under Alex Colville. Though Pratt was obviously influenced by Colville and probably affected by the training he received at the Glasgow School of Art in Scotland, he has developed a particular style of his own. The subjects he chooses come from the everyday world we know, but his paintings have a special quality that sets them apart and leads us on beyond time and space.

The Bed has a classical sense of order that brings a feeling of peace and security – the same feeling that we found in Plamondon's *Soeur Saint-Alphonse* and Ozias Leduc's *L'Enfant au Pain*. The subject is very simple, a bed in the recess of a room, and the painting appears to be a straightforward one.

Although the bed is not shut in an enclosure, it is protected by the arms of the wall jutting out into the room. The bed itself is plain and white and the cover neat and orderly. The bed and the space around it have a human size and scale. We feel safe within it, because it is a protected space that does not overpower us.

But behind the bed a window opens onto a view of the sea, which appears to go on and on and on. Our safe inside space is contained within this endless outside one. And now, as we look out of the window, we experience another feeling – a sense of floating in a dream-like and unearthly space.

The artist has achieved his effects very subtly, using a series of planes, one behind the other to move back into the picture space. The foot of the bed seems almost close enough to touch. The first level of wall surface comes next, followed by the headboard and the wall behind it. The window frame, the surface of the glass, and the sea beyond carry the eye into the far distance.

To control the feeling of backward movement into space, the canvas is divided by the many horizontal and vertical lines that define the bed, walls, and window frame. These create a series of repeated patterns and give the painting its feeling of mathematical order.

The simplicity of the patterns, the quiet colours, and the even light keep everything controlled and balanced. Even the meaning of the painting is balanced; we begin our lives and often end them in a bed. The bed is a symbol of life, ordered and defined by daily and yearly patterns. At night we sleep in a bed and revive ourselves for the activity of another day. In a room we find shelter from the summer and winter weather. A bed, a room, a house, all give us protection and security.

But they also exist in a larger world, a universe that moves on and on in time and space. The sea, because it flows beyond the horizon, has often been used as a symbol for eternity. Here, the simple white bed, sheltered by the warm pink walls, is like a cocoon that contains our life and shelters us from a world we know little about.

This particular bed is a symbol of the bed in which each of us sleeps, our own particular shelter in the vast universe we all share. Pratt takes us outwards, step by step, from the known into the unknown.

GLOSSARY

Cross references are indicated by words in SMALL CAPITALS.

ABSTRACT ART is based on the idea that forms and colours themselves have certain meanings and express values entirely independent of the actual subject matter of a work of art. This is an ancient theory that was used thousands of years ago in Egypt and the Middle East; it was also used in the art of the early Christian church and during the Middle Ages. Today it is the basis of many modern styles.

ABSTRACT EXPRESSIONISM. A form of ABSTRACT ART that is said to come directly and automatically from the subconscious mind. Thus, it takes the form of free shapes and combinations of colours that are not consciously controlled by the will of the artist. Although the style originated largely from the theories of Wassily Kandinsky, the term came into use during the 1950s to describe the work of a group of New York painters. See also ACTION PAINTING.

ACADEMY is the name originally given to the group that gathered around Plato, the Greek philosopher, for discussions on a wide range of subjects. During the fifteenth-century Renaissance in Italy, a number of academies were founded, including some devoted to art. Since that time academies have been established in many other countries as well. The French Academy, founded in 1643, became extremely powerful, and until the 1860s it was difficult for an artist to survive without being a member and showing his work in the official SALON. The Royal Academy in England, founded in 1768, and the Royal Canadian Academy, founded in 1880, also exerted great influence. The official academic schools and member artists taught according to accepted rules based on CLASSICAL theories, and only works painted in the academic style were exhibited. During the nineteenth century this style became dull and conservative and led to a complete break away from the academies.

ACRYLIC paint is a new synthetic product that can be used as if it were either watercolour or oil paint. Being soluble in water, it can be applied in thin washes, but it can also be applied in thick strokes to give the effect of a heavy texture.

ACTION PAINTING is a technique in which paint is dribbled or splashed onto the canvas. It is an extreme form of ABSTRACT EXPRESSIONISM and is based on the theory that the subconscious mind produces its own forms and patterns. The American artist Jackson Pollock is the principal figure connected with this technique.

AERIAL PERSPECTIVE. See PERSPECTIVE.

ALLEGORICAL PAINTING is a visual way of showing one thing and meaning another. It usually takes the form of a story in which each person and object has a meaning besides the one that is apparent.

ANONYMOUS. Artist unknown.

AQUATINT is a printing method related to engraving that gives strong effects of changing tones. For a full description see page 39.

ANTIQUE, THE. Art that originated in Greece and Rome. During the Renaissance, artists looked back to what was called classical antiquity as being the period of highest artistic achievement. Since then there have been frequent revivals of interest in the study of the Antique; one of these formed the basis for the teaching in the academies. See also ACADEMY; CLASSICAL.

ART NOUVEAU. A 'new art' form that was popular in Europe in the 1890s and had a strong influence on the early works of the Group of Seven. It was based on the curling, twisting forms of plants, particularly vines and creepers. These shapes were used, for example, as decoration in architecture, furniture, textile, and book design. Art Nouveau also had a considerable effect on the painting styles of many artists working at the beginning of the twentieth century.

ATTRIBUTION is the term used in assigning a work of art to a particular artist. An attribution can be made on the basis of a proven signature, documents related to the work or the artist, and careful consideration and analysis of the style. Evidence is often confirmed scientifically by means of x ray, paint analysis, and examination by microscope. For a full description see pages 57 to 58.

AUTOMATISM is the basis of ABSTRACT EXPRESSIONISM, the result of the subconscious mind automatically directing the hand.

BAROQUE ART is a term given to a style that evolved in Europe in the seventeenth century, though not all seventeenth-century art is Baroque. Because it is an extremely emotional art form, it is in complete contrast to the CLASSICAL style. In painting it combines the effects of rich colours; strong contrasts of light and shade; movement; diagonal compositions, which are more exciting than compositions with a horizontal or vertical emphasis; and the impression of weight, particularly weight in motion.

BESTIARIES. Ancient books of natural history that describe creatures from all parts of the world. They were composed and illustrated from many sources: myths, fables, fact, observation, and imagination. One of the best-known sources, though not the oldest, is a book of beasts that probably appeared in Egypt between the second and fifth centuries A.D. Possibly written in Greek, it was widely translated, and Physiologus's Latin version of the eighth century is the source from which many other bestiaries were written in many languages.

BURIN or GRAVER. The tool used in engraving that is pushed along the lines of the surface of the metal plate. The burin throws up a metal shaving, the burr, on either side of the furrow. This may be removed when the plate is polished, or it may be left to catch the ink and give a rich effect.

CAMERA OBSCURA, LUCIDA. Devices used by artists to assist the accuracy of their drawing, particularly of scenery. The *camera obscura* was invented in the sixteenth century, and the *camera lucida,* which is technically a more advanced device, appeared in 1807. Basically the principal of operation is the same as that of a camera. The light, shining off the scene to be drawn, goes through a small hole fitted with a lens into a box or tent where the artist sits. The image appears upside down on a screen opposite the hole. It is then reflected back by a mirror onto a sheet of paper so that the artist can trace around it.

CARTOGRAPHY. Mapmaking.

CARTOON is a term that has changed its meaning. In the modern sense it refers to a humorous or satirical drawing, but, derived from the Italian *cartone,* meaning 'large sheet of paper', it originally referred to a full-size drawing made in preparation for a painting. The cartoon was rubbed on the back with chalk and placed on the canvas or wall. The lines were then either traced over or pricked through, and by this process the design was transferred into its final position.

CHIAROSCURO (Italian, 'light-dark'). A term used in art to describe the balance of light and shadow in a painting or print. This can be used dramatically to give strong contrasts or more gradually for a gentler effect; the way in which it is used contributes to the general composition of the work.

CLASSICAL, classical, classicism are all terms that tend to be used rather loosely. In the strictest sense, Classical (with a capital C) refers to the art of Greece and Rome and particularly to that of the fifth century B.C. This was the period considered by many to have set the standards of artistic perfection; for this reason, Classical art has been copied and revived in various ways throughout the history of Western art. Styles based on the original Classical forms and theories are frequently referred to as classical (with a small *c*) or as types of classicism. The major characteristics of a classical style are clarity of forms and colours, balanced proportions and harmony of parts, careful drawing, and a general sense of order and discipline. It is an art that comes from the mind rather than from the emotions. See also ACADEMY; ANTIQUE, THE.

COLLAGE. A work of art made up of pieces of paper, cloth, and/or other materials stuck on a backing. This technique was used quite extensively by the Cubists and certain Dada artists. It was also a favourite method of Matisse, used frequently in his late work.

COMMERCIAL ART AND DESIGN. Those forms of art that are used for business purposes, such as advertising, magazine illustrations, and textiles, rather than as ends in themselves. Boldness and clarity of design and colour, concentration on essentials rather than on details, and emphasis on the purpose of the object rather than on any independent meaning are all characteristics of commercial art.

COMPLEMENTARY COLOUR. The three primary colours of the spectrum that cannot be made by mixing are red, blue, and yellow. Each primary colour has a complementary colour that is made by mixing the other two. Red and green are complementary, as are blue and orange, yellow and violet. According to the colour theory of the Impressionists, every primary has its complementary colour in the shadow cast by it. For example, a red object has green in its shadow.

COMPOSITION. The manner in which all the elements of a painting, such as form, colour, line and space, are treated and made into one harmonious whole.

CONSTRUCTIVISM. An art movement that was founded in Russia in the early twentieth century. The Constructivists created lightweight abstract sculpture made from glass, wire, sheet metal, and other materials; their work was usually transparent and often hanging. Believing that movement in space gives a greater sense of satisfaction than solid objects in space, the Constructivists achieved these effects in their sculpture. Later their ideas had considerable influence on architecture, decoration, and even painting.

CONVERSATION PIECE. A small informal group portrait, often showing members of a family having a conversation while gathered around a tea table or enjoying some other quiet domestic event. This type of portraiture was popular in the eighteenth century, particularly in Britain.

CUBISM. An art movement that was originally developed by Pablo Picasso and Georges Braque in the early years of this century. It has been called 'the parent of all abstract art forms' of the modern era. The aim of the Cubists was to analyze all forms into their basic geometric structure and then reduce these to the flat two-dimensional picture surface. (For the development of Cubism from the original aims of Paul Cézanne to the theory of Picasso and Braque, see page 161.) The first Cubist exhibition was held in 1907. Between the years 1909 and 1912 this art form entered an increasingly intellectual phase, sometimes known as High or Analytical Cubism. In the last phase, Synthetic Cubism, the aim changed considerably under Juan Gris. While in Analytical Cubism the forms of the world were reduced to patterns of flat geometrical shapes, in Synthetic Cubism new forms were created to represent objects in the world. As it has been said, 'Painting becomes creation parallel to nature rather than the depiction of nature.'

DADA. An art form that began in Europe during the First World War. Its aim was to outrage and shock people by its senselessness. The theory behind it was that the world had become senseless and that art should reflect this condition. What was the point, asked the Dadaists, of producing Fine Art of beauty and meaning that bore no relation to an ugly, meaningless situation?

DIPLOMA PIECES. Works of art that were required by the official academies for membership. Strict obedience to the accepted standards of subject matter and style was demanded. See also ACADEMY.

DRY-POINT. A simple type of ENGRAVING on a metal plate with a hard steel instrument like a pencil. This leaves a high burr (see BURIN) which gives a rich effect to the printed line. Dry-point is often used in combination with etching or engraving.

ECLECTIC. A term applied to an artist who works in several styles, either combining them into his own style or painting different works in different styles.

ENGRAVING. A term that is often used in reference to various printing methods and, like many other terms, is used rather loosely. The earliest dated print is from 1446. An original engraving is a work of art invented and produced by the engraver himself. A reproductive engraving is a copy of a work, such as a painting, drawing, or statue, by another artist. For a full description of line engraving, see page 37. See also AQUATINT; DRY-POINT; ETCHING; MEZZOTINT.

ETCHING. A form of ENGRAVING. The first dated etching is from 1513, though the method did not become really popular until the seventeenth century. For the method of etching, see page 37.

EXPRESSIONISM is a late nineteenth-century movement, particularly connected with Vincent van Gogh (1853-1890) and a number of German artists who were painting in the early years of this century. As a type of art, though, Expressionism has always existed as a way of conveying strong emotions through exaggeration and violent use of line and/or colour. See also FAUVISM.

EX-VOTO paintings are religious works of art produced 'out of gratitude' to the gods of pagan religions or to Christian saints, particularly St. Anne, the mother of the Virgin.

FAUVISM is a movement that developed out of IMPRESSIONISM and EXPRESSIONISM. The first exhibition was held in 1905, and the artists were labelled *Les Fauves*, meaning 'the wild beasts'. Although they used certain techniques of the Impressionists in applying their paint, they rejected pale pastel colours in favour of brilliant hues with which they made flat patterns. The intention of the Fauves was to express strong emotions as the Expressionists had done, but their work also existed in open rebellion against the dark, conservative work of the academies.

FOLK ART is a term that is often used interchangeably with naïve and primitive art. It describes the work of untrained artists who live in communities that have their own particular customs and traditions. See also NAÏVE ART; PRIMITIVE ART.

FORESHORTENING. The method used to show perspective in a single object or figure. The strange effects that are seen, for instance, in a photograph of an arm with a hand held up towards the camera show how distorted the appearance can be without artistic foreshortening.

FOUND OBJECT (OBJET TROUVÉ). Any object that is found or recognized for a particular quality, such as its beauty, its likeness to something else, or its individual character that would normally be overlooked, can become a work of art. The artistry lies in recognizing the visual value of the object.

FUTURISM. An art movement that developed in Italy in the early years of this century. It was a style concerned with capturing the effect of movement as it occurred, particularly in relation to machines. The Futurists hoped to bring art closer to life, which they saw in terms of force and movement.

GENRE PAINTING depicts the everyday life of ordinary people. It is an art form that was particularly popular in northern Europe from the seventeenth to the nineteenth century. It has always been enjoyed by those who prefer realism and scenes showing the visible world as we know it to abstract ideas or idealized life.

GLAZING. The process of applying a transparent coloured layer of paint over another colour so that the bottom layer shines through and gives a blended appearance. Great care has to be taken when cleaning paintings that have glazes so that the surface is not removed and the colour not distorted.

GOUACHE. Opaque watercolour paint, of which poster paint is one type.

GRAPHIC ARTS depend on drawing rather than on colour and include various types of engraving and pencil and pen drawings.

GROUND. The base upon which a painting is made. It is usually unwise to work directly on canvas or wood without first preparing the surface with a priming coat, usually white lead, and then a ground, of which there are various types.

HARD-EDGE. A type of ABSTRACT ART in which the shapes are clear and have sharp outlines. This style was particularly popular in New York during the 1940s and 1950s and came about partly as a rejection of ABSTRACT EXPRESSIONISM.

HATCHING. Shading with parallel lines. In cross-hatching one layer of lines crosses another layer at an angle.

IDEAL ART, IDEALISM. The theories of Plato provide the philosophical basis for this form of art. Plato believed that perfection only exists in the idea of a thing and that every individual form on earth differs in some respect from this perfect idea or ideal. In CLASSICAL ART artists strive to approach the ideal as closely as possible by relying on mathematical proportions, geometry, and a complete harmony of parts within the whole.

ILLUSIONISM is achieved by using every means possible to suggest that what is seen in the picture is a part of real life. This involves the use of 'tricks' to deceive the eye, such as mathematical PERSPECTIVE and FORESHORTENING. See also TROMPE L'OEIL.

IMPASTO. A term used to describe paint applied in thick strokes that add texture to the canvas.

IMPRESSIONISM, IMPRESSIONISTIC. Impressionism was a name given to the style of a group of artists painting in France in the 1870s and 1880s. The Impressionists held eight exhibitions between 1874 and 1886, but the style itself had a wide and continuing influence. (For its characteristics see page 119.) Because it was based largely on scientific theories, the style tended to prevent the artist from expressing strong ideas or feelings. For this reason the Post-Impressionists (see POST-IMPRESSIONISM) adapted the style to allow for more freedom of emotional and intellectual expression. The term impressionistic (with a small *i*) has a wider meaning. It is used to describe works of art from any period in which the artist's aim is to give a general impression of his subject rather than a detailed description of it.

INTAGLIO PRINTING METHODS. Processes in which the lines that are to be printed are cut into the printing plate. The design, therefore, lies below the surface of the plate and holds the printing ink, while the background remains untouched (opposite of RELIEF PRINTING METHODS where the background is cut away). See also AQUATINT; ENGRAVING; ETCHING; MEZZOTINT.

KINETIC ART is related to CONSTRUCTIVISM; both support the theory that light and movement are important elements in a work of art. Kinetic art is more closely related to sculpture than to painting, but now that the boundaries between the various types of visual arts are less clearly defined, new ways of suggesting movement in space have also affected painting.

LINEAR COMPOSITION depends on the effects of lines and the patterns made by the outlines of forms, rather than on the relationships between solid objects and masses.

LITHOGRAPHY. A method of printing, invented in 1798, that is still a popular technique. The design to be printed is drawn with a greasy chalk on a stone slab (zinc is often used today because it is a lighter material). The whole stone is then wetted and a greasy ink is rolled over the surface. The ink sticks to the original design, which has remained dry, but rolls off the wet stone. This method is widely used in commercial art, because almost any number of prints can be made from a single block.

LUMINISM. A term that describes the method used in certain nineteenth-century landscape paintings to convey a misty effect of light. Though it originated in Britain and Germany, luminism became particularly popular in the United States.

MAGIC REALISM. A comparatively new term used to describe a type of realism that seems to go almost beyond the bounds of real life. The style of painting is extremely precise and exacting, and the effect achieved is so clear that it becomes super-real and dream-like. Unlike SURREALISM, which places together unrelated objects, Magic Realism is completely logical.

MEZZOTINT. A form of printing invented in the seventeenth century that became extremely popular in the eighteenth century, particularly in England. It was usually used to reproduce other works of art rather than to make originals. In this process, the plate is first covered with a mass of dots that are dug up by a rocker, an instrument with sharp teeth that is rocked over the surface so that the points bite into the metal. The artist then scrapes away the burr (see BURIN), which holds the ink, to varying depths. The more he scrapes away, the less ink an area will hold. The highlights, where no ink is required, are polished smooth. See also AQUATINT; ENGRAVING; ETCHING.

MONUMENTAL, as it is used in art, does not refer to physical size but to the grandeur and impressiveness of the idea behind the work and the way in which the artist uses it. Even a small painting can give a sense of monumentality.

MURAL. A painting applied on the surface of a wall.

NAÏVE ART. Art produced by untrained artists. The term is often used interchangeably with FOLK and PRIMITIVE ART, though these terms can be used for more specific purposes.

NARRATIVE PAINTING, like GENRE PAINTING, depicts scenes of everyday life. In genre painting, however, there is usually no specific story suggested, although one can be imagined by the viewer. In narrative painting, there is a definite subject clearly suggested by the artist, frequently a sad and sentimental story. This type of work was particularly popular in the nineteenth century.

NEOCLASSICISM. A particular style that spread through Europe in the second half of the eighteenth century. It was a deliberate imitation of CLASSICAL art, rather than a spontaneous revival of classical ideas such as occurs regularly throughout the history of Western art. There were several reasons for the Neoclassical movement. During the second half of the eighteenth century there was great excitement over new archaeological discoveries. Pompeii and other centres in Italy that had been buried since Roman times by the eruptions of the volcano Vesuvius had recently been uncovered. Greek and Roman architecture, sculpture, and painting became instantly popular. People were also tired of the extravagances of the upper classes who had favoured the BAROQUE and ROCOCO styles. A return to the ideals of the Roman Empire, including patriotism, self-sacrifice, and political ambition, also served the causes of the leaders of the French Revolution. Jacques Louis David, the greatest of all Neoclassical artists, was also a revolutionary and used his art as political propaganda. The style itself was based on the classical principles of clarity and logic and emphasized linear patterns.

OEUVRE. The complete output of an artist.

OIL PAINTING. Since the fifteenth century, oil has been the chief medium for painting large pictures. Today other media, such as acrylics, are probably more popular. There are two basic methods of oil painting. Since the nineteenth century the *Alla Prima,* or direct, technique has been the most common. When using this method, the artist completes the entire painting in full colour, often with no previous drawing or underpainting. In the work of the Old Masters, however, the technique was slower and more elaborate. The design was first drawn and then painted in a single colour; on top of this the final colours were applied layer by layer in glazes (transparent colours that altered the effect of those below) or scumbles (opaque colours). See also GLAZING; SCUMBLING.

OP or OPTICAL ART. A style based on creating optical illusions. This type of art also depends on knowledge of human perception and raises philosophical questions about the reality of what we see. If what is depicted looks like one thing one moment and another thing the next, how can we define what is real and what is not?

PERSPECTIVE is one of the chief ways of achieving ILLUSIONISM and so is only considered important in forms of art that attempt to re-create an illusion of the visible world. It is a mathematical method of conveying a sense of logical space on a two-dimensional surface and is based on the fact that parallel lines appear to meet when receding into space. Their point of apparent meeting on the horizon is called the VANISHING POINT. AERIAL PERSPECTIVE does not rely on mathematics but on changes in tone and colour that can be seen in a receding view of a landscape. Owing to the density of the atmosphere, there are less obvious distinctions between tones seen at a distance. Colours become increasingly pale and tend to move towards blue.

PLEIN AIR PAINTING. A term applied to landscapes that are painted outdoors rather than in a studio. As a general practice it was first used by the Barbizon painters (see p. 111). and later it was carried to greater extremes by the Impressionists (see IMPRESSIONISM).

POP ART originated in England in the 1950s and later became popular in the United States. Its sources are commercial art, including advertisements, neon signs, and posters, and popular visual material, such as comic strips. Bright acrylic colours, flat shapes, and repetitions of forms are some of its characteristics.

POST-IMPRESSIONISM. A general term applied to various styles developed in Europe in the latter half of the nineteenth century. Although certain aspects of IMPRESSIONISM may be found in most Post-Impressionist styles, these styles were developed largely in reaction against it. The four major figures of Post-Impressionism in Europe are Vincent van Gogh, Paul Cézanne, Henri Matisse, and Paul Gauguin. The aims of these artists differed widely, but from their ideas stemmed the four main directions of modern art.

PRE-RAPHAELITE BROTHERHOOD. A name chosen by a group of English painters in 1848. Although their work does not resemble that of the Italian artists painting before Raphael, as their name suggests, they believed that Raphael represented the over-praised style of the High Renaissance. Their intent was to return to the simplicity and sincerity they believed existed in medieval and early Italian painting before that time. Their paintings were closely related to poetry and usually depicted narrative subjects. They stressed serious moral virtues, made great use of symbolism, and also believed in looking closely at nature and including every detail.

PRIMARY COLOURS. The three colours of the spectrum – red, blue, and yellow – that cannot be obtained by mixing. A secondary colour is obtained by mixing two of the primaries and a tertiary colour by mixing three. Black and white are not primary colours. See also COMPLEMENTARY COLOUR.

PRIMING. See GROUND.

PRIMITIVE ART is a term that is used very loosely and often interchangeably with FOLK and NAÏVE ART. It is, for example, widely used in connection with the untrained artists of the eighteenth and nineteenth centuries in the United States, the American Primitives. It was also used to describe the work of the early Italian painters of the thirteenth and fourteenth centuries. But a more logical use of the term, provided it is not misunderstood, is to apply it to the work of artists who have not come into contact with the art of the major civilizations. In this sense, primitive art includes African tribal art, Eskimo art, and North American Indian art. This use of the term became popular towards the end of the nineteenth century but tended to be misused. At that time it was suggested that primitive meant unformed, or in the process of some kind of maturing. But true primitive art has its own forms, images, and means of expression that are as advanced artistically as any art of the major civilizations.

PROVENANCE. A term given to the individual case history of a painting; a complete record of its existence and ownership.

RECESSION. The word used to describe the way in which objects appear to recede into the depth of the imaginary picture space; one of the chief aims of ILLUSIONISM.

RELIEF PRINTING METHODS. The opposite processes to INTAGLIO PRINTING METHODS. In the relief techniques, such as WOODCUTS and STONE-CUTS, the backgound of the design is removed and the printing surface is left at the original level of the block. Details are also cut way and are therefore white in the final print. Colour prints are made by cutting a special block for each colour as well as a key-block for the main linear structure.

RENAISSANCE. The rebirth of interest in Classical art and learning that began in Italy and spread throughout Europe. In art this period is normally divided into two main divisions: the Early Renaissance, largely centred in Florence and existing from approximately 1420 to 1500, and the High Renaissance, largely centred in Rome and existing from approximately 1500 to 1527.

REPLICA. At one time it was a common practice for an artist to paint, or have copied for him, two or more identical paintings, each a replica of the original.

ROCOCO. An eighteenth-century style consisting of small curving forms and dainty shapes that was applied to painting, architecture, sculpture, and visual design in general. Pastel colours, mirrors, gold and silver scrolls, and pretty, delicate decoration are all characteristics of Rococo. The style developed partly as a reaction against the extravagance and grandeur of BAROQUE ART.

ROMANTIC, ROMANTIC, ROMANTICISM are all terms that are used in several senses. The Romantic movement in the arts emerged in the early nineteenth century in Europe, though even two hundred years before this there were certain artists who were already showing characteristics of Romanticism in their work. (For a description of the historical circumstances and social changes that lead to the Romantic movement, see page 44.) A romantic attitude of mind is not, however, limited to the nineteenth century and is as strong today as it was then. The romantic believes in the power of the imagination and expresses himself through his emotions. This attitude exists in contrast to the classical frame of mind, which considers man's mind and power of reason to be his major strengths. See also CLASSICAL.

SALON. This name comes from the Salon d'Appolon in the Louvre in Paris, which was the official exhibition hall for the French Academy in the seventeenth century. Until 1863 it was the only place an artist could exhibit his work in order to gain official recognition. The exhibitions were judged on the basis of strict academic rules governing style and subject matter. In 1863 there was such an outcry against the system that Napoleon III agreed to open a salon for those artists who had been rejected; it was called the *Salon des Refusés*. Although the official Salon continued, this action paved the way for the gradual breakdown of the academic system. See also ACADEMY.

SCHOOL, as applied to art, is a term that has two meanings: one is geographical and can be used in a wide sense (for example, Italian School, Flemish School) or more narrowly (for example, Venetian School, Florentine School); the other meaning refers in a more detailed way to characteristics of style and/or specific artists (for example, School of Raphael).

SCUMBLING is the opposite of GLAZING. It is done by applying an opaque layer of paint of one colour over a layer of paint of another colour, allowing the lower layer to emerge in places. This gives a broken but rich effect of different colours.

SERIGRAPH or SILK-SCREEN. A popular method of printmaking that is widely used today. Basically it is a form of stencilling. A screen of fine silk is blocked out with a coating of lacquer or paper masks in those areas where the colour is not wanted. The paint that is then applied over the screen penetrates the open parts of the design. By using several masks, one after the other, prints can be produced in several colours, or colours can be mixed by printing one on top of another. Each print may differ slightly from the others owing to changes in the mask or the thickness of paint. This gives a less mechanical effect than LITHOGRAPHY, for example, where the result remains basically consistent.

SFUMATO. A term that describes the subtle changes of colour and tone, from light to dark, that can be achieved in oil painting. Leonardo da Vinci was a master of this art, and in his notes he remarked that light and shade should blend 'without lines or borders, in the manner of smoke'.

SILK-SCREEN. See SERIGRAPH.

STILL LIFE. A painting of a group of objects arranged for an aesthetic effect, giving the artist the opportunity for studies of form, colour, texture, and relationships. Probably the earliest still lifes date back to the Roman examples discovered at Pompeii and Herculaneum. Small still lifes were included in religious paintings of the fifteenth century in northern Europe, and later, when still-life painting became a subject in its own right, it remained more popular in the North than in Italy. In academic art, the subject occupied a very low position in the order of importance of subject matter.

STONE-CUT. A RELIEF PRINTING METHOD that has been widely used among the Eskimos.

SURREALISM. An art movement developed in the 1920s that was, in some respects, related to DADA. In a wider sense, however, Surrealism has a long history as an art form concerned with the weird and the fantastic. Hieronymus Bosch (see p. 180) could be considered one of the most

famous artists of the surreal. In the early part of this century, many artists became interested in the workings of the subconscious mind, and from this emerged two kinds of Surrealism: one is more accurately named AUTOMATISM or TACHISME, and it was this idea that appealed to Paul-Emile Borduas (see p. 190); the other variety of Surrealism, and the one to which the name is usually applied, deals with an illogical dream-like world, where the objects depicted can be quite easily identified but bear no relationship to each other. Salvador Dali is particularly famous in this field.

SYMBOLISM originally emerged in the French poetry of the late nineteenth century, but the theory was adopted by a number of visual artists as well. The aim of the Symbolists was to express in art their belief in mystical and spiritual ideas.

SYNTHETISM is the same as SYMBOLISM. It is, in fact, the correct term to apply to Symbolist works in visual art, although Symbolism is probably more frequently used both for painting and poetry.

TACHISME. See ACTION PAINTING; AUTOMATISM.

TEMPERA. A painting technique that has been used for centuries and was the chief method of easel painting until the fifteenth century. It consists of mixing ground colours with egg yolk, or sometimes the whole egg. This mixture, which dries very quickly, can be combined with water and then glazed over with an oil and paint mix. Tempera painting has recently become popular again.

THEOSOPHY. An ancient form of mystical philosophy that interested a number of artists in the early years of the twentieth century and influenced their painting. For a further description see page 141.

TOPOGRAPHY. The aim of topography is to give a detailed visual description of a scene, particulary of buildings, towns, ruins, and natural views. It differs from landscape painting because its purpose is to be correct and exacting rather than pleasing. During the eighteenth century a number of artists specialized in topography, recording scenes for tourists to buy as souvenirs. Military artists were also employed as topographers to make visual records for the armed forces.

TRIPTYCH. A painting divided into three parts. (A picture or relief with two or more panels is called a polyptych.) In the past these were usually made as altar-pieces with side wings that could be folded over the centre panel. The triptych has occasionally been used by twentieth-century artists.

TROMPE L'OEIL (French, 'deceive the eye'). In extreme examples such exacting care is taken to paint every small detail with the utmost realism that it is hard to distinguish the painted object from the real one. See also ILLUSIONISM.

UNDERPAINTING, sometimes done in a neutral colour, is the method used to lay-in the design and composition and indicate the tone values of the final painting.

VALUES. The relative tones from light to dark of any object.
VANISHING POINT. See PERSPECTIVE.

WATERCOLOUR PAINTING. A technique in which ground-up colours held together by gums and soluble in water are used as the medium. This type of painting has been particularly popular in England and was used by some of the most famous English painters of the eighteenth century.

WOODCUT. A RELIEF PRINTING METHOD that dates from the end of the fourteenth century.

SELECTED LIST OF PUBLIC ART GALLERIES IN CANADA

This list includes the major public art galleries in each province. Most of the larger institutions have their own collections of Canadian art; several of the minor ones rely on travelling exhibitions. In addition to those listed here, there are many smaller galleries, institutions, and private collectors who own Canadian paintings. Information on these may be obtained through the galleries listed here or through the *Canadian Museums Association, Room 500, 56 Sparks Street, Ottawa, Ontario*, K I P 5 R 4. Most provinces are also now making collections of the work of their own contemporary artists and hold exhibitions periodically in provincial buildings. Private commercial galleries also exhibit the work of Canadian artists.

ALBERTA

Banff
Archives of the Canadian Rockies
Peter Whyte Gallery

Calgary
Alberta College of Art Gallery
Glenbow-Alberta Institute
University of Calgary Art Gallery

Edmonton
The Edmonton Art Gallery
Provincial Museum of Alberta
University Art Gallery and Museum, University of Alberta

Lethbridge
Southern Alberta Art Gallery
University of Lethbridge Art Gallery

BRITISH COLUMBIA

Burnaby
Burnaby Art Gallery
The Simon Fraser Gallery, Simon Fraser University

Vancouver
Fine Arts Gallery, University of British Columbia
The Vancouver Art Gallery

Victoria
Art Gallery of Greater Victoria
British Columbia Provincial Museum
Emily Carr Arts Centre
Open Space Gallery

MANITOBA

Brandon
Brandon Allied Arts Centre

Leaf Rapids
Leaf Rapids National Exhibition Centre

Winnipeg
Gallery 111, University of Manitoba
Provincial Archives of Manitoba
Winnipeg Art Gallery

NEW BRUNSWICK

Fredericton
Beaverbrook Art Gallery
University of New Brunswick Art Centre

Moncton
Galerie d'art, Université de Moncton
Moncton Museum Incorporated

Sackville
Owens Art Gallery, Mount Allison University

Saint John
The New Brunswick Museum

NEWFOUNDLAND

St. John's
The Art Gallery, Memorial University of Newfoundland
Arts and Culture Centre / Maritime Museum, Reference Library and Art Gallery

NORTHWEST TERRITORIES

Fort Smith
The Northern Life Museum

NOVA SCOTIA

Glace Bay
Miners' Museum and National Exhibition Centre

Halifax
Anna Leonowens Gallery
Art Gallery of Nova Scotia
Dalhousie University Art Gallery
Mount Saint Vincent University Art Gallery
Nova Scotia Museum
Public Archives of Nova Scotia
Saint Mary's University Art Gallery

Wolfville
Acadia University Art Gallery

ONTARIO

Brantford
The Art Gallery of Brant

Chatham
Thames Art Centre

Guelph
University of Guelph Art Gallery

Hamilton
The Art Gallery of Hamilton
McMaster University Art Gallery

Kingston
  The Agnes Etherington Art Centre, Queen's University

Kitchener-Waterloo
  The Kitchener-Waterloo Art Gallery

Kleinburg
  The McMichael Canadian Collection

London
  London Art Gallery
  McIntosh Gallery, University of Western Ontario

Oakville
  Oakville Centennial Gallery

Oshawa
  The Robert McLaughlin Gallery

Ottawa
  Canadian War Museum
  The National Gallery of Canada
  National Museum of Man
  Public Archives of Canada

Owen Sound
  Tom Thomson Memorial Gallery and Museum of Fine Art

Peterborough
  Art Gallery of Peterborough

St. Catharines
  Rodman Hall Art Centre

Sarnia
  Sarnia Public Library and Art Gallery

Stratford
  The Gallery/Stratford

Sudbury
  Laurentian University Museum and Arts Centre

Toronto
  Art Gallery of Ontario
  Canadiana Department of the Royal Ontario Museum
  Hart House, University of Toronto
  Metropolitan Toronto Central Library / Archives
  Royal Ontario Museum
  York University Art Gallery

Windsor
  The Art Gallery of Windsor

PRINCE EDWARD ISLAND

Charlottetown
  Confederation Centre Art Gallery and Museum

QUEBEC

Joliette
  Musée d'art de Joliette

Montreal
  Château de Ramezay
  McCord Museum
  The Montreal Museum of Fine Arts
  Musée d'art contemporain
  Saidye Bronfman Centre of the Y.M.-Y.W.H.A.
  Sir George Williams Art Galleries

Pointe Claire
  Pointe Claire Cultural Centre Art Gallery

Quebec City
  Hôtel-Dieu
  Musée du Québec
  Université Laval

Rimouski
  Musée régional de Rimouski

Sherbrooke
  Galerie d'art et centre culturel, Université de Sherbrooke

Trois-Rivières
  Centre culturel de Trois-Rivières

Ste-Anne de Beaupré
  Musée historical

SASKATCHEWAN

Moose Jaw
  Moose Jaw Art Museum

Regina
  Dunlop Art Gallery, Regina Public Library
  Norman Mackenzie Art Gallery, University of Regina
  Saskatchewan Arts Board / Centre of the Arts

Saskatoon
  Saskatoon Gallery and Conservatory Corporation
  (Mendel Art Gallery)

Swift Current
  Swift Current National Exhibition Centre

YUKON TERRITORY

Whitehorse
  Art Gallery of the Whitehorse Public Library

SELECTED BIBLIOGRAPHY OF CANADIAN ART

This selected list contains books of a general nature which, with the exception of a few, have been published since 1940. Several good monographs on individual artists are also available but are too numerous to mention here.

Two lists of periodicals are included: the first is Canadian, though some of the publications are not entirely devoted to art; the second is international, but these magazines often contain articles on Canadian art and artists.

Exhibition catalogues published by the major art galleries are one of the most useful sources of information, particularly in the case of contemporary art. Most of the larger art galleries in Canada have now also issued catalogues of their collections, though these are lists of works and their provenance and seldom contain the critical information that is available in the exhibition catalogues.

Barbeau, Charles Marius. *Painters of Quebec*. Toronto: Ryerson Press, 1946.

Bell, Michael. *Painters in a New Land; From Annapolis Royal to the Klondike*. Toronto: McClelland and Stewart, 1973.

Biéler, André and Harrison, Elizabeth, eds. *Conference of Canadian Artists*. Kingston: Queen's University, 1941.

Boggs, Jean Sutherland. *The National Gallery of Canada*. Toronto: Oxford University Press, 1971.

Brooker, Bertram, ed. *Yearbook of the Arts in Canada*, Vols. I, II. Toronto: Macmillan Co., 1928-9, 1936.

Buchanan, D.W. *Canadian Painters from Paul Kane to the Group of Seven*. Oxford and London: Phaidon Press, 1945.

– . *The Growth of Canadian Painting*. London and Toronto: Collins, 1950.

Canada, Department of Northern Affairs and National Resources. *Eskimo Graphic Art*. Ottawa: Department of Northern Affairs and National Resources, 1960.

Colgate, William. *Canadian Art; Its Origin and Development*. Toronto: Ryerson Press, 1967.

Detroit, Institute of Arts. *The French in America, 1520-1880*. Exhibition catalogue. Detroit: Institute of Arts, 1951.

Dickason, Olive Patricia. *Indian Arts in Canada*. Ottawa: Department of Indian Affairs and Northern Development, 1974.

Duval, Paul. *Canadian Drawings and Prints*. Toronto: Burns and MacEachern, 1952.

– . *Canadian Watercolour Painting*. Toronto: Burns and MacEachern, 1954.

– . *Four Decades; The Canadian Group of Painters and their Contemporaries, 1930-1970*. Toronto: Clarke, Irwin and Co., 1972.

– . *Group of Seven Drawings*. Toronto: Burns and MacEachern, 1965.

– . *High Realism in Canada*. Toronto: Clarke, Irwin and Co., 1974.

– . *A Vision of Canada; The McMichael Canadian Collection*. Toronto: Clarke, Irwin and Co., 1973.

Editions La Barre du Jour. *Les Automatistes*. Paul-Emile Borduas, Claude Gauvreau, Marcel Fournier, Jean Stafford, Claude Bertrand, *et al.*, contributors. Montreal: Editions La Barre du Jour, 1969.

Farr, Dorothy and Luckyj, Natalie, eds. *From Women's Eyes: Women Painters in Canada*. Exhibition catalogue. Kingston: The Agnes Etherington Art Centre, 1975.

Gagnon, Maurice. *Sur un état actuel de la peinture canadienne*. Montreal: Société des Editions Pascal, 1945.

Graham. Mayo, ed. *Some Canadian Women Artists/Quelques artistes canadiennes*. Exhibition catalogue. Ottawa: The National Gallery of Canada, 1975.

Greenhill, Ralph. *Early Photography in Canada*. Toronto: Oxford University Press, 1965.

Harper, J. Russell. *Early Painters and Engravers in Canada*. Toronto: University of Toronto Press, 1970.

– . *Everyman's Canada; Paintings and Drawings from the McCord Museum of McGill University*. Exhibition catalogue. Ottawa: The National Gallery of Canada, 1962.

– . *Painting in Canada, A History*. Toronto: University of Toronto Press, 1966.

Hill, Charles. *Canadian Painting in the Thirties*. Exhibition catalogue. Ottawa: The National Gallery of Canada, 1975.

Housser, F.B. *A Canadian Art Movement; The Story of the Group of Seven*. Toronto: Macmillan Co., 1926.

Houston, James A. *Eskimo Prints*. Barre Massachusetts: Barre Publishing Co., 1967.

Hubbard, Robert H. *An Anthology of Canadian Art*. Toronto: Oxford University Press, 1960.

– . *The National Gallery of Canada, Catalogue of Paintings and Sculpture, Volume III: Canadian School*. Ottawa: The National Gallery of Canada, 1960.

– . *The Development of Canadian Art*. Ottawa: The National Gallery of Canada, 1963.

Kilbourn, Elizabeth. *Great Canadian Painting; A Century of Art*. The Canadian Centennial Library. Toronto: McClelland and Stewart, 1966.

Larmour, W.T. *The Art of the Canadian Eskimo/L'art des Esquimaux du Canada*. Ottawa: Department of Indian Affairs and Northern Development, 1967.

MacDonald, Colin S. *A Dictionary of Canadian Artists*. Vols. I, II, III, IV (Adams-Myles). Ottawa: Canadian Paperbacks, 1967, 1968, 1969 –

MacDonald, Thoreau. *The Group of Seven*. Toronto: Ryerson Press, 1944.

McInnes, Graham C. *Canadian Art*. Toronto: Macmillan Co., 1950.

– . *A Short History of Canadian Art*. Toronto: Macmillan Co., 1939.

MacTavish, Newton. *The Fine Arts in Canada*. Toronto: Macmillan Co., 1925.

Mellen, Peter. *The Group of Seven*. Toronto: McClelland and Stewart, 1970.

Montréal, Musée d'art contemporain. *Borduas et les automatistes: Montréal 1945-1955*. Exhibition catalogue. Montreal: Musée d'art contemporain, 1971.

— . *Panorama de la peinture au Québec,* 1940-1966. Exhibition catalogue. Montreal: Musée d'art contemporain, 1967.

Morris, Jerrold A. *The Nude in Canadian Painting.* Toronto: New Press, 1972.

Morisset, Gérard. *Coup d'oeil sur les arts en Nouvelle-France.* Quebec: Les Presses de Charrier et Dugal, 1941.

— . *Peintres et tableaux.* Vols. I, II. Quebec: Les Editions du Chevalet, 1936, 1937.

— . *La Peinture traditionelle au Canada français.* Ottawa: Le Cercle du Livre de France, 1960.

Ostiguy, Jean René. *Un siècle de peinture canadienne,* 1870-1970. Quebec: Les Presses de l'université Laval, 1971.

Ottawa, The National Gallery of Canada. *Quebec; A Collection of Unpublished Photographs of Paintings, Sculptures and Architecture from Quebec.* Exhibition catalogue. Ottawa: The National Gallery of Canada, 1960–?

Ottawa, The National Gallery of Canada. *Three Hundred Years of Canadian Art/Trois cent ans d'art canadien.* Exhibition catalogue. Ottawa: The National Gallery of Canada, 1967.

Paris, Musée d'art moderne de la ville de Paris. *Canada trajectoires 73.* Exhibition catalogue. Paris: Musée d'art moderne de la ville de Paris, 1973.

Paris, Musée de l'homme. *Chefs-d'oeuvre des arts indiens et esquimaux du Canada/Masterpieces of Indian and Eskimo Art from Canada.* Exhibition catalogue. Paris: Musée de l'homme, 1969.

Paris, Musée national d'art moderne. *Canada; art d'aujourd'hui.* Exhibition catalogue. Paris: Musée national d'art moderne, 1968.

Patterson, Nancy Lou. *Canadian Native Art; Arts and Crafts of Canadian Indians and Eskimos.* Don Mills: Collier-Macmillan Canada, 1973.

Les Presses de l'université de Montréal. *Peinture canadienne-française; debats.* Conférences J.A. de Sève, 11-12. Montreal; Les Presses de l'université de Montréal, 1971.

Quebec, Musée du Québec. *Trésors des communautés religieuses de la ville de Québec.* Exhibition catalogue. Quebec: Ministère des affaires culturelles, 1973.

Reid, Dennis. *A Concise History of Canadian Painting.* Toronto: Oxford University Press, 1973.

— . *The Group of Seven/Le groupe des sept.* Exhibition catalogue. Ottawa: The National Gallery of Canada, 1970.

— . *The MacCallum Bequest, of paintings by Tom Thomson and other Canadian Painters and the Mr. and Mrs. H.R. Jackman Gift of the murals from the late Dr. MacCallum's cottage painted by some of the members of the Group of Seven/Le legs MacCallum, peintures par Tom Thomson et par d'autres peintres canadiens et le don de M. et Mme. H.R. Jackman de panneaux décoratifs du chalet de feu le Dr. MacCallum peints par quelques-uns des membres du Groupe des sept.* Exhibition catalogue. Ottawa: The National Gallery of Canada, 1969.

Robert, Guy. *L'art au Quebec depuis* 1940. Montreal: Editions de la presse, 1973.

Robillard, Yves, ed. *Quebec underground,* 1962-1972. Vols. I, II, III. Montreal: Médiart, 1973.

Robson, A.H. *Canadian Landscape Painters.* Toronto: Ryerson Press, 1932.

Roch, Ernst, ed. *Arts of the Eskimo: Prints.* Montreal: Signum Press in association with Oxford University Press, Toronto, 1974.

The Roundstone Council for the Arts. *Canadian Artists in Exhibition* 1972-1973; 1973-1974/*Artistes canadiens: expositions* 1972-1973; 1973-1974. Desmeules, Raynald, trans. Toronto: The Roundstone Council for the Arts, 1974.

Spendlove, F. St. George. *The Face of Early Canada.* Toronto: Ryerson Press, 1958.

Time Canada. *The Canadian Canvas/Peintres canadiens actuels.* Toronto: Time Canada, 1974.

Toronto, Art Gallery of Ontario. *The Canadian Collection.* Toronto: McGraw-Hill, 1970.

— . *Impressionism in Canada,* 1895-1935. Exhibition catalogue. Toronto: Art Gallery of Ontario, 1973.

Townsend, William, ed. *Canadian Art Today.* London: Studio International, 1970.

Vancouver, The Vancouver Art Gallery. *The Arts in French Canada/Les arts au Canada français.* Exhibition catalogue. Vancouver: The Vancouver Art Gallery, 1959.

Viau, Guy. *Modern Painting in French Canada.* Series on the Arts, Humanities, and Sciences in French Canada, Vol. III. Quebec: Department of Cultural Affairs, 1967.

West Baffin Eskimo Co-operative. *Eskimo Graphic Art/Les arts graphiques esquimaux.* Ottawa: West Baffin Eskimo Co-operative/Queen's Printer, 1961–

Withrow, William. *Contemporary Canadian Painting.* Toronto: McClelland and Stewart, 1972.

PERIODICALS

CANADIAN

artscanada. Toronto, 1967-
Bulletin des recherches historiques. Lévis, 1895-1968.
Canadian Architect and Builder. Toronto, 1887-1895.
Canadian Art. Ottawa, 1943-1966 (Now artscanada).
The Canadian Forum. Toronto, 1920-
Canadian Magazine. Toronto, 1837-1939 (Early issues called
Canadian Monthly).
Canadian Review of Music and Art. Toronto, 1942-1948.
Liberté. Montreal, 1959-
Maritime Art Magazine. Halifax, 1940-1943.
Rapport de l'Archiviste de la Province de Québec. Quebec.
Royal Society of Canada. Ottawa.
Saturday Night. Toronto, 1887-
Vie des Arts. Montreal, 1955-

INTERNATIONAL

Art International. Lugano, Switzerland, 1956-
Art in America. New York, 1913-
Arts Magazine. New York, 1926-
Art News. New York, 1902-
Magazine of Art. New York, 1909-1953.
The Studio. London, 1893-1964 (Now Studio International).
Studio International. London, 1964-

CREDITS

Illustrations are listed in alphabetical order. Principal sources and photographers are credited under the following abbreviations:

GALLERIES

A.E.A.C.
The Agnes Etherington Art Centre,
Queen's University, Kingston
A.G.H.
The Art Gallery of Hamilton
A.G.O.
Art Gallery of Ontario, Toronto
A.G.M.U.
The Art Gallery, Memorial University of
Newfoundland, St. John's
A.G.W.
The Art Gallery of Windsor
B.A.G.
Beaverbrook Art Gallery, Fredericton
C.C.A.G.
Confederation Centre Art Gallery and Museum,
Charlottetown
E.A.G.
The Edmonton Art Gallery
M.M.F.A.
The Montreal Museum of Fine Arts
N.G.C.
The National Gallery of Canada, Ottawa
P.A.C.
Public Archives of Canada, Ottawa
R.M.G.
The Robert McLaughlin Gallery, Oshawa
R.O.M.
Royal Ontario Museum, Toronto
T.G.I.
Thomas Gilcrease Institute of American History
and Art, Tulsa, Oklahoma
V.A.G.
The Vancouver Art Gallery
W.A.G.
Winnipeg Art Gallery

PHOTOGRAPHERS

B.M.J.H.
Brian Merrett and Jennifer Harper, Incorporated,
Montreal
E.M.
Ernest Mayer, Winnipeg
J.D.
J. Dow Camerawork Associates, Edmonton

W.B.E.
W.B. Edwards Incorporated, Quebec City

Abstract: W.A.G., Gift of the Douglas Duncan Estate; E.M.
Approaching Storm: E.A.G., Gift of Dr. Harold Orr, Dr. Allan
    Coates Rankin, and Mr. George H. Steer, 1949; J.D.
At the Foot of the Rocky Mountains: McCord Museum,
    Montreal
Ave Maria: A.G.H., Gift of the Women's Committee, 1963

Backyard: C.C.A.G.
The Bed: B.A.G., Wallace S. Bird Memorial Collection
Behind Bonsecours Market, Montreal: N.G.C.
British Naval Squadron off Nova Scotia: N.G.C.

The Canada Southern Railway at Niagara: N.G.C.
The Cataract of Niagara: P.A.C., Historical Branch
Cheval Marin: T.G.I.
The Christ Child: Congrégation de Notre-Dame, Montreal;
    Photograph from *A People's Art* by J. Russell Harper,
    reproduced courtesy of University of Toronto Press
Circular Motion (En Deuxième Phase; Rythmique Circulaire).
    York University Art Gallery; Peter Patterson, Photo Design
Composition #1: V.A.G.

Dalton Camp Having a Medieval Vision: A.G.M.U.
Dazzle Red: A.G.O., Purchase, Corporations' Subscription
    Endowment, 1966
Decay and Growth: Norman Mackenzie Art Gallery,
    University of Regina; A.G.O.
Decorative Panel, Forest Undergrowth III: N.G.C.,
    Gift of Mr. and Mrs. H.R. Jackman, Toronto, 1967
Doc Snider's House: N.G.C., Gift of Dr. P.D. Ross, Ottawa,
    1932
Draped Head: Hart House, University of Toronto; Photograph
    from *Four Decades* by Paul Duval, reproduced courtesy of
    Clarke, Irwin and Company Limited, Toronto

L'Enfant au Pain: N.G.C.
Enigma: A.E.A.C.
L'Etoile Noire: M.M.F.A., Donated by Gérard Lortie, 1960
*Exercising Flying Cows Over the Governor General's
    Grounds:* Collection of the Artist; B.M.J.H.
Ex-Voto de l'Ange gardien: Hôtel-Dieu, Quebec City; Photo-
    graph from *Painting in Canada, A History* by J. Russell
    Harper, reproduced courtesy of University of Toronto Press
Ex-Voto de Monsieur Edouin: Commemorative Chapel,
    Ste-Anne de Beaupré; W.B.E.

The Falls of Montmorency: R.O.M.
The Ferry, Quebec: N.G.C.

QUOTATIONS

reproduced courtesy of McClelland and Stewart Limited, Toronto
Sunday Morning #2: Collection of Joan S. Currie; Eberhard E. Otto Photography Limited, Toronto
Sunrise on the Saguenay: N.G.C., The Royal Canadian Academy, diploma work, deposited 1881

Tanglewood: W.A.G; E.M.
The Three Kings: Private Collection; Photograph from *A People's Art* by J. Russell Harper, reproduced courtesy of University of Toronto Press
The Three Robinson Sisters: A.G.O., Loaned by Mr. and Mrs. J.B. Robinson, 1944
Les Trois Pommes: Private Collection; Photograph from *Painting in Canada, A History* by J. Russell Harper, reproduced courtesy of University of Toronto Press
Trout Stream in the Forest: N.G.C., The Royal Canadian Academy, diploma work, deposited 1882; B.M.J.H.
Turned Out of the Herd: E.A.G., Ernest E. Poole Foundation Collection; J.D.

Ulysses: V.A.G.
Untitled: V.A.G.
Untitled Mural: C.C.A.G.
The Upper Ottawa: N.G.C.

Végétaux Marins: Art Collection Society of Kingston; M.M.F.A.
A Venetian Bather: N.G.C.
Venus Simultaneous: A.G.O.
A View of the Bridge on the River La Puce: N.G.C.
A View of the River La Puce near Quebec, North America: N.G.C.
View of Victoria Hospital, Second Series: N.G.C.; B.M.J.H.
Visitors Are Invited to Register: Saskatoon Gallery and Conservatory Corporation; General Graphic Services Limited.
A Visit to Otelne in his Lodge: A.E.A.C.
Vu des Etalons: T.G.I.

Windigo: Glenbow-Alberta Institute, Calgary
Winter, Charlevoix County: A.G.O.
Winter Theme No. 7: N.G.C.
The Woolsey Family: N.G.C., Gift of Major Edgar C. Woolsey, Ottawa, 1952
A Wreath of Flowers: N.G.C.

Young Canadian: Hart House, University of Toronto; TDF Artists Limited

p. 9
from *Book of Beasts* by T.H. White (London: Jonathan Cape, 1969).

pp. 89-90
from *Robert Harris, 1849-1919: An Unconventional Biography* by Moncrieff Williamson (Toronto: McClelland and Stewart, 1970).

p. 127
from 'The Hot Mush School' by H.F. Gadsby, *Toronto Star,* Dec. 12, 1913.

p. 129
from 'The Group System in Art' by Hector Charlesworth, *Saturday Night,* Jan. 24, 1925.

pp. 129-130
from 'Pictures That Can Be Heard' by Hector Charlesworth, *Saturday Night,* March 18, 1916.

pp. 144-146
from *Growing Pains* by Emily Carr (Toronto: Clarke, Irwin a 1966).

pp. 148-149, 151-152
from *Lionel Lemoine FitzGerald, Bertram Brooker; Their Drawings,* exhibition catalogue edited by Patricia E. Bovey (Winnipeg: Winnipeg Art Gallery, 1975).

p. 154
from *David Milne, 1882—1953; An Exhibition Prepared to Mark Canada's Centennial Year, 1967,* introduction by David P. Silcox (Kingston: The Agnes Etherington Art Centre, 1967)

p. 168
from 'From This Point I Looked Out' by Goodridge Roberts, *Queen's Quarterly,* Vol. LX-3, Autumn, 1953.

p. 203
from *In Search of Form* by Jack Shadbolt (Toronto: McClelland and Stewart, 1968).

pp. 236-237
from *Some Canadian Women Artists/Quelques artistes canadiennes,* exhibition catalogue edited by Mayo Graham (Ottawa: The National Gallery of Canada, 1975).